DOVER · THRIFT · EDITIONS

Infamous Speeches

From Robespierre to Osama bin Laden

Edited by

BOB BLAISDELL

DOVER PUBLICATIONS, INC.

Mineola, New York

DOVER THRIFT EDITIONS

GENERAL EDITOR: MARY CAROLYN WALDREP
EDITOR OF THIS VOLUME: SUZANNE E. JOHNSON

Copyright

Copyright © 2011 by Dover Publications, Inc.
All rights reserved.

Bibliographical Note

Infamous Speeches: From Robespierre to Osama bin Laden is a new compilation, first published by Dover Publications, Inc., in 2011.

Library of Congress Cataloging-in-Publication Data

Infamous speeches : from Robespierre to Osama bin Laden / edited by
Bob Blaisdell.
    p. cm. — (Dover thrift editions)
  ISBN-13: 978-0-486-47849-4
  ISBN-10: 0-486-47849-1
 1. Speeches, addresses, etc.   2. World history—Sources.   3. World politics—
Sources.   4. Extremists—History—Sources.   I. Blaisdell, Robert.
  PN6122.I54 2011
  808.85—dc22

                                                                              2010036702

Manufactured in the United States by Courier Corporation
47849101
www.doverpublications.com

Note

ALL OF THE SPEECHES included in this anthology are, or have been, infamous, and several have even been regarded and admired as masterpieces of oratory. Not all of the speakers are history's villains, though many are, and it would no doubt be unpleasant to find oneself shoulder to shoulder with murderous maniacs when all one did was argue for one's religious beliefs (William Jennings Bryan), or misjudge Hitler's intentions (Neville Chamberlain). Certainly at some point in their lives or careers the speechmakers attained power and influence, and some of them were, or are, in spite of the speeches herein, upstanding men or women. It's also useful to remind oneself that some of the worst and most poisonous people who ever lived did not commit themselves to words for the public. There is, after all, some sort of daring and nerve required to lie to thousands of listeners and to history. In public utterance, there is always the potential for fame or risk of infamy. Because Stalin committed himself to a bit of public speaking, we know more about the Soviet Union; we know more about the terrible allure of Hitler because of his public words. Knowing the historical aftermaths of most of these speeches gives us a perspective that in several instances would have been hard to have had at the time; we now know a lot more about the guilt or wrongs or crimes by, among others, Deng Xiaoping and Saddam Hussein.

Unsurprisingly, there is more oil and honey in these speeches than we might find in more admirable, braver, truer speeches. The truths that are delivered are often resting precariously on lies and deception. King Leopold II of Belgium, who seems never to have wasted a tear of remorse for his destruction of millions of African lives and dozens of cultures, presented himself as one of the world's noblest philanthropists: "To open to civilisation the only part of our globe where it has not yet penetrated, to pierce the darkness which envelops entire populations, is, I dare to say, a crusade worthy of this century of progress." There are, on the other hand, a few completely candid speeches, but they are disturbing all the same, such as George Wallace's call for continued segregation in Alabama.

Much of the history is fascinating, but it can seem, as Voltaire remarked, "nothing more than a picture of crimes and miseries," and there is a great deal of unpleasantness in store here for any reader. What do we make of the unrepentant and unpunished, the remorselessness of Hitler and Stalin and Amin, or the thorough cynicism of politicians preferring, for instance, legalities over justice, or maintaining their own power at the cost of human lives? What is it that makes the reprehensible Jefferson Davis or Mao Tse-Tung continue, in some circles today, to be revered? So while there are unfortunately for the human race no doubt thousands of alternative candidates for inclusion in such an anthology as this, my most serious misgivings, given that my particular prejudices and interests have weighed my selections, are including speeches by people who were not advocating violence, persecution, or intolerance, but were simply talking through their hat or lying through their teeth. Propaganda-spinners and liars aren't in the same league as mass-murdering dictators—but they're all together in this collection.

For each selection I have provided a short introductory note, with the date and place and the official or customary reference to the speech in the heading as well as a sample and telling quotation in parenthesis. I have deleted almost all editorialized references to laughter, applause, and cheering unless the speakers responded to those audience responses at the moment.

I would like to thank a friend, the writer and editor Daniel Evan Weiss, and my father, F. William Blaisdell, for their suggestions of numerous speeches; my daughter, Odette Blaisdell, helped with some of the typing. Finally, I express my appreciation to the librarians of the New York City Public Library and especially those at Columbia University's Arthur W. Diamond Law Library and Lehman Social Sciences Library for helping me track down elusive sources.

—BOB BLAISDELL
New York City, June 2010

Contents

MAXIMILIEN MARIE ISIDORE ROBESPIERRE

"The Principles of Political Morality"

Address to the National Convention

("Terror is only justice prompt, severe and inflexible...
an emanation of virtue;...a natural consequence of
the general principle of democracy, applied to the most
pressing wants of the country")

Paris, France

February 5, 1794

Maximilien Marie Isidore Robespierre (1758–1794) was among the French Revolution's most important leaders and most spellbinding of orators. As a member of the deadly Committee of Public Safety, he continues his advocacy for the "Reign of Terror" against those fighting or challenging the social and legal upheavals the Revolution has wrought. Robespierre saw enemies everywhere and desired the power of terror to obliterate them. Five and a half months later, after his foes gained power, he was executed.

Citizens/Representatives of the People:

We laid before you some time ago the principles of our exterior political system; we come today to develop the principles of our interior political morality.

After having long pursued the path which chance pointed out, carried away in a manner by the efforts of contending factions, the Representatives of the French people have shown a character and a government. A sudden change in the success of the nation announced to Europe the regeneration which was operated in the national representation. But to this point of time, even now that I address you, it must be allowed that we have been impelled through the tempest of a revolution, rather by a love of goodness and a

1

feeling of the wants of our country, than by an exact theory, and precise rules of conduct, which we had not even leisure to sketch.

It is time to designate clearly the purposes of the revolution and the point which we wish to attain. It is time we should examine ourselves the obstacles which yet are between us and our wishes, and the means most proper to realize them, a simple and important idea that appears not yet to have been contemplated. Eh! How could a base and corrupt government have dared to realize it? A king, a proud senate, a Caesar, a Cromwell; of these the first care was to cover their dark designs under the cloak of religion, to covenant with every vice, caress every party, destroy men of integrity, oppress and deceive the people in order to attain the end of their treacherous ambition. If we had not had a task of the first magnitude to accomplish; if all our concern had been to raise a party or create a new aristocracy, we might have believed, as certain writers more ignorant than wicked asserted, that the plan of the French Revolution was to be found written in the works of Tacitus and of Machiavelli; we might have sought the duties of the representatives of the people in the history of Augustus, of Tiberius, or of Vespasian, or even in that of certain French legislators; for tyrants are substantially alike and only differ by trifling shades of treachery and cruelty.

For our part we now come to make the whole world partake in your political secrets, in order that all friends of their country may rally at the voice of reason and public interest, and that the French nation and her representatives be respected in all countries which may attain a knowledge of their true principles; and that intriguers who always seek to supplant other intriguers may be judged by public opinion upon settled and plain principles.

It is necessary to take every precaution to place the interests of freedom in the hands of truth, which is eternal, rather than in those of men, who come and go; so that if the government forgets the interests of the people or falls into the hands of men corrupted, according to the natural course of things, the light of acknowledged principles should unmask their treasons, and that every new faction may read its death in the very thought of a crime.

Happy the people that attains this end; for, whatever new machinations are plotted against their liberty, what resources does not public reason present when guaranteeing freedom!

What is the end of our revolution? The tranquil enjoyment of liberty and equality; the reign of that eternal justice, the laws of which are graven, not on marble or stone, but in the hearts of men, even in the heart of the slave who has forgotten them, and in that of the tyrant who disowns them.

We wish to substitute in our country morality for egotism, integrity for "honor," principles for customs, deeds for decorum, the empire of reason over the tyranny of fashion, a contempt of vice for a contempt of misfortune, pride for insolence, magnanimity for vanity, the love of glory for the love of money, good people for good company, merit for intrigue, genius for wit, truth for flash, the attractions of happiness for the ennui of sensuality, the grandeur of man for the littleness of the great, a people magnanimous, powerful, happy, for a people amiable, frivolous and miserable; that is to say, all the virtues and miracles of a Republic instead of all the vices and absurdities of a monarchy.

We wish, in a word, to fulfill the intentions of nature and the destiny of man, realize the promises of philosophy, and acquit providence of a long reign of crime and tyranny. That France, once illustrious among enslaved nations, may, by eclipsing the glory of all free countries that ever existed, become a model to nations, a terror to oppressors, a consolation to the oppressed, an ornament of the universe and that, by sealing the work with our blood, we may at least witness the dawn of the bright day of universal happiness. This is our ambition; this is the end of our efforts.

What kind of government can realize these wonders? Only a democratic or republican government—these two words are synonyms, despite the abuses in common speech, because an aristocracy is no closer than a monarchy to being a republic. A democracy is not a state where the people, continually assembled, regulate all the public affairs themselves; much less is it one where a hundred thousand groups of people, segregated by measures, hasty and contradictory, decide the fate of the whole nation: such a government has never existed except to bring back the people under the yoke of despotism.

Democracy is a state in which the sovereign people, guided by laws which are of their own making, do for themselves all that they can do well, and by their delegates do all that they cannot do for themselves.

It is therefore in the principles of a democratic government that you are to seek the rules of your political conduct.

But, in order to found and consolidate among us democracy, to reach the peaceful reign of constitutional laws, we must terminate the war of liberty against tyranny, and weather successfully the tempests of the revolution. This is the end of the revolutionary government you have framed. You should therefore again regulate your conduct by the tempestuous circumstances in which the Republic exists, and the plan of your administration should be the result of the spirit of the revolutionary government combined with the general principles of democracy.

Now, what is the fundamental principle of popular or democratic government, that is to say, the essential mainspring which sustains it and gives it motion? It is virtue. I speak of the public virtue that worked so many wonders in Greece and Rome and ought to produce even more astonishing things in republican France—that virtue which is nothing else than the love of the nation and its laws.

But as the essence of the republic or of democracy is equality, it follows that love of country necessarily embraces the love of equality.

Again, it is true that this sublime passion supposes a preference for the interest of the public over all private considerations; it results from this then that the love of country supposes or produces all virtues. For what are they but a strength of mind which commands such sacrifices? And how could the slave of avarice and ambition, for example, sacrifice his idol for his country?

Not only is virtue the soul of democracy; it can exist in no other government. In a monarchy, I know only one individual who could love his country, and for that, he does not need a bit of virtue; that one is the king. The reason is that of all those who live in his dominions, the king is the only one who has a country. Is he not the sovereign, at least in fact? Is not he in the place of the people? And so what is a fatherland if not a country where the citizen is a member of the sovereignty?

By consequence of this same principle, in the aristocratic governments, the word "fatherland" signifies nothing more than the patriarchal families that have usurped sovereignty.

It is only in a democracy where the state is truly a country of all the individuals who compose it, and can count as many zealous defenders of its cause as there are citizens. Here is the source of the superiority of free people over all others. If Athens and Sparta triumphed over all the tyrants of Asia, and the Swiss over the tyrants of Spain and Austria, it is unnecessary to seek another cause.

But the French are the first people of the world who have established real democracy, by calling all men to equality and full rights of citizenship; and there, in my judgment, is the true reason why all the tyrants in league against the Republic will be vanquished.

There are important consequences to be drawn immediately from the principles we have just explained.

Since virtue and equality are the soul of the republic, and that your aim is to found, to consolidate the republic, it follows, that the first rule of your political conduct should be, to let all your measures tend to maintain equality and encourage virtue, for the first care of the legislator should be to strengthen the principles on which the government rests. Hence all that tends to excite a love of country, to purify manners, to exalt the mind, to direct the passions of the human heart towards the public good, you should adopt and establish. All that tends to concentrate and debase them into selfish egotism, to awaken an infatuation for littlenesses, and a disregard for greatness, you should reject or repress. In the system of the French Revolution that which is immoral is impolitic, and what tends to corrupt is counter-revolutionary. Weaknesses, vices, prejudices are the road to monarchy. Carried away, too often perhaps, by the force of ancient habits, as well as by the innate imperfection of human nature, to false ideas and pusillanimous sentiments, we have more to fear from the excesses of weakness, than from excesses of energy. The warmth of zeal is not perhaps the most dangerous rock that we have to avoid; but rather that languour which ease produces and a distrust of our own courage. Therefore continually wind up the sacred spring of republican government, instead of letting it run down. I need not say that I am not here justifying any excess. The most sacred principles may be abused: the wisdom of government should guide its operations according to circumstances, it should time its measures, choose its means; for the manner of bringing about great things is an essential part of the talent of producing them, just as wisdom is an essential attribute of virtue.

We do not pretend to cast the French Republic in the model of that of Sparta; we do not want to give it either austerity or the corruption of cloisters. We come to present to you, in all its purity, the moral and political principle of popular government. You have then a compass that can guide you through the midst of storms of all the passions, and from the whirlwinds of intrigues that surround you. You have the touchstone by which you can try out all your laws and all the propositions that you make. By ceaselessly comparing them by this principle, you can from now on avoid the reef of large assemblies, the danger of surprises and precipitous measures that are incoherent and contradictory. You can give to all your measures the systematic unity, wisdom and dignity that should characterize representatives of the world's leading people.

It is not necessary to detail the natural consequences of the principle of democracy; it is the principle itself, simple yet copious, which deserves to be developed.

Republican virtue may be considered as it respects the people and as it respects the government. It is necessary in the one and in the other. When however, the government alone is deprived of it, there exists a resource in that of the people; but when the people themselves are corrupted liberty is already lost.

Happily virtue is natural in the people, despite aristocratic prejudices. A nation is truly corrupt, when, after having by degrees lost its character and liberty, it passes from democracy into aristocracy or monarchy; this is the death of the political body by decrepitude. When, after 400 years of glory, the avarice finally chased out of Sparta the customs along with the laws of Lycurgus, Agis died in vain to restore them. Demosthenes unsuccessfully thundered against Philip, and Philip found the vices of Athens degenerated its advocates more eloquently than Demosthenes. There is now, in Athens, a population as numerous as in the time of Militiades and Aristides, but there are no more "Athenians." What does it matter that Brutus killed the tyrant? Tyranny still lives in those hearts, and Rome does not exist except in Brutus.

But, when, by prodigious effects of courage and of reason, a whole people break off the chains of despotism to turn them into trophies to liberty; when, by their moral temperament, they rise in a manner from the arms of death, to resume all the strength of youth when, in turns forgiving and inexorable, intrepid and docile, they can neither be checked by impregnable ramparts, nor by innumerable armies of tyrants leagued against them, and yet of themselves stop at the voice of the law; if then they do not reach the heights of their destiny it can only be the fault of those who govern.

Again, it may be said, that, in one sense, to love justice and equality the people need no great effort of virtue; it is sufficient that they love themselves.

But the magistrate is obliged to sacrifice his own interest to the interest of the people, and the pride of power to equality. It is necessary that the law speak with all its energy, especially to its representatives. It is necessary that the government conduct itself to have all its parts in harmony with it. If there is a representative body, a primary authority, constituted by the people, it is its duty to superintend and ceaselessly repress the public functionaries. But what will repress it, except its own virtue? The more exalted this source of public order is, the more pure it ought to be. It is necessary then that the representative body begin by suppressing in its bosom all private passions and interests to the general will and good of the public. Happy are those representatives when their glory and their interest attach themselves, as much as their duties, to the cause of liberty.

We deduce from all this a great truth—that the characteristic of popular government is to be trustful towards the people and rigorous with itself.

Here the development of our theory would reach its limit, if you had only to steer the ship of the Republic through calm waters. But the tempest rages, and the state of the revolution in which you find yourselves imposes upon you another task.

This great purity of the principles of the French Revolution, the sublimity indeed of its object, are what constitute our strength and our weakness; our strength as it gives us our ascendancy which truth will command over imposture, and the rights of the public interest over private interests; our weakness, because it gives scope to the machinations of men, of all those who in their hearts meditate plunder of the people, and all those who wish their former plunderings should go unpunished, and those who have abhorred liberty as a personal calamity, and those who embraced the Revolution as a trade and the Republic as booty: Hence the defection of so many ambitious and avaricious men, who, after starting with us, abandoned us on the way, because they had not undertaken the journey to arrive at our goal. One might say that these two opposing peoples, who have been imagined as disputing with each other the empire of nature, are combating at this great epoch of human history to set without return the destiny of the world, and that France is the theater of this important contest. Externally, all the tyrants surround you; internally all the friends of tyranny conspire; they will conspire until hope for the crime has been taken away. It is necessary to annihilate the internal and external enemies of the Republic or perish with them. Now, in this situation, the first maxim of your policy ought to be to lead the people by reason and the people's enemies by terror.

If virtue be the basis of a popular government in times of peace, the basis of that government during a revolution is virtue combined with terror: virtue, without which terror is destructive; terror, without which virtue is impotent. Terror is only justice prompt, severe and inflexible; it is then an emanation of virtue; it is less a distinct principle than a natural consequence of the general principle of democracy, applied to the most pressing wants of the country.

It has been said that terror is the basis of despotic government. Does yours then resemble despotism? Yes, as the steel that glistens in the hands of the heroes of liberty resembles the sword with which the servants of tyranny are armed. Let the despot govern by terror his debased subjects; he is right as a despot: conquer by terror the enemies of liberty and you will be right as founders of the Republic. The government in a revolution is the despotism of liberty against tyranny. Is force only intended to protect crime? Is it not destined that the lightning of heaven strike those proud heads?

The law of self-preservation, with every being whether physical or moral, is the first law of nature. Crime butchers innocence to secure a throne, and innocence struggles with all its might against the attempts of crime. If tyranny reigned one single day not a patriot would survive it. How long yet will the madness of despots be called justice, and the justice of the people barbarity or rebellion? How tenderly oppressors and how severely the oppressed are treated! Nothing more natural: whoever does not abhor crime cannot love virtue.

It is necessary, meanwhile, that one or the other must be crushed. Let mercy be shown the royalists, exclaim some men. Grace to the villains! No: give grace to the innocents, to the weak, to the unhappy; grace to humanity!

The protection of government is only due to peaceable citizens; and all citizens in the Republic are Republicans. The royalists, the conspirators, are strangers, or rather enemies. Is not this dreadful contest, which liberty maintains against tyranny, indivisible? Are not the internal enemies the allies of those outside? The assassins who lay waste the interior; the intriguers who purchase the consciences of the delegates of the people: the traitors who sell them; the mercenary libelers paid to dishonor the cause of the people, to smother public virtue, to fan the flame of civil discord, and bring about a political counter revolution by means of a moral one; all these men, are they less culpable or less dangerous than the tyrants whom they serve? All those who interpose their killing-softness between these villains and the avenging sword of national justice resemble those who throw themselves between the servants of tyrants and the bayonets of our soldiers; all the transports of their false sensibility appear to me nothing but sighs for the success of England and Austria.

Eh! For whom ought they show their tenderness? Shouldn't it be for the 200,000 heroes, the chosen ones of the nation, mowed down by the sword of the enemies of liberty or destroyed by the dagger of royalist or federal assassins? No, they were plebeians, these patriots. To have a right to their tender interest, it is necessary to have been at least the widow of a general who has betrayed his country twenty times; he who wishes to gain their attention, it is necessary to prove almost that he has sacrificed 10,000 Frenchmen, just as a Roman general, to gain a triumph, had to have killed 10,000 enemies. A narrative of the measures committed by the tyrants against the defenders of liberty is heard with sangfroid; our women horribly mutilated, our children massacred on the bosom of their mothers; our prisoners expiating in the most cruel torments sublime and astonishing acts of heroism; yet the tardy punishment of those monsters fattened on the purest blood of the country, is called a horrible butchery.

One suffers with patience the misery of the generous female-citizens who have sacrificed to the most beautiful of causes their brothers, their children, their husbands; but it is the wives of conspirators who receive the generous consolation; it is accepted that they can with impunity bias justice, plead against liberty the cause of their relations and their accomplices. They have been established practically as a privileged corporation, and quartered on the people.

With what good nature we are again duped by words! How aristocracy and moderation govern us once more by the deadly maxims they have given us!

Aristocracy defends itself by intrigue better than patriotism by its services. They desire to govern the revolution by palace cavils; they treat the conspiracies against the public as if they were the lawsuits of private citizens. Tyranny kills and liberty pleads; and the code framed by the conspirators is the law by which they are judged.

When public safety is at stake, the testimony of the universe is not admitted to supply the place of personal evidence, nor presumptive proof admitted when the positive cannot be adduced.

Delays in giving sentence produce the effect of impunity; the uncertainty of punishment encourages crimes; and yet the severity of punishment is complained of, the confinement of enemies of the Republic is cried up as a grievance. Precedents are looked for in the history of tyrants, and that of the people lies neglected; neither are they drawn from the nature and imperiousness of circumstances when liberty is menaced. In Rome, when the counsel discovered the conspiracy and smothered it at the same instant by the death of Cataline's conspirators, he was accused of having violated the customs. By whom? By the ambitious Caesar, who wished to swell his party with the horde of conspirators, by the Pisons, the Clodiusses, and all those bad citizens who themselves dreaded the virtue of a true Roman and the severe laws.

To punish the oppressors of humanity is clemency; to forgive them is cruelty. The severity of tyrants has barbarity for its principle; that of a republican government is founded on beneficence.

Therefore let him beware who should dare to influence the people by that terror which is made only for their enemies! Let him beware, who, regarding the inevitable errors of civicism in the same light, with the premeditated crimes of treachery, or the attempts of conspirators, suffers the dangerous intriguer to escape and pursues the peaceable citizen! Death to the villain who dares abuse the sacred name of liberty or the powerful arms intended for her defense, to carry mourning or death to the patriotic heart! This abuse has existed, one cannot doubt it. It has been exaggerated, no doubt, by the aristocracy. But if in all the Republic there existed only one virtuous man persecuted by the enemies of liberty, the government's duty would be to seek him out vigorously and give him a signal revenge.

But is it necessary to conclude that the persecutions suffered by the patriots by the hypocritical zeal of the counter-revolutionaries, that counter-revolutionaries ought to be given liberty, and renounce the severity? These new crimes by the aristocracy are a proof of the necessity of that system. What do the daring attempts of our enemies prove but the weakness with which they have been pursued? They are caused in great measure by the doctrine of mildness that has lately been preached to reassure them. If you are able to listen to such advice, your enemies would accomplish their goal, and receive from your very hands the prize of their last infamies.

What inconsistency there would be in regarding some victories achieved by patriotism as putting an end to all our dangers? Examine our real situation and you will be sensible that vigilance and energy are more necessary than ever. A secret opposition against all the operations of the government; the fatal influence of foreign courts, though hidden, is nevertheless active and to be feared. It is evident that crime that has been intimidated has only covered its operations with more care and cunning.

The internal enemies of the French people are divided into two factions, which form the two armies. They march under different colors, by different routes; but they go toward the same goal, the disorganization of the popular government, the overthrow of the convention, that is, the triumph of tyranny. One of these factions endeavors to make us swerve to the side of a fatal weakness; the other drives us to excess. The one desires to transform liberty into a drunken reveler; the other into a prostitute.

Inferior intriguers, often even good citizens misled, take one or the other side; but the chiefs of both belong to the cause of royalty or aristocracy, and cooperate against the patriots. Villains while at war with one another bear less hatred to each other than they abhor honest men. The country is their prey; they fight to divide it; but they are leagued against those who defend it.

One faction has been called moderates; there is perhaps more fancy than truth in the appellation of ultra-revolutionist, by which the others are distinguished. This appellation, which can in no wise be applied to those with good intentions are sometimes carried beyond the bounds of wholesome policy of the revolution, by zeal or ignorance, does not characterize those treacherous beings in the pay of tyrants, whose task it is to throw an odium on the revolution by a false or exaggerated application of the sacred principles of our revolution.

The feigned revolutionary falls perhaps more often on this side than on that side of the revolution. He is, however, now moderate, now revolutionary to madness, according to circumstances. In the Prussian, English, Austrian, and even Moscovy committees it is every day settled what he will think the next day. He opposes energetic measures and executes them when he has not been able to defeat them: Severe against innocence, but indulgent to crime. Denouncing both the guilty who are not rich enough to buy his silence or powerful enough to deserve his service, but ever cautious not to expose himself by undertaking the cause of slandered virtue: unveiling at times plots already discovered, and unmasking traitors already unmasked, or even beheaded; but loud in the praise of living conspirators, who command an influence. Ever ready to embrace the opinion of the moment, but not less attentive never to enlighten it, much less to shock it. Ever ready to adopt high-toned measures, provided they have great inconveniences attached to them; slandering such as only hold out advantages, or adding to them such amendments as may render them harmful. Telling truth with sparseness, just so as to acquire a right to lie with impunity; and distilling good drop by drop, but pouring out evil at a torrent; full of fire for such high-sounding resolutions that mean nothing; more than indifferent to such as can do honor to the cause of the people and be beneficial to the country. Laying great show of patriotism; much attached, like the pious, he would rather wear out a hundred red caps than be guilty of a good action.

What difference is there between these and the moderates? They are servants of the same master, or, if you please, accomplices in villainy, who pretend to quarrel with each other the better to conceal their crimes. Judge them not by the difference of their professions, but by the identicalness in the result of their goals. He who attacks the convention in violent declamations and he that deceives to betray it, are they not agreed? He who by unjust severity obliges patriotism to tremble for its safety makes interest to obtain a pardon for aristocracy and treachery. There were monsters who, while they instigated France to attempt the conquest of the world, had no other view than to assist tyrants in the conquest of France. The hypocritical foreigner who for five years did not cease to proclaim Paris the capital of the universe was only translating into another jargon the anathemas of the vile federalists, who devoted Paris to destruction. To preach up atheism is only one way of absolving superstition and accusing philosophy; and war declared against the deity is only a diversion in favor of royalty.

What other means are there of combating liberty?

Will the example of the first champions of the aristocracy be followed, praising the sweets of slavery and the advantages of monarchy, the supernatural genius and the incomparable virtues of kings?

Will the rights of man and the eternal principles of justice be proclaimed as empty sounds?

Will nobility and priestcraft be dragged from their graves or will the right of the high bourgeoisie to enjoy the privileges of both orders be claimed?

No. It is more convenient to assume the mask of patriotism, to disfigure by disgraceful parodies the sublime drama of the revolution, to endanger the cause of liberty by a hypocritical moderation or by studied extravagances.

Hence aristocracy instituted popular societies; counter-revolutionary pride concealed under rags its schemes and daggers. Fanaticism overthrows its own altars; royalism chants the victories of the republic; nobility, haunted by its recollection of lost influence, tenderly embraces equality to smother it; tyranny dyed with the blood of the defenders of liberty strews flowers on their tomb. If all hearts are not regenerated, how many faces wear masks? How many traitors only meddle with our affairs to ruin them!

Do you wish to put them to the proof, require of them real services instead of oaths and declamations.

Is it necessary to take action? They talk on and on. Is it necessary to deliberate? They wait to start taking action. Are the times peaceable? They oppose every useful change. Are the times tempestuous? They propose reforming everything, in order to throw all into confusion. If you endeavour to repress the seditious, they tell you of the clemency of Caesar. Do you wish to rescue patriots from persecution? Then the firmness of Brutus is their theme. They find out that such a one belonged to the nobility, while he is serving the republic, and they forget everything except that he was treasonous. Is peace desirable? They enlarge on the advantage of victory. Is war necessary? They are eloquent about the blessings of peace. Is the territory to be defended? They are for punishing the tyrants beyond the mountains and seas. Are our fortresses to be retaken? They are now for storming churches and scaling the heavens. They forget the Austrians in order to make war on the devoted. Is it necessary to assist our cause by securing the fidelity of our allies, then they declaim against all the governments that exist and would propose to pass a decree of accusation against the Grand Mogul himself. Do the people flock to the capital to return thanks to the gods for their victories? They break into pitiful mourning-songs for our past misfortunes. Is there news of achieving success? They spread in the midst of us hatreds, divisions, persecutions, and discouragement. Is it necessary to render the sovereignty of the people active and concentrate its force by a firm and respectable government? They find that the principles of government are an infringement on the sovereignty of the people. Are the rights of the people to be pleaded against the oppression of the government? They speak of nothing but respect for the laws and of the obedience due to the constituted authorities.

They have found an admirable expedient to second the efforts of the republican government; that is, completely to disorganize and degrade it, and to make war on all patriots who have contributed to our success.

Do you look for ways to provision our armies? Do you endeavor to wrest from avarice or timidity the provisions they hold and conceal? They very patriotically lament the public misfortunes and announce an approaching famine. The wish of averting evil is a means with them of increasing it. In the north, fowls were killed, and a scarcity of eggs produced, under the pretext that fowls eat grain; in the south, it was proposed to destroy the mulberry and orange trees, under the pretext that silk is an article of luxury and oranges superfluous.

You could never have imagined some of the excesses committed by hypocritical counter-revolutionaries in order to blight the cause of the revolution. Would you believe that in the regions where superstition has held the greatest sway, the counter-revolutionaries are not content with burdening religious observances under all the forms that could render them odious, but have spread terror among the people by sowing the rumor that all children under ten and all old men over seventy are going to be killed? This rumor was spread particularly through the former province of Brittany and in the departments of the Rhine and the Moselle. It is one of the crimes imputed to the former public prosecutor of the criminal court of Strasbourg. That man's tyrannical follies make everything that has been said of Caligula and Heliogabalus credible; one can scarcely believe it, despite the evidence. He pushed his delirium to the point of commandeering women for his own use—we are told that he even employed that method in selecting a wife. Whence came this sudden swarm of foreigners, priests, nobles, intriguers of all kinds, which at the same instant spread over the length and breadth of the Republic, seeking to execute, in the name of philosophy, a plan of counter-revolution which has only been stopped by the force of public reason? Execrable conception, worthy of the genius of foreign courts leagued against liberty, and of the corruption of all the internal enemies of the Republic!

It is thus, that to the miracles constantly produced by the virtue of a great people, intrigue always unites the lowest crimes, crime commanded by the tyrants, and which afterward form the subject of their ridiculous manifestoes, to keep their ignorant subjects in the abject state of oppression and in the chains of slavery.

Eh! What relation is there between liberty and the infamy of its enemies? The sun, though obscured by a passing cloud, is he less the great vivifying principle of nature? Does the scum, which the ocean throws on its shores, diminish its grandeur?

In deceitful hands all the remedies for our ills turn into poisons. Everything you can do, everything you can say, they will turn against you, even the truths which we come here to present this very day.

They do all in their power, for example, after having sewn the seeds of civil war, by a violent attack on all religious prejudices; they will even endeavor to turn the measures which a wholesome policy has dictated in favor of religious freedom into arming fanaticism and aristocracy. If you had permitted the conspiracy to proceed, it would sooner or later have produced a dreadful and universal opposition to the progress of the revolution; if you check it, they will endeavor to protect the priests and moderates. You must not even be astonished if those priests who have most openly confessed their religious quackery should be found the authors of this system.

If the patriots, carried away by the warmth of an honest zeal have at any time been the dupes of their intrigues, they throw the blame on the patriots; for the first principle in their Machiavelian doctrine is to ruin the Republic by ruining the Republicans, just as a country is subjugated by the destruction of the army that defends it. Hence one of their favorite maxims may be understood, which is, that the lives of men must not be regarded—a regal maxim, which means that all friends of liberty should be put in their power.

It is to be observed that the fate of men who seek the public good only is to be the victim of those who consult their own interest only, which proceeds from two causes. The first, that the intriguers attack with the vices of the ancient government; the second, that the patriots only defend themselves with the virtues of the new.

Such an internal situation ought to seem to you worthy of all your attention, above all if you reflect that at the same time you have the tyrants of Europe to combat, a million and two hundred thousand men under arms to maintain, and that the government is obliged continually to repair, with energy and vigilance, all the ill which the innumerable multitude of our enemies has prepared for us during the course of five years.

What is the remedy for all these evils? We know no other than the development of that general motive force of the Republic—virtue.

Democracy perishes by two kinds of excess: either the aristocracy of those who govern, or else the popular scorn for the authorities whom the people themselves have established, scorn which makes each clique, each individual take unto himself the public power and bring the people through excessive disorders, to annihilation or to the power of one man.

The double task of the moderates and the false revolutionaries is to toss us back and forth perpetually between these two perils.

But the people's representatives can avoid them both, because government is always the master at being just and wise; and, when it has that character, it is certain of the confidence of the people.

It is very true that the goal of all our enemies is to dissolve the Convention. It is true that the tyrant of Great Britain and his allies promise their parliament and subjects that they will deprive you of your energy and of the public confidence which you have merited; that is the first lesson taught all their agents.

But it is a truth that ought to be regarded as trivial in politics that a large body invested with the confidence of a great people can only be destroyed by its own misconduct. Your enemies are convinced of this, and therefore do not doubt but they will endeavor to awaken among you all those passions which will back up their sinister designs.

What can they do against the national representation unless they succeed in influencing the adoption of impolitic measures which may furnish pretexts for their criminal declamations? They must therefore necessarily wish to have two kinds of agents, the ones endeavoring to degrade it by their slanders, the others, who even in its bosom will strive to deceive it, to hazard the glory and interests of the republic.

To attack it with success, it was politic to begin the war against the representatives in the departments which had shown confidence in your measures, and go against the Committee of Public Safety. They were therefore attacked by men who appeared to disagree among themselves.

What could they do better than paralyze the government of the convention and destroy all its spirits at a time when the fate of the republic and of tyrants rested on its measures?

Far from us be the idea that there yet exists among us a man so vile as to wish to serve the cause of tyrants! But still farther from us be the crime, which could not be forgiven us, of deceiving the National Convention and betraying the French people by guilty silence! For there is one circumstance much in favor of a free people, that truth while it is the bane of despots is the life of freemen. It is certain that there is yet one danger which our liberty has to run, the only danger perhaps to be feared: it is the plan which has existed of rallying all the enemies of the republic by bringing into action a party spirit; of persecuting all patriots, discouraging and causing the ruin of the faithful agents of the republican government, to oppose its operations. It has been endeavored to deceive the convention upon persons and things; it has been misled as to the causes of the abuses which are exaggerated in order to prevent the possibility of applying a remedy; terror has been a weapon in the hands of their enemies to mislead or paralyze it; they look to divide; it is endeavored particularly to create divisions among the representatives sent to the departments and the Committee of Public Safety; the first were to be induced to counteract the central authority, in order to lead to disorder and confusion; on their return it was endeavored to sour their minds, to render them the instruments of a faction. Foreigners make good use of all private passions, even of misled patriotism.

At first a more direct road was intended to have been pursued, that of slandering the Committee of Public Safety. It was hoped they would be unable to bear the weight of their arduous duty. The victories and good fortune of the French people have been their shield. Since that time it has been attempted by praises to condemn them to inaction and destroy the fruits of their labors. All those vague declamations against the necessary agents of the Committee, all the plans of disorganization disguised under the appellation of reforms, rejected by the Convention, and again brought forward now by foreign influence; the warmth with which the intrigues unmasked by the Committee, have been been praised; the terror with which good citizens have been struck, the indulgence with which conspirators are treated, all that system of imposture and intrigue, of which the principal author is a man, you expelled from among you, is aimed at the welfare of the National Convention and tends to realize the wishes of all the enemies of France.

It is since the time when that system was announced in libelous writings and was begun to be in practice, that aristocracy and royalism have begun to raise their insolent heads, that patriotism has again been persecuted in a position of the republic; that the national authority experience an opposition on which intriguers began to lose the habit. Indeed, if these indirect attacks had had no other inconvenience than to divide the attention and energy of those who have borne the important burden which men have laid on them, and to draw off their attention from the important measures of public safety, in order to counteract dangerous intrigues, even then they might be considered as essentially serving the interests of our enemies.

But let us keep courage; this is the sanctuary of truth; here sit the founders of the republic, the avengers of humanity, the destroyers of tyrants.

Here to destroy an abuse it is sufficient to point it out. It is enough for us to appeal, in the name of our country, from the persuasions of self-love or the weakness of individuals to the virtue and glory of the National Convention.

We call for a solemn discussion upon all the subjects of its [the Convention's] inquietude, and on all that can influence the progress of the Revolution. We entreat that no private interest or secret motive be permitted here to usurp the place of the general will of the assembly, and the eternal power of reason.

We shall content ourselves this day with proposing that you should sanction with your formal approbation on the moral and political truths on which your internal administration and the stability of the republic should be founded, as you have already sanctioned the principles of your conduct towards foreign peoples: Thus you will rally all good citizens, you will deprive conspirators of all hope; you will assure your measures, and confound the intrigues and slanders of kings; you will do honor to your cause and character in the eyes of all people.

Give to the French people this new pledge of your zeal in protecting patriotism, of your inflexible justice towards the guilty, and of your devotion to the cause of the people. Order that the principles of political morality which we have just developed be proclaimed, in your name, claimed, in your name within and beyond the borders of the republic.

NAPOLEON BONAPARTE

Address to his Troops at the Beginning
of the Russian Campaign

May 1812

Napoleon Bonaparte (1769–1821) was born in Corsica, which came under French power in 1770. He shined as an officer during the years of the French Revolution and by 1796 was the commander of the Army of the Interior. He was so successful in battle that he led an army to Egypt and took control of that country. In 1800, with the government in disarray, he became France's First Consul and then in 1804 Emperor. Militarily dominating much of Europe, he decided to challenge Russia, and thereby led a half a million men to their destruction. In 1814 he abdicated his emperorship, and after an ill-fated return in 1815, he was exiled.

Soldiers:

The second war of Poland has commenced. The first war terminated at Friedland and Tilsit. At Tilsit, Russia swore eternal alliance with France, and war with England. She has openly violated her oath, and refuses to offer any explanation of her strange conduct till the French Eagle shall have passed the Rhine, and, consequently, shall have left her allies at her discretion. Russia is impelled onward by fatality. Her destiny is about to be accomplished. Does she believe that we have degenerated? That we are no longer the soldiers of Austerlitz? She has placed us between dishonor and war. The choice cannot for an instant be doubtful.

Let us march forward, then, and crossing the Niemen, carry the war into her territories. The second war of Poland will be to the French army as glorious as the first. But our next peace must carry with it its own guarantee, and put an end to that arrogant influence which, for the last fifty years, Russia has exercised over the affairs of Europe.

PRESIDENT ANDREW JACKSON

"Indian Removal"

Seventh Annual Message to Congress

("they cannot live in contact with a civilized
community and prosper")

Washington, D.C.

December 7, 1835

Andrew Jackson (1767–1845) made his name as the general who defeated the British at the Battle of New Orleans in the War of 1812. Though an important and well-regarded president (he served two terms), he was known for his belligerence toward the native peoples and continually encouraged the take-over of their treaty-granted lands by white settlers. He describes in this excerpt from his presidential address the supposed generosity of the government forcing the removal of the Cherokees, who had been prospering in Georgia for many years. This betrayal was one of many in a series of treaties broken by the U.S. government. In 1837, after Jackson's leaving office, several thousand Native Americans died on "The Trail of Tears."

The plan of removing the aboriginal people who yet remain within the settled portions of the United States to the country west of the Mississippi River approaches its consummation. It was adopted on the most mature consideration of the condition of this race, and ought to be persisted in till the object is accomplished, and prosecuted with as much vigor as a just regard to their circumstances will permit, and as fast as their consent can be obtained. All preceding experiments for the improvement of the Indians have failed. It seems now to be an established fact they cannot live in contact with a civilized community and prosper. Ages of fruitless endeavors have at length brought us to a knowledge of this principle of intercommunication with them. The past we cannot recall, but the future we can provide for. Independently of the treaty stipulations into which we have entered with the various tribes for the usufructuary rights they have ceded to us, no one can doubt the moral duty of the Government of the United States to protect and if possible to preserve and perpetuate the scattered remnants of this race which are left within our borders. In the discharge of this duty an extensive region in the West has been assigned for their permanent residence. It has been divided into districts and allotted among them. Many have already removed and others are preparing to go, and with the exception of two small bands living in Ohio and Indiana, not exceeding 1,500 persons, and of the Cherokees, all the tribes on the east side of the Mississippi, and extending from Lake Michigan to Florida, have entered into engagements which will lead to their transplantation.

The plan for their removal and reestablishment is founded upon the knowledge we have gained of their character and habits, and has been dictated by a spirit of enlarged liberality. A territory exceeding in extent that relinquished has been granted to each tribe. Of its climate, fertility, and capacity to support an Indian population the representations are highly favorable. To these districts the Indians are removed at the expense of the United States, and with certain supplies of clothing, arms, ammunition, and other indispensable articles; they are also furnished gratuitously with provisions for the period of a year after their arrival at their new homes. In that time, from the nature of the country and of the products raised by them, they can subsist themselves by agricultural labor, if they choose to resort to that mode of life; if they do not they are upon the skirts of the great prairies, where countless herds of buffalo roam, and a short time suffices to adapt their own habits to the changes which a change of the animals destined for their food may require. Ample arrangements have also been made for the support of schools; in some instances council houses and churches are to be erected, dwellings constructed for the chiefs, and mills for common use. Funds have been set apart for the maintenance of the poor; the most necessary mechanical arts have been introduced, and blacksmiths, gunsmiths, wheelwrights, millwrights, etc., are supported among them. Steel and iron, and sometimes salt, are purchased for them, and plows and other farming utensils, domestic animals, looms, spinning wheels, cards, etc., are presented to them. And besides these beneficial arrangements, annuities are in all cases paid, amounting in some instances to more than $30 for each individual of the tribe, and in all cases sufficiently great, if justly divided and prudently expended, to enable them, in addition to their own exertions, to live comfortably. And as a stimulus for exertion, it is now provided by law that "in all cases of the appointment of interpreters or other persons employed for the benefit of the Indians a preference shall be given to persons of Indian descent, if such can be found who are properly qualified for the discharge of the duties."

Such are the arrangements for the physical comfort and for the moral improvement of the Indians. The necessary measures for their political advancement and for their separation from our citizens have not been neglected. The pledge of the United States has been given by Congress that the country destined for the residence of this people shall be forever "secured and guaranteed to them." A country west of Missouri and Arkansas has been assigned to them, into which the white settlements are not to be pushed. No political communities can be formed in that extensive region, except those which are established by the Indians themselves or by the Untied States for them and with their concurrence. A barrier has thus been raised for their protection against the encroachment of our citizens, and guarding the Indians as far as possible from those evils which have brought them to their present condition. Summary authority has been given by law to destroy all ardent spirits found in their country, without waiting the doubtful result and slow process of a legal seizure. I consider the absolute and unconditional interdiction of this article among these people as the first and great step in their melioration. Halfway measures will answer no purpose. These cannot successfully contend against the cupidity of the seller and the overpowering appetite of the buyer. And the destructive effects of the traffic are marked in every page of the history of our Indian intercourse.

Some general legislation seems necessary for the regulation of the relations which will exist in this new state of things between the Government and the people of the United States, and these transplanted Indian tribes; and for the establishment among the latter, and with their own consent, of some principles of intercommunication, which their juxtaposition will call for; that moral may be substituted for physical force; the authority of a few and simple laws for the tomahawk; and that an end may be put to those bloody wars, whose prosecution seems to have made part of their social system.

After the further details of this arrangement are completed, with a very general supervision over them, they ought to be left to the progress of events. These, I indulge the hope, will secure their prosperity and improvement and a large portion of the moral debt we owe them will then be paid....

JOHN C. CALHOUN

U.S. Senator from South Carolina

On the Reception of Abolition Petitions

("We of the South will not, cannot,
surrender our institutions")

Washington, D.C.

February 6, 1837

Calhoun (1782–1850) was a fearless, conscienceless defender of the justice of slavery. He was vice president of the United States from 1825 to 1832, and then served in the U.S. Senate as well as a taking a spell as Secretary of State under President John Tyler. After his death, he became a patron devil of the Southern slaveholding interests who, having taken him at his word ("Abolition and the Union cannot co-exist") instigated secession and the Civil War. In this speech, outraged by the abolitionists' moral objections to slavery, Calhoun blusters: "... let me not be understood as admitting, even by implication, that the existing relations between the two races in the slaveholding States is an evil:—far otherwise; I hold it to be a good, as it has thus far proved itself to be to both, and will continue to prove so if not disturbed by the fell spirit of abolition."

If the time of the Senate permitted, I would feel it to be my duty to call for the reading of the mass of petitions on the table, in order that we might know what language they hold towards the slaveholding states and their institutions; but as it will not, I have selected, indiscriminately from the pile, two; one from those in manuscript, and the other from the printed, and without knowing their contents will call for the reading of them, so that we may judge, by them, of the character of the whole.

(Here the Secretary, on the call of Mr. Calhoun, read the two petitions.)

Such is the language held towards us and ours. The peculiar institution of the South—that, on the maintenance of which the very existence of the slaveholding States depends, is pronounced to be sinful and odious, in the sight of God and man; and this with a systematic design of rendering us hateful in the eyes of the world— with a view to a general crusade against us and our institutions. This, too, in the legislative halls of the Union; created by these confederated States, for the better protection of their peace, their safety, and their respective institutions;—and yet, we, the representatives of twelve of these sovereign States against whom this deadly war is waged, are expected to sit here in silence, hearing ourselves and our constituents day after day denounced, without uttering a word; for if we but open our lips, the charge of agitation is resounded on all sides, and we are held up as seeking to aggravate the evil which we resist. Every reflecting mind must see in all this a state of things deeply and dangerously diseased.

I do not belong to the school which holds that aggression is to be met by concession. Mine is the opposite creed, which teaches that encroachments must be met at the beginning, and, that those who act on the opposite principle are prepared to become slaves. In this case, in particular, I hold concession or compromise to be fatal. If we concede an inch, concession would follow concession—compromise would follow compromise, until our ranks would be so broken that effectual resistance would be impossible. We must meet the enemy on the frontier, with a fixed determination of maintaining our position at every hazard. Consent to receive these insulting petitions, and the next demand will be that they be referred to a committee in order that they may be deliberated and acted upon. At the last session we were modestly asked to receive them, simply to lay them on the table, without any view to ulterior action. I then told the Senator from Pennsylvania (*Mr. Buchanan*), who so strongly urged that course in the Senate, that it was a position that could not be maintained; as the argument in favor of acting on the petitions if we were bound to receive, could not be resisted. I then said, that the next step would be to refer the petition to a committee, and I already see indications that such is now the intention. If we yield, that will be followed by another, and we will thus proceed, step by step, to the final consummation of the object of these petitions. We are now told that the most effectual mode of arresting the progress of abolition is, to reason it down; and with this view it is urged that the petitions ought to be referred to a committee. That is the very ground which was taken at the last session in the other House, but instead of arresting its progress it has since advanced more rapidly than ever. The most unquestionable right may be rendered doubtful, if once admitted to be a subject of controversy, and that would be the case in the present instance. The subject is beyond the jurisdiction of Congress—they have no right to touch it in any shape or form, or to make it the subject of deliberation or discussion.

In opposition to this view it is urged that Congress is bound by the constitution to receive petitions in every case and on every subject, whether within its constitutional competency or not. I hold the doctrine to be absurd, and do solemnly believe, that it would be as easy to prove that it has the right to abolish slavery, as that it is bound to receive petitions for that purpose. The very existence of the rule that requires a question to be put on the reception of petitions is conclusive to show that there is no such obligation. It has been a standing rule from the commencement of the Government, and clearly shows the sense of those who formed the constitution on this point. The question on the reception would be absurd, if, as is contended, we are bound to receive; but I do not intend to argue the question; I discussed it fully at the last session, and the arguments then advanced neither have been nor can be answered.

As widely as this incendiary spirit has spread, it has not yet infected this body, or the great mass of the intelligent and business portion of the North; but unless it be speedily stopped, it will spread and work upwards till it brings the two great sections of the Union into deadly conflict. This is not a new impression with me. Several years since, in a discussion with one of the Senators from Massachusetts (*Mr. Webster*), before this fell spirit had showed itself, I then predicted that the doctrine of the proclamation and the Force Bill,—that this Government had a right, in the last resort, to determine the extent of its own powers, and enforce its decision at the point of the bayonet, which was so warmly maintained by that Senator, would at no distant day arouse the dormant spirit of abolitionism. I told him that the doctrine was tantamount to the assumption of unlimited power on the part of the Government, and that such would be the impression on the public mind in a large portion of the Union. The consequences would be inevitable. A large portion of the Northern States believed slavery to be a sin, and would consider it as an obligation of conscience to abolish it if they should feel themselves in any degree responsible for its continuance,—and that this doctrine would necessarily lead to the belief of such responsibility. I then predicted that it would commence as it has with this fanatical portion of society, and that they would begin their operations on the ignorant, the weak, the young, and the thoughtless,—and gradually extend upwards till they would become strong enough to obtain political control, when he and others holding the highest stations in society, would, however reluctant, be compelled to yield to their doctrines, or be driven into obscurity. But four years have since elapsed, and all this is already in a course of regular fulfilment.

Standing at the point of time at which we have now arrived, it will not be more difficult to trace the course of future events now than it was then. They who imagine that the spirit now abroad in the North, will die away of itself without a shock or convulsion, have formed a very inadequate conception of its real character; it will continue to rise and spread, unless prompt and efficient measures to stay its progress be adopted. Already it has taken possession of the pulpit, of the schools, and, to a considerable extent, of the press; those great instruments by which the mind of the rising generation will be formed.

They who imagine that the spirit now abroad in the North will die away of itself without a shock or convulsion, have formed a very inadequate conception of its real character; it will continue to rise and spread, unless prompt and efficient measures to stay its progress be adopted. Already it has taken possession of the pulpit, of the schools, and, to a considerable extent, of the press; those great instruments by which the mind of the rising generation will be formed.

However sound the great body of the non-slaveholding States are at present, in the course of a few years they will be succeeded by those who will have been taught to hate the people and institutions of nearly one-half of this Union, with a hatred more deadly than one hostile nation ever entertained toward another. It is easy to see the end. By the necessary course of events, if left to themselves, we must become, finally, two people. It is impossible under the deadly hatred which must spring up between the two great sections, if the present causes are permitted to operate unchecked, that we should continue under the same political system. The conflicting elements would burst the Union asunder, powerful as are the links which hold it together.

Abolition and the Union cannot co-exist. As the friend of the Union, I openly proclaim it,—and the sooner it is known the better. The former may now be controlled, but in a short time it will be beyond the power of man to arrest the course of events. We of the South will not, cannot, surrender our institutions. To maintain the existing relations between the two races, inhabiting that section of the Union, is indispensable to the peace and happiness of both. It cannot be subverted without drenching the country in blood, and extirpating one or the other of the races. Be it good or bad, it has grown up with our society and institutions, and is so interwoven with them, that to destroy it would be to destroy us as a people. But let me not be understood as admitting, even by implication, that the existing relations between the two races in the slaveholding States is an evil:—far otherwise; I hold it to be a good, as it has thus far proved itself to be to both, and will continue to prove so if not disturbed by the fell spirit of abolition. I appeal to facts. Never before has the black race of Central Africa, from the dawn of history to the present day, attained a condition so civilized and so improved, not only physically, but morally and intellectually. It came among us in a low, degraded, and savage condition, and in the course of a few generations it has grown up under the fostering care of our institutions, reviled as they have been, to its present comparatively civilized condition. This, with the rapid increase of numbers, is conclusive proof of the general happiness of the race, in spite of all the exaggerated tales to the contrary. In the mean time, the white or European race has not degenerated. It has kept pace with its brethren in other sections of the Union where slavery does not exist. It is odious to make comparison; but I appeal to all sides whether the South is not equal in virtue, intelligence, patriotism, courage, disinterestedness, and all the high qualities which adorn our nature. I ask whether we have not contributed our full share of talents and political wisdom in forming and sustaining this political fabric; and whether we have not constantly inclined most strongly to the side of liberty, and been the first to see and first to resist the encroachments of power. In one thing only are we inferior—the arts of gain; we acknowledge that we are less wealthy than the Northern section of this Union, but I trace this mainly to the fiscal action of this Government, which has extracted much from and spent little among us. Had it been the reverse—if the exaction had been from the other section, and the expenditure with us—this point of superiority would not be against us now, as it was not at the formation of this Government.

But I take higher ground. I hold that in the present state of civilization, where two races of different origin, and distinguished by color, and other physical differences, as well as intellectual, are brought together, the relation now existing in the slaveholding States between the two, is, instead of an evil, a good—a positive good. I feel myself called upon to speak freely upon the subject where the honor and interests of those I represent are involved. I hold then, that there never has yet existed a wealthy and civilized society in which one portion of the community did not, in point of fact, live on the labor of the other. Broad and general as is this assertion, it is fully borne out by history. This is not the proper occasion, but if it were, it would not be difficult to trace the various devices by which the wealth of all civilized communities has been so unequally divided, and to show by what means so small a share has been allotted to those by whose labor it was produced, and so large a share given to the nonproducing classes. The devices are almost innumerable, from the brute force and gross superstition of ancient times, to the subtle and artful fiscal contrivances of modern. I might well challenge a comparison between them and the more direct, simple, and patriarchal mode by which the labor of the African race is, among us, commanded by the European.

I may say with truth, that in few countries so much is left to the share of the laborer, and so little exacted from him, or where there is more kind attention paid to him in sickness or infirmities of age. Compare his condition with the tenants of the poor houses in the more civilized portions of Europe—look at the sick, and the old and infirm slave, on one hand, in the midst of his family and friends, under the kind superintending care of his master and mistress, and compare it with the forlorn and wretched condition of the pauper in the poor house. But I will not dwell on this aspect of the question; I turn to the political; and here I fearlessly assert that the existing relation between the two races in the South, against which these blind fanatics are waging war, forms the most solid and durable foundation on which to rear free and stable political institutions. It is useless to disguise the fact. There is and always has been in an advanced stage of wealth and civilization, a conflict between labor and capital. The condition of society in the South exempts us from the disorders and dangers resulting from this conflict; and which explains why it is that the political condition of the slaveholding States has been so much more stable and quiet than that of the North. The advantages of the former, in this respect, will become more and more manifest if left undisturbed by interference from without, as the country advances in wealth and numbers.

We have, in fact, but just entered that condition of society where the strength and durability of our political institutions are to be tested; and I venture nothing in predicting that the experience of the next generation will fully test how vastly more favorable our condition of society is to that of other sections for free and stable institutions, provided we are not disturbed by the interference of others, or shall have sufficient intelligence and spirit to resist promptly and successfully such interference. It rests with ourselves to meet and repel them.

I look not for aid to this government, or to the other states; not but there are kind feelings toward us on the part of the great body of the non-slaveholding states; but, as kind as their feelings may be, we may rest assured that no political party in those States will risk their ascendancy for our safety. If we do not defend ourselves, none will defend us; if we yield we will be more and more pressed as we recede; and if we submit we will be trampled under foot. Be assured that emancipation itself would not satisfy these fanatics: that gained, the next step would be to raise the negroes to a social and political equality with the whites; and, that being effected, we would soon find the present condition of the two races reversed. They, and their northern allies, would be the masters, and we the slaves; the condition of the white race in the British West India Islands, bad as it is, would be happiness to ours; there the mother country is interested in sustaining the supremacy of the European race. It is true that the authority of the former master is destroyed, but the African will there still be a slave, not to individuals but to the community,—forced to labor, not by the authority of the overseer, but by the bayonet of the soldiery and the rod of the civil magistrate.

Surrounded as the slaveholding States are with such imminent perils, I rejoice to think that our means of defence are ample, if we shall prove to have the intelligence and spirit to see and apply them before it is too late. All we want is concert, to lay aside all party differences, and unite with zeal and energy in repelling approaching dangers. Let there be concert of action, and we shall find ample means of security without resorting to secession or disunion. I speak with full knowledge and a thorough examination of the subject, and for one, see my way clearly. One thing alarms me—the eager pursuit of gain which overspreads the land, and which absorbs every faculty of the mind and every feeling of the heart. Of all passions avarice is the most blind and compromising—the last to see and the first to yield to danger. I dare not hope that any thing I can say will arouse the South to a due sense of danger; I fear it is beyond the power of mortal voice to awaken it in time from the fatal security into which it has fallen.

JEFFERSON DAVIS
"On Withdrawal from the Union"
Farewell Address to the U.S. Senate
("This is done . . . from the high and solemn motive of defending and protecting the rights we inherited, and which it is our sacred duty to transmit unshorn to our children.")
Senate Chamber, Washington, D.C.
January 21, 1861

The former Secretary of War and Vice President of the United States was a year older than Abraham Lincoln and also born in Kentucky. Davis here announces his resignation from the United States Senate on the principle of defending slavery for his home state of Mississippi, which had seceded from the Union on January 9. A few weeks later, in February 1861, Davis (1808–1889) became the President of the Confederate States of America.

The Civil War began in April. After the war's end in 1865, he was arrested and served two years in prison. He seems never to have repented for his support of slavery, his treason against the United States, or his leadership of a war that cost more than a half-million lives.

I rise, Mr. President, for the purpose of announcing to the Senate that I have satisfactory evidence that the State of Mississippi, by a solemn ordinance of her people in convention assembled, has declared her separation from the United States. Under these circumstances, of course my functions are terminated here. It has seemed to me proper, however, that I should appear in the Senate to announce that fact to my associates, and I will say but very little more. The occasion does not invite me to go into argument; and my physical condition would not permit me to do so if it were otherwise; and yet it seems to become me to say something on the part of the State I here represent, on an occasion so solemn as this.

It is known to Senators who have served with me here, that I have for many years advocated, as an essential attribute of State sovereignty, the right of a State to secede from the Union. Therefore, if I had not believed there was justifiable cause; if I had thought that Mississippi was acting without sufficient provocation, or without an existing necessity, I should still, under my theory of the Government, because of my allegiance to the State of which I am a citizen, have been bound by her action. I, however, may be permitted to say that I do think she has justifiable cause, and I approve of her act. I conferred with her people before that act was taken, counseled them then that if the state of things which they apprehended should exist when the convention met, they should take the action which they have now adopted.

I hope none who hear me will confound this expression of mine with the advocacy of the right of a State to remain in the Union, and to disregard its constitutional obligations by the nullification of the law. Such is not my theory. Nullification and secession, so often confounded, are indeed antagonistic principles. Nullification is a remedy which it is sought to apply within the Union, and against the agent of the States. It is only to be justified when the agent has violated his constitutional obligation, and a State, assuming to judge for itself, denies the right of the agent thus to act, and appeals to the other States of the Union for a decision; but when the States themselves, and when the people of the States, have so acted as to convince us that they will not regard our constitutional rights, then, and then for the first time, arises the doctrine of secession in its practical application.

A great man who now reposes with his fathers, and who has been often arraigned for a want of fealty to the Union, advocated the doctrine of nullification, because it preserved the Union. It was because of his deep-seated attachment to the Union, his determination to find some remedy for existing ills short of a severance of the ties which bound South Carolina to the other States, that Mr. John C. Calhoun advocated the doctrine of nullification, which he proclaimed to be peaceful, to be within the limits of State power, not to disturb the Union, but only to be a means of bringing the agent before the tribunal of the States for their judgment.

Secession belongs to a different class of remedies. It is to be justified upon the basis that the States are sovereign. There was a time when none denied it. I hope the time may come again, when a better comprehension of the theory of our Government, and the inalienable rights of the people of the States, will prevent any one from denying that each State is a sovereign, and thus may reclaim the grants which it has made to any agent whomsoever.

I therefore say I concur in the action of the people of Mississippi, believing it to be necessary and proper, and should have been bound by their action if my belief had been otherwise; and this brings me to the important point which I wish on this last occasion to present to the Senate. It is by this confounding of nullification and secession that the name of a great man, whose ashes now mingle with his mother earth, has been invoked to justify coercion against a seceded State. The phrase "to execute the laws," was an expression which General Jackson applied to the case of a State refusing to obey the laws while yet a member of the Union. That is not the case which is now presented. The laws are to be executed over the United States, and upon the people of the United States. They have no relation to any foreign country. It is a perversion of terms; at least it is a great misapprehension of the case, which cites that expression for application to a State which has withdrawn from the Union. You may make war on a foreign State. If it be the purpose of gentlemen, they may make war against a State which has withdrawn from the Union; but there are no laws of the United States to be executed within the limits of a seceded State. A State finding herself in the condition in which Mississippi has judged she is, in which her safety requires that she should provide for the maintenance of her rights out of the Union, surrenders all the benefits, (and they are known to be many,) deprives herself of the advantages, (they are known to be great,) severs all the ties of affection, (and they are close and enduring,) which have bound her to the Union; and thus divesting herself of every benefit, taking upon herself every burden, she claims to be exempt from any power to execute the laws of the United States within her limits.

I well remember an occasion when Massachusetts was arraigned before the bar of the Senate, and when then the doctrine of coercion was rife and to be applied against her because of the rescue of a fugitive slave in Boston. My opinion then was the same that it is now. Not in a spirit of egotism, but to show that I am not influenced in my opinion because the case is my own, I refer to that time and that occasion as containing the opinion which I then entertained, and on which my present conduct is based. I then said, if Massachusetts, following her through a stated line of conduct, chooses to take the last step which separates her from the Union, it is her right to go, and I will neither vote one dollar nor one man to coerce her back; but will say to her, God speed, in memory of the kind associations which once existed between her and the other States.

It has been a conviction of pressing necessity; it has been a belief that we are to be deprived in the Union of the rights which our fathers bequeathed to us, which has brought Mississippi into her present decision. She has heard proclaimed the theory that all men are created free and equal, and this made the basis of an attack upon her social institutions; and the sacred Declaration of Independence has been invoked to maintain the position of the equality of the races. That Declaration of Independence is to be construed by the circumstances and purposes for which it was made. The communities were declaring their independence; the people of those communities were asserting that no man was born—to use the language of Mr. Jefferson—booted and spurred to ride over the rest of mankind; that men were created equal—meaning the men of the political community; that there was no divine right to rule; that no man inherited the right to govern; that there were no classes by which power and place descended to families, but that all stations were equally within the grasp of each member of the body-politic. These were the great principles they announced; these were the purposes for which they made their declaration; these were the ends to which their enunciation was directed. They have no reference to the slave; else, how happened it that among the items of arraignment made against George III was that he endeavored to do just what the North has been endeavoring of late to do—to stir up insurrection among our slaves? Had the Declaration announced that the Negroes were free and equal, how was the Prince to be arraigned for stirring up insurrection among them? And how was this to be enumerated among the high crimes which caused the colonies to sever their connection with the mother country? When our Constitution was formed, the same idea was rendered more palpable, for there we find provision made for that very class of persons as property; they were not put upon the footing of equality with white men—not even upon that of paupers and convicts; but, so far as representation was concerned, were discriminated against as a lower caste, only to be represented in the numerical proportion of three fifths.

Then, Senators, we recur to the compact which binds us together; we recur to the principles upon which our Government was founded; and when you deny them, and when you deny to us the right to withdraw from a Government which thus perverted threatens to be destructive of our rights, we but tread in the path of our fathers when we proclaim our independence, and take the hazard. This is done not in hostility to others, not to injure any section of the country, not even for our own pecuniary benefit; but from the high and solemn motive of defending and protecting the rights we inherited, and which it is our sacred duty to transmit unshorn to our children.

I find in myself, perhaps, a type of the general feeling of my constituents towards yours. I am sure I feel no hostility to you, Senators from the North. I am sure there is not one of you, whatever sharp discussion there may have been between us, to whom I cannot now say, in the presence of my God, I wish you well; and such, I am sure, is the feeling of the people whom I represent towards those whom you represent. I therefore feel that I but express their desire when I say I hope, and they hope, for peaceful relations with you, though we must part. They may be mutually beneficial to us in the future, as they have been in the past, if you so will it. The reverse may bring disaster on every portion of the country; and if you will have it thus, we will invoke the God of our fathers, who delivered them from the power of the lion, to protect us from the ravages of the bear; and thus, putting our trust in God and in our own firm hearts and strong arms, we will vindicate the right as best we may.

In the course of my service here, associated at different times with a great variety of Senators, I see now around me some with whom I have served long; there have been points of collision; but whatever of offense there has been to me, I leave here; I carry with me no hostile remembrance. Whatever offense I have given which has not been redressed, or for which satisfaction has not been demanded, I have, Senators, in this hour of our parting, to offer you my apology for any pain which, in heat of discussion, I have inflicted. I go hence unencumbered of the remembrance of any injury received, and having discharged the duty of making the only reparation in my power for any injury offered.

Mr. President, and Senators, having made the announcement which the occasion seemed to me to require, it only remains to me to bid you a final adieu.

KING LEOPOLD II
King of Belgium
Opening Address at the Geographical
Conference on Africa

Brussels, Belgium

September 12, 1876

King Leopold II (1835–1909), frustrated by his small nation's lack of power or wealth, managed, through his agents, including the explorer Henry Morton Stanley, to take over as a personal domain a region in Africa seventy-six times the size of Belgium. He never visited the Congo, but he managed to exploit it for rubber and other natural resources for twenty-three years and in the process bring death and destruction to millions of Africans. Presenting himself here as an advocate for civilizing and Christianizing the people and freeing the region from Arab slave-traders, he would soon have his police force, Force Publique, enslave native people as laborers to build his personal financial empire. Adam Hochschild's history, King Leopold's Ghost (1998), tells the story of Leopold's cynical and cruel quest.

Gentlemen:

Permit me to thank you warmly for the amiable readiness with which you have accepted my invitation. Besides the satisfaction to which I look forward in listening here to the discussion of the problems in the solution of which we are interested, I feel the most vivid pleasure in meeting the distinguished men whose labours and valorous efforts in favour of civilisation I have seen for years.

The subject which unites us today is one of those which deserve in the highest degree to occupy the friends of humanity. To open to civilisation the only part of our globe where it has not yet penetrated, to pierce the darkness which envelops entire populations, is, I dare to say, a crusade worthy of this century of progress; and I am happy to see how much public sentiment is favourable to its accomplishment—the current is with us.

Amongst those who have studied Africa most, many have come to think that it would be an advantage for the common end they pursue to be able to meet and confer, with a view to regulating the movement, to combine the efforts, to share in all the resources, and to avoid useless repetition.

It has appeared to me that Belgium, a central and neutral State, would be a well-chosen ground for such a meeting, and it is that which has encouraged me to summon you all here at my home in the little Conference which I have the great satisfaction in opening today.

Need I tell you that in summoning you to Brussels I have not been guided by egoistical views? No, gentlemen; if Belgium is small, she is happy and satisfied with her lot, and I have no other ambition than to serve her well. But I cannot go so far as to affirm that I should be insensible to the honour which would result for my country that an important movement in a question which will mark our epoch should date from Brussels. I would be happy to have Brussels become in some sort, the headquarters of this civilising movement.

I have ventured to think, therefore, that it would be convenient for you to come to discuss and determine in common the means to follow, and the means to employ to plant, definitely, the standard of civilisation in the soil of Central Africa, to decide on what must be done to interest the public in your noble enterprise, and lead it to the contribution of its obolus. For, gentlemen, in works of this kind it is the assistance of great numbers which makes success, and it is the sympathy of the masses which it is necessary to solicit, and to know how to obtain.

What resources would there not be, indeed, if everyone to whom a franc was nothing, or a very small thing, would consent to pay one into the fund destined for the suppression of the slave trade in the interior of Africa!

Great progress has already been made; the unknown has been stormed from many sides, and if those here present who have enriched science by so many important discoveries wished to recall the principal points again for us, their accounts would be powerful encouragement to everyone.

Amongst the questions which are yet to be examined or referred to are the following:

(1) The precise designation of the basis of operation to be acquired, amongst others, on the coast of Zanzibar, and near the mouth of the Congo, either by conventions with the chiefs, or by purchase or hire from the holders.

(2) The designation of routes to follow successively towards the interior, and of stations—hospital, scientific, and pacificatory—to be organised as a means of abolishing slavery, of establishing concord amongst the chiefs, of procuring for them just and disinterested arbitrators, etc.

(3) The creation, the work being well defined, of an international and central committee, and of national committees, to carry out its

execution, each in that which concerns itself, and to make known its aims to the public everywhere, and make the appeal to charitable sentiment which no good cause has ever made in vain.

Such, gentlemen, are some points which seem to merit your attention. If there are others, they will suggest themselves from your discussions, and you will not fail to elucidate them.

My desire is to serve, in whatever way you indicate to me, the great cause for which you have done so much already. For this end I put myself at your disposal, and I wish you a hearty welcome.

OTTO VON BISMARCK
Chancellor of the German Empire
"A Plea for Imperial Armament"
("We Germans fear God, and nothing else
in the world!")
Reichstag, Berlin
February 6, 1888

Otto Edward Leopold, Prince von Bismarck-Schonhausen (1815–1898) was a Prussian reactionary and royalist. A clever diplomat and political chess-player, he believed nevertheless in the superior effectiveness of "iron and blood." Having helped bring about the unification of Germany in 1870 after the Franco-Prussian War, he was given the title "Prince" and named the Imperial Chancellor of the German Empire, an office he held until 1890. As Chancellor, he attempted to curb papal influence by placing restrictions on Roman Catholics, which led to the emigration of thousands of citizens. During his chancellorship, Germany partook in the detestable "Scramble for Africa." He continually prepared Germany for war, but in the midst of the 1888 Bulgarian Crisis, made it clear he preferred to participate in or provoke only the ones it could win: "It is not fear which makes us peaceable, but the consciousness of our strength—the consciousness that if we were attacked at the most unfavorable time, we are strong enough for defense and for keeping in view the possibility of leaving it to the providence of God to remove in the meantime the necessity for war."

If I rise to speak today it is not to urge on your acceptance the measure the President has mentioned (the army appropriation). I do not feel anxious about its adoption, and I do not believe that I can do anything to increase the majority by which it will be adopted—by which it is all-important at home and abroad that it should be adopted. Gentlemen of all parties have made up their minds how they will vote and I have the fullest confidence in the German Reichstag that it will restore our armament to the height from which we reduced it in the period between 1867 and 1882; and this not with respect to the conditions of the moment, not with regard to the apprehensions which may excite the stock exchanges and the mind of the public; but with a considerate regard for the general condition of Europe. In speaking, I will have more to say of this than of the immediate question.

I do not speak willingly, for under existing conditions a word unfortunately spoken may be ruinous, and the multiplication of words can do little to explain the situation, either to our own people or to foreigners. I speak unwillingly, but I fear that if I kept silent there would be an increase rather than a diminution of the expectations which have attached themselves to this debate, of unrest in the public mind, of the disposition to nervousness at home and abroad. The public might believe the question to be so difficult and critical that a minister for foreign affairs would not dare to touch upon it. I speak, therefore, but I can say truly that I speak with reluctance. I might limit myself to recalling expressions to which I gave utterance from this same place a year and a day ago. Little change has taken place in the situation since then. I chanced today on a clipping from the *Liberal Gazette*, a paper which I believe stands nearer to my friend, Representative Richter, than it does to me. It pictures one difficult situation to elucidate another, but I can take only general notice of the main points there touched on, with the explanation that if the situation has since altered, it is for the better rather than for the worse.

We had then our chief apprehension because of a war which might come to us from France. Since then, one peace-loving President has retired from administration in France, and another peace-loving President has succeeded him. It is certainly a favorable symptom that in choosing its new chief executive France has not put its hand into Pandora's box, but that we have assurance of a continuation under President Carnot of the peaceful policy represented by President Grevy. We have, moreover, other changes in the French administration whose peaceful significance is even stronger than that of the change in the presidency—an event which involved other causes. Such members of the ministry as were disposed to subordinate the peace of France and of Europe to their personal interests have been shoved out, and others, of whom we have not this to fear, have taken their places. I think I can state, also—and I do it with pleasure, because I do not wish to excite but to calm the public mind—that our relations with France are more peaceful, much less explosive than a year ago.

The fears which have been excited during the year have been occasioned more by Russia than by France, or I may say that the occasion was rather the exchange of mutual threats, excitement, reproaches, and provocations which have taken place during the summer between the Russian and the French press. But I do not believe that the situation in Russia is materially different now from what it was a year ago. The *Liberal Gazette* has printed in display type what I said then: "Our friendship with Russia sustained no interruption during our war and it is elevated above all doubt today. We expect neither assault nor attack nor unfriendliness from Russia." Perhaps this was printed in large letters to make it easier to attack it. Perhaps also with the hope that I had reached a different conclusion in the meantime and had become convinced that my confidence in the Russian policy of last year was erroneous. This is not the case. The grounds which gave occasion for it lie partly in the Russian press and partly in the mobilization of Russian troops. I cannot attach decided importance to the attitude of the press. They say that it means more in Russia than it does in France. I am of the contrary opinion. In France the press is a power which influences the conclusions of the administration. It is not such a power in Russia, nor can it be; but in both cases the press is only spots of printer's ink on paper against which we have no war to wage. There can be no ground of provocation for us in it. Behind each article is only one man—the man who has guided the pen to send the article into the world. Even in a Russian paper, we may say in an independent Russian paper, secretly supported by French subsidies, the case is not altered. The pen which has written in such a paper an article hostile to Germany has no one behind it but the man whose hand held the pen, the man who in his cabinet produced the lucubration and the protector which every Russian newspaper is wont to have—that is to say the official more or less important in Russian party politics who gives such a paper his protection. But both of them do not weigh a feather against the authority of his Majesty, the Czar of Russia....

Since the great war of 1870 was concluded, has there been any year, I ask you, without its alarm of war? Just as we were returning, at the beginning of the seventies, they said: When will we have the next war? When will the Revanche be fought? In five years at latest. They said to us then: "The question of whether we will have war and of the success with which we shall have it (it was a representative of the Centre who upbraided me with it in the Reichstag) depends today only on Russia. Russia alone has the decision in her hands."

Perhaps I will return to this question later. In the meantime, I will continue the pictures of these forty years and recall that in 1876 a war-cloud gathered in the South; that in 1877, the Balkan War was only prevented by the Berlin Congress from putting the whole of Europe in a blaze, and that quite suddenly after the Congress a new vision of danger was disclosed to us in the East because Russia was offended by our action at the conference. Perhaps, later on, I will recur to this also if my strength will permit.

Then followed a certain reaction in the intimate relations of the three emperors which allowed us to look for some time into the future with more assurance; yet on the first signs of uncertainty in their relations, or because of the lapsing of the agreements they had made with each other, our public opinion showed the same nervous and, I think, exaggerated excitement with which we had to contend last year—which, at the present time, I hold to be specially uncalled for. But because I think this nervousness uncalled for now, I am far from concluding that we do not need an increase of our war footing. On the contrary! Therefore, I have unrolled before you this tableau of forty years—perhaps not to your amusement! If not, I beg your pardon, but had I omitted a year from that which you yourselves had experienced with shuddering, the impression might have been lost that the state of anxiety before wars, before continually extending complications, the entanglements of which no one can anticipate,— that this condition is permanent with us; that we must reckon upon it as a permanency; and that independently of the circumstances of the moment, with the self-confidence of a great nation which is strong enough under any circumstances to take its fate into its own hands against any coalition; with the confidence in itself and in God which its own power and the righteousness of its cause, a righteousness which the care of the government will always keep with Germany—that we shall be able to foresee every possibility and, doing so, to look forward to peace.

The long and the short of it is that in these days we must be as strong as we can; and if we will, we can be stronger than any other country of equal resources in the world. I will return to that. And it would be a crime not to use our resources. If we do not need an army prepared for war, we do not need to call for it. It depends merely on the not very important question of the cost—and it is not very important, though I mention it incidentally. I have no mind to go into figures, financial or military, but France during the last few years has spent in improving her forces three thousand millions, while we have spent hardly fifteen hundred millions including that we are now asking for. But I leave the ministers of war and of finance to deal with that. When I say that we must strive continually to be ready for all emergencies, I advance the proposition that, on account of our geographical position, we must make greater efforts than other powers would be obliged to make in view of the same ends. We lie in the middle of Europe. We have at least three fronts on which we can be attacked. France has only an eastern boundary; Russia only its western, exposed to assault. We are, moreover, more exposed than any other people to the danger of hostile coalition because of our geographical position, and because, perhaps, of the feeble power of cohesion which, until now, the German people has exhibited when compared with others. At any rate, God has placed us in a position where our neighbors will prevent us from falling into a condition of sloth—of wallowing in the mire of mere existence. On one side of us he has set the French, a most warlike and restless nation; and he has allowed to become exaggerated in the Russians fighting tendencies which had not become apparent in them during the earlier part of the century. So we are spurred forward on both sides to endeavors which perhaps we would not make otherwise. The pikes in the European carp-pond will not allow us to become carp, because they make us feel their stings in both our sides. They force us to an effort which, perhaps, we would not make otherwise, and they force us also to a cohesion among ourselves as Germans which is opposed to our innermost nature; otherwise we would prefer to struggle with each other. But when we are enfiladed by the press of France and Russia, it compels us to stand together, and through such compression it will so increase our fitness for cohesion that we may finally come into the same condition of indivisibility which is natural to other people—which thus far we have lacked. We must respond to this dispensation of Providence, however, by making ourselves so strong that the pike can do nothing more than encourage us to exert ourselves. We had, years ago, in the times of the Holy Alliance (I recall an old American song which I learned from my dead friend, Motley[1]: "In good old colonial times/When we lived under a king!")

We had then patriarchal times and with them a multitude of balustrades on which we could support ourselves, and a multitude of dykes to protect us from the wild European floods. That was the German confederation, and the true beginning, and continuance, and conclusion of the German confederation was the Holy Alliance, for whose service it was made. We depended on Russia

---

[1] The great American historian Thomas Lathrop Motley (1814–1877) was indeed Bismarck's friend.

and Austria, and, above everything, we relied on our own modesty, which did not allow us to speak before the rest of the company had spoken. We have lost all that, and we must help ourselves. The Holy Alliance was shipwrecked in the Crimean War—through no fault of ours! The German confederation has been destroyed by us because our existence under it was neither tolerable for us nor for the German people. Both have ceased to exist. After the dissolution of the German confederation, after the war of 1866, we would have been obliged to reckon on isolation for Prussia or North Germany, had we been obliged to stop at reckoning with the fact that, on no side would they forgive us the new and great successes which we had obtained. Never do other powers look with pleasure on the triumphs of a neighbor. Our connection with Russia was not disturbed, however, by the events of 1866. In 1866 the memory of the politics of Count von Buol and of Austrian politics during the Crimean War was too fresh in Russia to allow them to think of supporting the Austrian against the Prussian monarchy, or of renewing the campaign which Czar Nicholas had conducted for Austria in 1849. For us, therefore, there remained a natural inclination towards Russia, which, foreseen in the last century, had in this its recognized origin in the politics of Czar Alexander I. To him Prussia owes thanks indeed. In 1813 he could easily have turned on the Polish frontiers and concluded peace. Later he could have brought about the fall of Prussia. We have then, as a fact, to thank, for the restoration of the old footing, the good will of Czar Alexander I; or, if you are inclined to be skeptical, say to the need felt in Russian politics for Prussia. This feeling of gratitude has controlled the administration of Frederick William the Third.

The balance which Russia had on its account with Prussia was used up through the friendship, I may say through the serviceability of Prussia during the entire reign of Czar Nicholas and, I may add, settled at Olmutz. At Olmutz, Czar Nicholas did not take the part of Prussia, did not shield us from adverse experience, did not guard us against humiliation; for, on the whole, he leaned towards Austria more than towards Prussia. The idea that during his administration we owed thanks to Russia results from a historical legend. But while Czar Nicholas lived, we, on our side, did not violate the tradition with Russia. During the Crimean War, as I have already told you, we stood by Russia in spite of threats and of some hazard. His Majesty, the late King, had no desire to play a decided part in the war with a strong army, as I think he could easily have done. We had concluded treaties by which we were bound to put a hundred thousand men in the field by a set time. I advised his Majesty that we should put not a hundred thousand but two hundred thousand in the field and to put them there *a cheval* so that we could use them right and left; so that his Majesty would have been the final arbiter of the fortunes of the Crimean War. But his late Majesty was not inclined to warlike undertakings, and the people ought to be grateful to him for it. I was younger and less experienced then than I am now. We bore no malice for Olmutz, however, during the Crimean War. We came out of the Crimean War as a friend of Russia, and while I was ambassador to Russia I enjoyed the fruit of this friendship in a very favorable reception at court and in Russian society. Our attitude towards Austria in the Italian War was not to the taste of the Russian cabinet, but it had no unfavorable consequences. Our Austrian War of 1866 was looked upon with a certain satisfaction. No one in Russia then grudged Austria what she got. In the year 1870 we had, in taking our stand and making our defense, the satisfaction of coincidently rendering a service to our Russian friends in the Black Sea. The opening of the Black Sea by the contracting powers would never have been probable if the Germans had not been victorious in the neighborhood of Paris. Had we been defeated, for example, I think the conclusion of the London agreement would not have been so easily in Russia's favor. So the war of 1870 left no ill humor between us and Russia....

The bill will bring us an increase of troops capable of bearing arms—a possible increase, which if we do not need it, we need not call out, but can leave the men at home. But we will have it ready for service if we have arms for it. And that is a matter of primary importance. I remember the carbine which was furnished by England to our Landwehr in 1813, and with which I had some practice as a huntsman—that was no weapon for a soldier! We can get arms suddenly for an emergency, but if we have them ready for it, then this bill will count for a strengthening of our peace forces and a reinforcement of the peace league as great as if a fourth great power had joined the alliance with an army of seven hundred thousand men—the greatest yet put in the field.

I think, too, that this powerful reinforcement of the army will have a quieting effect on our own people, and will in some measure relieve the nervousness of our exchanges, of our press, and of our public opinion. I hope they all will be comforted if they make it clear to themselves that after this reinforcement and from the moment of the signature and publication of the bill, the soldiers are there! But arms are necessary, and we must provide better ones if we wish to have an army of triarians—of the best manhood that we have among our people; of fathers of family over thirty years old!

And we must give them the best arms that can be had! We must not send them into battle with what we have not thought good enough for our young troops of the line. But our steadfast men, our fathers of family, our Samsons, such as we remember seeing hold the bridge at Versailles, must have the best arms on their shoulders, and the best clothing to protect them against the weather, which can be had from anywhere. We must not be niggardly in this. And I hope it will reassure our countrymen if they think now it will be the case—as I do not believe—that we are likely to be attacked on both sides at once. There is a possibility of it, for, as I have explained to you in the history of the Forty Years' War, all manner of coalitions may occur. But if it should occur we could hold the defensive on our borders with a million good soldiers. At the same time, we could hold in reserve a half million or more, almost a million, indeed; and send them forward as they were needed. Someone has said to me: "The only result of that will be that the others will increase their forces also." But they cannot. They have long ago reached the maximum. We lowered it in 1867 because we thought that, having the North German confederation, we could make ourselves easier and exempt men over thirty-two. In consequence our neighbors have adopted a longer term of service—many of them a twenty-year term. They have a maximum as high as ours, but they cannot touch us in quality. Courage is equal in all civilized nations. The Russians or the French acquit themselves as bravely as the Germans. But our people, our seven hundred thousand men, are veterans trained in service, tried soldiers who have not yet forgotten their training. And no people in the world can touch us in this, that we have the material for officers and under-officers to command this army. That is what they cannot imitate. The whole tendency of popular education leads to that in Germany as it does in no other country. The measure of education necessary to fit an officer or under-officer to meet the demands which the soldier makes on him exists with us to a much greater extent than with any other people. We have more material for officers and under-officers than any other country, and we have a corps of officers that no other country can approach. In this and in the excellence of our corps of under-officers, who are really the pupils of our officers' corps, lies our superiority. The course of education which fits an officer to meet the strong demands made on his position for self-denial, for the duty of comradeship, and for fulfilling the extraordinarily difficult social duties whose fulfillment is made necessary among us by the comradeship which, thank God, exists in the highest degree among officers and men without the least detriment to discipline—they cannot imitate us in that—that relationship between officers and men which, with a few unfortunate exceptions, exists in the German army. But the exceptions confirm the rule, and so we can say that no German officer leaves his soldiers under fire, but brings them out even at the risk of his own life; while, on the other hand, no German soldier, as we know by experience, forsakes his officer.

If other armies intend to supply with officers and sub-officers as many troops as we intend to have at once, then they must educate the officers, for no untaught fool is fit to command a company, and much less is he fit to fulfill the difficult duties which an officer owes to his men, if he is to keep their love and respect. The measure of education which is demanded for that, and the qualities which, among us especially, are expressed in comradeship and sympathy by the officer,—*that* no rule and no regulation in the world can impress on the officers of other countries. In *that* we are superior to all, and in that they cannot imitate us! On that point I have no fear.

But there is still another advantage to be derived from the adoption of this bill: The very strength for which we strive shows our peaceful disposition. That sounds paradoxical, but still it is true.

No man would attack us when we have such a powerful war-machine as we wish to make the German army. If I were to come before you today and say to you—supposing me to be convinced that the conditions are different from what they are—if I were to say to you: "We are strongly threatened by France and Russia; it is evident that we will be attacked; my conviction as a diplomat, considering the military necessities of the case, is that it is expedient for us to take the defensive by striking the first blow, as we are now in a position to do; an aggressive war is to our advantage, and I beg the Reichstag for a milliard or half a milliard to begin it at once against both our neighbors"—indeed, gentlemen, I do not know that you would have sufficient confidence in me to consent! I hope you would not.

But if you were to do it, it would not satisfy me. If we in Germany should wish to wage war with the full exertion of our national strength, it must be a war with which all who engage in it, all who offer themselves as sacrifices in it—in short, the whole nation takes part as one man; it must be a people's war; it must be a war carried on with the enthusiasm of 1870, when we were ruthlessly attacked. I well remember the ear-splitting, joyful shouts at the Cologne railway station; it was the same from Berlin to Cologne; and it was the same here in Berlin. The waves of public feeling in favor of war swept us into it whether we wished or not. It must always be so if the power of a people such as ours is to be exerted to the full. It will be very difficult, however, to make it clear to the provinces and states of the confederation and to their peoples, that war is now unavoidably necessary. They would ask: "Are you sure of that? Who knows?" In short, when we came to actual hostilities, the weight of such imponderable considerations would be much heavier against us than the material opposition we would meet from our enemies. "Holy Russia" would be irritated; France would bristle with bayonets as far as the Pyrenees. It would be the same everywhere. A war which was not decreed by the popular will could be carried on if once the constituted authorities had finally decided on it as a necessity; it would be carried on vigorously, and perhaps successfully, after the first fire and the sight of blood. But it would not be a finish fight in its spirit with such fire and *élan* behind it as we would have in a war in which we were attacked. Then all Germany from Memel to Lake Constance would flame out like a powder mine; the country would bristle with arms, and no enemy would be rash enough to join issues with the *Juror Teutonicus* (Berserker madness) thus roused by attack.

We must not lose sight of such considerations, even if we are now superior to our future opponents, as many military critics besides our own consider us to be. All our own critics are convinced of our superiority. Naturally every soldier believes it. He would come very near to being a failure as a soldier if he did not wish for war and feel full assurance of victory. If our rivals sometimes suspect that it is fear of the result which makes us peaceful, they are grievously in error. We believe as thoroughly in the certainty of our victory in a righteous cause as any lieutenant in a foreign garrison can believe in his third glass of champagne—and perhaps we have more ground for our assurance! It is not fear which makes us peaceable, but the consciousness of our strength—the consciousness that if we were attacked at the most unfavorable time, we are strong enough for defense and for keeping in view the possibility of leaving it to the providence of God to remove in the meantime the necessity for war.

I am never for an offensive war, and if war can come only through our initiative, it will not begin. Fire must be kindled by someone before it can burn, and we will not kindle it. Neither the consciousness of our strength, as I have just represented it, nor the trust in our alliances will prevent us from continuing with our accustomed zeal our accustomed efforts to keep the peace. We will not allow ourselves to be led by bad temper; we will not yield to prejudice. It is undoubtedly true that the threats, the insults, the provocations which have been directed against us, have aroused great and natural animosities on our side. And it is hard to rouse such feelings in the Germans, for they are less sensitive to the dislike of others towards them than any other nation. We are taking pains, however, to soften these animosities, and in the future as in the past we will strive to keep the peace with our neighbors—especially with Russia. When I say "especially with Russia," I mean that France offers us no security for the success of our efforts, though I will not say that it does not help. We will never seek occasion to quarrel. We will never attack France. In the many small occasions for trouble which the disposition of our neighbors to spy and to bribe has given us, we have made pleasant and amicable settlements. I would hold it grossly criminal to allow such trifles either to occasion a great national war or to make it probable. There are occasions when it is true that the "more reasonable gives way." I name Russia especially, and I have the same confidence in the result I had a year ago when my expression gave this "Liberal" paper here occasion for black type. But I have it without running after—or, as a German paper expressed it, "grovelling before Russia." That time has gone by. We no longer sue for favor either in France or in Russia. The Russian press and Russian public opinion have shown the door to an old, powerful, and attached friend as we were. We will not force ourselves upon them. We have sought to regain the old confidential relationship, but we will run after no one. But that does not prevent us from observing—it rather spurs us on to observe with redoubled care—the treaty rights of Russia. Among these treaty rights are some which are not conceded by all our friends: I mean the rights which at the Berlin Congress Russia won in the matter of Bulgaria.

In consequence of the resolution of the Congress, Russia, up to 1885, chose as prince a near relative of the Czar concerning whom no one asserted or could assert that he was anything else than a Russian dependent. It appointed the minister of war and a greater part of the officials. In short, it governed Bulgaria. There is no possible doubt of it. The Bulgarians, or a part of them, or their prince—I do not know which—were not satisfied. There was a *coup d'etat* and there has been a defection from Russia. This has created a situation which we have no call to change by force of arms—though its existence does not change theoretically the rights which Russia gained from the conference. But if Russia should seek to establish its rights forcibly I do not know what difficulties might arise and it does not concern us to know. We will not support forcible measures and will not advise them. I do not believe there is any disposition towards them. I am sure no such inclination exists. But if through diplomatic means, through the intervention of the Sultan as the suzerain of Bulgaria, Russia seeks its rights, then I assume that it is the province of loyal German statesmanship to give an unmistakable support to the provisions of the Berlin Treaty, and to stand by the interpretation which without exception we gave it—an interpretation on which the voice of the Bulgarians cannot make me err. Bulgaria, the Statelet between the Danube and the Balkans, is certainly not of sufficient importance to justify plunging Europe into war from Moscow to the Pyrenees, from the North Sea to Palermo—a war the issue of which no one could foresee, at the end of which no one could tell what the fighting had been about. So I can say openly that the position of the Russian press, the unfriendliness we have experienced from Russian public opinion, will not prevent us from supporting Russia in a diplomatic attempt to establish its rights as soon as it makes up its mind to assert them in Bulgaria. I say deliberately—"As soon as Russia expresses the wish." We have put ourselves to some trouble heretofore to meet the views of Russia on the strength of reliable hints, but we have lived to see the Russian press attacking, as hostile to Russia, the very things in German politics which were prompted by a desire to anticipate Russia's wishes. We did that at the Congress, but it will not happen again. If Russia officially asks us to support measures for the restoration in Bulgaria of the situation approved by the Congress with the Sultan as suzerain, I would not hesitate to advise his Majesty, the Emperor that it should be done. This is the demand which the treaties make on our loyalty to a neighbor, with whom, be the mood what it will, we have to maintain neighborly relations and defend great common interests of monarchy, such as the interests of order against its antagonists in all Europe, with a neighbor, I say, whose sovereign has a perfect understanding in this regard with the allied sovereigns. I do not doubt that when the Czar of Russia finds that the interests of his great empire of a hundred million people requires war, he will make war. But his interests cannot possibly prompt him to make war against us. I do not think it at all probable that such a question of interest is likely to present itself. I do not believe that a disturbance of the peace is imminent—if I may recapitulate—and I beg that you will consider the pending measure without regard to that thought or that apprehension, looking on it rather as a full restoration of the mighty power which God has created in the German people—a power to be used if we need it! If we do not need it, we will not use it and we will seek to avoid the necessity for its use. This attempt is made somewhat more difficult by threatening articles in foreign newspapers and I may give special admonition to the outside world against the continuance of such articles. They lead to nothing. The threats made against us, not by the government but in the newspapers, are incredibly stupid, when it is remembered that they assume that a great and proud power such as the German Empire is capable of being intimidated by an array of black spots made by a printer on paper, a mere marshalling of words. If they would give up that idea, we could reach a better understanding with both our neighbors. Every country is finally answerable for the wanton mischief done by its newspapers, and the reckoning is liable to be presented some day in the shape of a final decision from some other country. We can be bribed very easily—perhaps too easily—with love and good will. But with threats, never!

We Germans fear God, and nothing else in the world!

It is the fear of God which makes us love peace and keep it. He who breaks it against us ruthlessly will learn the meaning of the warlike love of the Fatherland which in 1813 rallied to the standard the entire population of the then small and weak kingdom of Prussia; he will learn, too, that this patriotism is now the common property of the entire German nation, so that whoever attacks Germany will find it unified in arms, every warrior having in his heart the steadfast faith that God will be with us.

JOSEPH CHAMBERLAIN
"The Future of the British Empire"
("I am told on every hand that Imperial Federation
is a vain and empty dream")
London, England
November 6, 1895

Joseph Chamberlain (1836–1914) was a leading advocate for British imperialism. As Great Britain's Secretary of State for the Colonies, he speaks here at a dinner celebrating the completion of the Natal-Transvaal Railway in England's colony in South Africa.

I thank you sincerely for the hearty reception you have given to this toast. I appreciate very much the warmth of your welcome, and I see in it confirmation of the evidence which is afforded by the cordial and graceful telegram from the Premier of Natal, which has been read by your chairman, and by other public and private communications that I have received, that any man who makes it his first duty, as I do, to draw closer together the different portions of the British Empire will meet with hearty sympathy, encouragement, and support. I thank my old friend and colleague, Sir Charles Tupper, for the kind manner in which he has spoken of me. He has said much, no doubt, that transcends my merits, but that is a circumstance so unusual in the life of a politician that I do not feel it in my heart to complain. I remember that Dr. Oliver Wendell Holmes, who was certainly one of the most genial Americans who ever visited these shores, said that when he was young he liked his praise in teaspoon-fuls, that when he got older he preferred it in table spoonfuls, and that in advanced years he was content to receive it in ladles. I confess that I am arriving at the period when I sympathise with Dr. Oliver Wendell Holmes. Gentlemen, the occasion which has brought us together is an extremely interesting one. We are here to congratulate Natal, its Government and its people, and to congratulate ourselves on the completion of a great work of commercial enterprise and civilisation, which one of our colonies, which happens to be the last to have been included in the great circle of self-governing communi-ties, has brought to a successful conclusion, giving once more a proof of the vigour and the resolution which have distinguished all the nations that have sprung from the parent British stock.

This occasion has been honoured by the presence of the represen-tatives of sister colonies, who are here to offer words of sympathy and encouragement; and, in view of the representative character of the gathering, I think, perhaps, I may be permitted, especially as this is the first occasion upon which I have publicly appeared in my capacity as Minister for the colonies to offer a few words of a general application.

I think it will not be disputed that we are approaching a criti-cal stage in the history of the relations between ourselves and the self-governing colonies. We are entering upon a chapter of our colo-nial history, the whole of which will probably be written in the next few years, certainly in the lifetime of the next generation, and which will be one of the most important in our colonial annals, since upon the events and policy which it describes will depend the future of the British Empire. That Empire, gentlemen, that world-wide domin-ion to which no Englishman can allude without a thrill of enthu-siasm and patriotism, which has been the admiration, and perhaps the envy, of foreign nations, hangs together by a thread so slender that it may well seem that even a breath would sever it. There have been periods in our history, not so very far distant, when leading statesmen, despairing of the possibility of maintaining anything in the nature of a permanent union, have looked forward to the time when the vigorous communities to which they rightly entrusted the control of their own destinies would grow strong and independent, would assert their independence, and would claim entire separation from the parent stem. The time to which they looked forward has arrived sooner than they expected. The conditions to which they referred have been more than fulfilled; and now these great communities, which have within them every element of national life, have taken their rank amongst the nations of the world; and I do not suppose that anyone would consider the idea of compelling them to remain within the empire as within the region of intelligent speculation. Yet, although, as I have said, the time has come, and the conditions have been fulfilled, the results which these statesmen anticipated have not followed. They felt, perhaps, overwhelmed by the growing burdens of the vast dominions of the British Crown. They may well have shrunk from the responsibilities and the obligations which they involve; and so it happened that some of them looked forward not only without alarm, but with hopeful expectation, to a severance of the union which now exists.

But if such feelings were ever entertained they are entertained no longer. As the possibility of separation has become greater, the desire for separation has become less. While we on our part are prepared to take our share of responsibility, and to do all that may fairly be expected from the mother country, and while we should look upon a separation as the greatest calamity that could befall us our fellow-subjects on their part see to what a great inheritance they have come by mere virtue of their citizenship; and they must feel that no separate existence, however splendid, could compare with that which they enjoy equally with ourselves as joint heirs of all the traditions of the past, and as joint partakers of all the influence, resources, and power of the British Empire.

I rejoice at the change that has taken place. I rejoice at the wider patriotism, no longer confined to this small island, which embraces the whole of Greater Britain and which has carried to every clime British institutions and the best characteristics of the British race. How could it be otherwise? We have a common origin, we have a common history, a common language, a common literature, and a common love of liberty and law. We have common principles to assert, we have common interests to maintain. I said it was a slender thread that binds us together. I remember on one occasion having been shown a wire so fine and delicate that a blow might break it; yet I was told that it was capable of transmitting an electrical energy that would set powerful machinery in motion. May it not be the same with the relations which exist between the colonies and ourselves; and may not that thread of union be capable of carrying a force of sentiment and of sympathy which will yet be a potent factor in the history of the world? There is a word which I am almost afraid to mention, lest at the very outset of my career I should lose my character as a practical statesman. I am told on every hand that Imperial Federation is a vain and empty dream. I will not contest that judgment, but I will say this: that that man must be blind indeed who does not see that it is a dream which has vividly impressed itself on the mind of the English-speaking race, and who does not admit that dreams of that kind, which have so powerful an influence upon the imagination of men, have somehow or another an unaccountable way of being realised in their own time. If it be a dream, it is a dream that appeals to the highest sentiments of patriotism, as well as to our material interests. It is a dream which is calculated to stimulate and to inspire every one who cares for the future of the Anglo-Saxon people. I think myself that the spirit of the time is, at all events, in the direction of such a movement. How far it will carry us no man can tell; but, believe me, upon the temper and the tone in which we approach the solution of the problems which are now coming upon us depend the security and the maintenance of that world-wide dominion, that edifice of Imperial rule, which has been so ably built for us by those who have gone before.

Gentlemen, I admit that I have strayed somewhat widely from the toast which your chairman has committed to my charge. That toast is "The Prosperity of South Africa and the Natal and Transvaal Railway." As to South Africa, there can be no doubt as to its prosperity. We have witnessed in our own time a development of natural and mineral wealth in that country altogether beyond precedent or human knowledge; and what we have seen in the past, and what we see in the present, is bound to be far surpassed in the near future. The product of the mines, great as it is at present, is certain to be multiplied many fold, and before many years are over the mines of the Transvaal may be rivalled by the mines of Mashonaland or Matabeleland; and in the train of this great, exceptional, and wonderful prosperity, in the train of the diamond-digger and of the miner, will come a demand for labour which no man can measure—a demand for all the products of agriculture and of manufacture, in which not South Africa alone, but all the colonies and the mother country itself must have a share.

The climate and soil leave nothing to be desired, and there is only one thing wanted—that is, a complete union and identity of sentiment and interest between the different States existing in South Africa. Gentlemen, I have no doubt that that union will be forthcoming although it may not be immediately established. I do not shut my eyes to differences amongst friends which have unfortunately already arisen, and which have not yet been arranged. I think these differences, if you look below the surface, will be found to be due principally to the fact that we have not yet achieved in South Africa that local federation which is the necessary preface to any serious consideration of the question of Imperial federation. But, gentlemen, in these differences, my position, of course, renders it absolutely necessary that I should take no side. I pronounce no opinion, and it would not become me to offer any advice; although, if the good offices of my department were at any time invoked by those who are now separated, all I can say is that they would be heartily placed at their service.

Gentlemen, I wish success to the Natal Railway, and to every railway in South Africa. There is room for all. There is prosperity for all enough to make the mouth of an English director positively water. There is success for all, if only they will not waste their resources in internecine conflict. I have seen with pleasure that a conference is being held in order to discuss, and I hope to settle, these differences. I trust that they may be satisfactorily arranged. In the meantime I congratulate our chairman, as representing this prosperous colony, upon the enterprise they have displayed, upon the difficulties they have surmounted, and on the success they have already achieved. And I hope for them—confidently hope—the fullest share in that prosperity which I predict without hesitation for the whole of South Africa.

ALBERT JEREMIAH BEVERIDGE
U.S. Senator from Indiana
("If this be imperialism, its final end will be
the empire of the Son of Man")
Washington, D.C.
January 9, 1900

Beveridge (1862–1927) served as a senator from 1899 to 1911. He was a loud advocate for American imperialism, unapologetic racism, and war. In 1898, after the Spanish-American War, Spain conceded the Philippines to the United States. After visiting the Philippines himself, Beveridge, in the extended excerpts below, argues for the complete take-over of the country. The native people, he declares, "are not a self-governing race; they are Orientals, Malays, instructed by Spaniards in the latter's worst estate." After decades of American colonial administration, the United States granted the Republic of the Philippines independence in 1946.

Mr. President, I address the Senate at this time because Senators and Members of the House on both sides have asked that I give to Congress and the country my observations in the Philippines and the far East, and the conclusions which those observations compel; and because of hurtful resolutions introduced and utterances made in the Senate, every word of which will cost and is costing the lives of American soldiers.

Mr. President, the times call for candor. The Philippines are ours, "territory belonging to the United States," as the Constitution calls them. And just beyond the Philippines are China's illimitable markets. We will not retreat from either. We will not repudiate our duty in the archipelago. We will not abandon our opportunity in the Orient. We will not renounce our part in the mission of our race. And we will move forward to our work, not howling out regrets, like slaves whipped to their burdens, but with gratitude for a task worthy of our strength, and thanksgiving to Almighty God that He has deemed us worthy of His work.

This island empire is the last land left in all the oceans. If it should prove a mistake to abandon it, the blunder, once made, would be irretrievable. If it proves a mistake to hold it, the error can be corrected when we will. Every other progressive nation stands ready to relieve us.

But to hold it will be no mistake. Our increasing trade henceforth must be with Asia. More and more Europe will manufacture what it needs, secure from its colonies what it consumes. Where shall we turn for consumers of our surplus? Geography answers the question. China is our natural customer. She is nearer to us than to England, Germany or Russia, the commercial powers of the present and the future. They have moved nearer to China by securing permanent bases on her borders. The Philippines give us a base at the door of all the East.

Lines of navigation from our ports to the Orient and Australia; from the Isthmian Canal to Asia; from all Oriental ports to Australia, converge at and separate from the Philippines. These islands are a self-supporting, dividend-paying fleet, permanently anchored at a spot selected by the strategy of Providence, commanding the Pacific. And the Pacific is the ocean of the commerce of the future. Most future wars will be conflicts for commerce. The power that rules the Pacific, therefore, is the power that rules the world. And, with the Philippines, that power will be the American Republic.

China's trade is the important commercial fact of our future. Her foreign commerce was $285,738,300 in 1897, of which we, her neighbor, had less than 9 percent, of which only a little more than half was merchandise sold to China by us. We ought to have 50 percent, and we shall. And China's foreign commerce is only beginning. Her resources, her possibilities, her wants, all are undeveloped. She has only 340 miles of railway. I have seen trains loaded with natives and all the activities of modern life already appearing along the line. But she needs, and in fifty years will have 200,000 miles of railway.

Who can estimate her commerce then? That statesman commits a crime against American trade who fails to put America where she may command that trade. Germany's Chinese trade is increasing like magic. She has established ship lines and secured a tangible foothold on China's soil. Russia's Chinese trade is growing rapidly. She is spending the revenues of the Empire to finish her railroad into Peking itself, and she is in physical possession of Manchuria. Japan's Chinese trade is multiplying in volume and value. She is bending her energy to her merchant marine, and is located along China's very coast. But the Philippines command the commercial situation of the entire East. Can America best trade with China from San Francisco or New York? From San Francisco, of course. But if San Francisco were closer to China than New York is to Pittsburgh, what then? And Manila is nearer to Hong-Kong than Havana is to Washington. Yet American statesmen plan to surrender this commercial advantage in the Orient which Providence and our soldiers' lives have won for us. When History comes to write the story of that suggested treason to American supremacy and therefore to the spread of American civilization, let her in mercy write that those who so proposed were blind and nothing more.

But if they did not command China, India, the Orient, the whole Pacific for purposes of offense, defense, and trade, the Philippines are so valuable in themselves that we should hold them. I have cruised more than 2,000 miles through the archipelago, every moment a surprise at its loveliness and wealth. I have ridden hundreds of miles over the islands, every foot of the way a revelation of vegetable and mineral riches.

No land in America surpasses in fertility the plains and valleys of Luzon. Rice and coffee, sugar and cocoanuts, hemp and tobacco, and many products of the temperate as well as the tropic zone grow in various sections of the archipelago. The forests of Negros, Mindanao, Mindora, Paluan, and parts of Luzon are invaluable and intact. The wood of the Philippines can supply the furniture of the world for a century to come. At Cebu the best informed man in the island told me that 40 miles of Cebu's mountain chain are practically mountains of coal. Pablo Majia, one of the most reliable men on the islands, confirmed the statement. Some declare that the coal is only lignite; but ship captains who have used it told me that it is better steamer fuel than the best coal of Japan.

In one of the islands valuable deposits of copper exist untouched. In many places there are indications of gold. The mineral wealth of the Philippines will one day surprise the world. I base this statement partly on personal observation, but chiefly on the testimony of foreign merchants in the Philippines, who have practically investigated the subject, and upon the unanimous opinion of natives and priests. And the mineral wealth is but a small fraction of the agricultural wealth of these islands.

And the wood, hemp, copra, and other products of the Philippines supply what we need and can not ourselves produce. Spain's export trade, with the islands undeveloped, was $11,534,731 annually. Ultimately our trade, when the islands shall be developed, will be $125,000,000 annually; for who believes that we cannot do ten times as well as Spain?

Behold the markets they command. It is as if a half-dozen of our states were set down between Oceana and the Orient, and those states themselves undeveloped and unspoiled of their primitive wealth and resources.

Nothing is so natural as trade with one's neighbors. The Philippines make us the nearest occidental neighbor of all the East. Nothing is more natural than to trade with those you know—this is the philosophy of all advertising. The Philippines bring us permanently face to face with the eagerly sought-for customers. National prestige, national propinquity, these and commercial activity are the elements of commercial success. The Philippines give the first.

The character of the American people supplies the last. It is a providential conjunction of all the elements of trade, of duty, and of power. If we are willing to go to war rather than let England have a few feet of frozen Alaska, which affords small market and commands none, what should we not do rather than let England, Germany or Japan have all the Philippines? And no man on the spot can fail to see that this would be their fate if we retired.

The climate is the best tropic climate in the world. This is the belief of those who have lived in many tropic countries, with scores of whom I talked on this point. My own experience with tropical conditions has not been extensive; yet, speaking from that experience, I testify that the climate of Iloilo, Jolo, Cebu, and even of Manila, greatly surpasses that of Hong Kong. And yet on the bare and burning rock of Hong Kong our constructing race has builded one of the noblest cities of all the world, and made the harbor it commands the focus of the commerce of the East. And the glory of that achievement illumines with a rarer splendor than that of Waterloo the flag that floats above the harbor; for from Hong Kong's heights civilization is irradiating all the Orient. If this be imperialism, its final end will be the empire of the Son of Man....

It will be hard for Americans who have not studied them to understand the people. They are a barbarous race, modified by three centuries of contact with a decadent race. The Filipino is the South Sea Malay, put through a process of three hundred years of dishonesty in dealing, disorder in habits of industry, and cruelty, caprice, and corruption in government. It is barely possible that 1,000 men in all the archipelago are now capable of self-government in the Anglo-Saxon sense. I know many clever and highly educated men among them, but there are only three commanding intellects and characters—Arellano, Mabini, and Aguinaldo. Arellano, the chief justice of their supreme court, is a profound lawyer and a brave and incorruptible man. Mabini, who, before his capture, was the literary and diplomatic associate of Aguinaldo, is the highest type of subtlety and the most constructive mind that race has yet produced.

Aguinaldo is a clever, popular leader, able, brave, resourceful, cunning, ambitious, unscrupulous, and masterful. He is full of decision, initiative and authority, and has the confidence of the masses. He is a natural dictator. His ideas of government are absolute orders, implicit obedience, or immediate death. He understands the character of his countrymen. He is a Malay Sulla; not a Filipino Washington....

I shall close these few extracts, which are a fair sample of a great number of others, all of which I am willing to submit to the Senate at any time, by reading a few suggestions made to me by the first statesman of the far East, who has had practical experience with similar problems. In the course of a long interview, he said:

You must establish government over the islands, because it is incalculably to your interest in the future, and because, if you do not, another power will undoubtedly take them, involving the world in a war for which you will be responsible.

As to the form of government, you should have a governor general of great ability, firmness, and purity; under him sub officers of districts, and under them still lower officials for the municipalities, all appointed by their superiors and not chosen by the people. You should employ the ablest natives in the government service in some way so as to enlist them on your side. The courts are the most important consideration of all. Don't put the natives in charge of them, whatever else you do. In the armed forces, don't give any natives superior positions for a long time. Don't do too much for

them in the beginning. Do it gradually, as the years go by. I think
your course is clear. Don't treat with them until you defeat them.
You must do that. You cannot treat and fight.

Make English the language of the courts, schools and everywhere
possible. Let me impress on you the necessity of conferring your
benefits on these people quite gradually. If you give them too much
they cannot appreciate nor understand nor rightly use it, and it will
thus be thrown away; but if you give them the blessing of free institutions gradually, you furnish a source of constant gratitude. In the
other way you exhaust yourself at the beginning, and besides, fail in
your good intentions.

Here, then, Senators, is the situation. Two years ago there was no
land in all the world which we could occupy for any purpose. Our
commerce was daily turning toward the Orient, and geography and
trade developments made necessary our commercial empire over the
Pacific. And in that ocean we had no commercial, naval, or military base. Today, we have one of the three great ocean possessions
of the globe, located at the most commanding commercial, naval,
and military points in the eastern seas, within hail of India, shoulder
to shoulder with China, richer in its own resources than any equal
body of land on the entire globe, and peopled by a race which civilization demands shall be improved.

Shall we abandon it? That man little knows the common people
of the Republic, little understands the instincts of our race, who
thinks we shall not hold fast and hold it for ever, administering just
government by simplest methods. We may trick up devices to shift
our burden and lessen our opportunity; they will avail us nothing
but delay. We may tangle conditions by applying academic arrangements of self-government to a crude situation; their failure will
drive us to our duty in the end.

The military situation, past, present, and prospective, is no reason
for abandonment. Our campaign has been as perfect as possible with
the force at hand. We have been delayed, first, by a failure to comprehend the immensity of our acquisition; second, by insufficient
force; third, by our efforts for peace. In February, after the treaty of
peace, General Otis had only 3,722 officers and men whom he had a
legal right to order into battle. The terms of enlistment of the rest of
his troops had expired, and they fought voluntarily and not on legal
military compulsion. It was one of the noblest examples of patriotic
devotion to duty in the history of the world.

Those who complain, do so in ignorance of the real situation. We
attempted a great task with insufficient means; we became impatient
that it was not finished before it could fairly be commenced; and I

pray we may not add that other element of disaster, pausing in the work before it is thoroughly and for ever done. That is the gravest mistake we could possibly make, and that is the only danger before us. Our Indian wars would have been shortened, the lives of soldiers and settlers saved, and the Indians themselves benefited, had we made continuous and decisive war; and any other kind of war is criminal, because ineffective. We acted toward the Indians as though we feared them, loved them, hated them—all at the same time—with a mingling of foolish sentiment, inaccurate thought, and paralytic purpose. Let us now be instructed by our own experience.

This war is like all other wars. It needs to be finished before it is stopped. I am prepared to vote either to make our work thorough or even now to abandon it. A lasting peace can be secured only by overwhelming forces in ceaseless action until universal and absolutely final defeat is inflicted on the enemy. To halt before every armed force, every guerrilla band opposing us is dispersed or exterminated, will prolong hostilities and leave alive the seeds of perpetual insurrection.

The news that 60,000 American soldiers have crossed the Pacific; that, if necessary, the American Congress will make it 100,000 or 200,000 men; that, at any cost, we will establish peace and govern the islands, will do more to end the war than the soldiers themselves. But the report that we even discuss the withdrawal of a single soldier at the present time, and that we even debate the possibility of not administering government throughout the archipelago ourselves, will be misunderstood and misrepresented and will blow into a flame once more the fires our soldiers' blood has almost quenched.

Mr. President, reluctantly and only from a sense of duty, I am forced to say that American opposition to the war has been the chief factor in prolonging it. Had Aguinaldo not understood that in America, even in the American Congress, even here in the Senate, he and his cause were supported; had he not known that it was proclaimed on the stump and in the press by a faction in the United States, that every shot his misguided followers fired into the breasts of American soldiers was like the volleys fired by Washington's men against the soldiers of King George, his insurrection would have dissolved before it entirely crystallized.

The utterances of American opponents of the war are read to the ignorant soldiers of Aguinaldo and repeated in exaggerated form among the common people. Attempts have been made by wretches claiming American citizenship to ship arms and ammunition from Asiatic ports to the Filipinos, and these acts of infamy were coupled by the Malays with American assaults on our Government at home.

The Filipinos do not understand free speech, and therefore our tolerance of American assaults on the American Government means to them that the Government is in the minority or it would not permit what appears to them such treasonable criticism. It is believed and stated in Luzon, Panay, and Cebu that the Filipinos have only to fight, harass, retreat, break up into small parties, if necessary, as they are doing now, but by any means hold out until the next Presidential election, and our forces will be withdrawn. All this has aided the enemy more than climate, arms, and battle. I have heard these reports myself; I have talked with the people; I have seen our mangled boys in the hospital and field; I have stood on the firing line and beheld our dead soldiers, their faces turned to the pitiless southern sky, and in sorrow, rather than anger, I say to those whose voices in America have cheered those misguided natives on to shoot our soldiers down, that the blood of those dead and wounded boys of ours is on their hands. In sorrow, rather than anger, I say these words, for I earnestly believe that our brothers knew not what they did.

But, Senators, it would be better to abandon the Philippines, and count our blood and treasure already spent a profitable loss, than to apply any academic arrangement of self-government to these children. They are not yet capable of self-government. How could they be? They are not a self-governing race; they are Orientals, Malays, instructed by Spaniards in the latter's worst estate.

They know nothing of practical government, except as they have witnessed the weak, corrupt, cruel, and capricious rule of Spain. What magic will anyone employ to dissolve in their minds and characters those impressions of governors and governed which three centuries of misrule has created? What alchemy will change the oriental quality of their blood, in a year, and set the self-governing currents of the American pouring through their Malay veins? How shall they, in a decade, be exalted to the heights of self-governing peoples which required a thousand years for *us* to reach?

Let men beware how they employ the term "self-government." It is a sacred term. It is the watchword at the door of the inner temple of liberty, for liberty does not always mean self-government. Self-government is a method of liberty—the highest, simplest, best— and it is acquired only after centuries of study and struggle and experiment and instruction in all the elements of the progress of man. Self-government is no cheap boon, to be bestowed on the merely audacious. It is the degree which crowns the graduate of liberty, not the reward of liberty's infant class, which has not yet mastered the alphabet of freedom. Savage blood, oriental blood, Malay blood, Spanish example—in these do we find the elements of self-government?

We must act on the situation as it exists, not as we would wish it. I have talked with hundreds of these people, getting their views as to the practical workings of self-government. The great majority do not understand participation in any government whatever. The most enlightened among them declare that self-government will succeed because the employers of labor will control the vote of their employees, and that this will insure intelligent voting. I was assured that we could depend upon good men always being in office, because the officials who constitute the government will nominate their successors, choose those among the people who will do the voting, and determine how and where elections will be held.

The most ardent advocate of self-government that I met was anxious that I should know that such a government would be tranquil, because as he said, "if anyone criticized it, the government would shoot the offender." A few of them have a sort of verbal understanding of the democratic theory, but the above are examples of the notions concerning the practical workings of self-government entertained by the aristocracy, the rich planters and traders, and heavy employers of labor—the men who would run the government.

Example for decades will be necessary to instruct them in American ideas and methods of administration. Example, example; always example—this alone will teach them.

Our government must be simple and strong. It must be a uniform government. Different forms for different islands will produce perpetual disturbance, because the people of each island will think that the people of the other islands are more favored than they. In Panay I heard murmurings that we were giving Negroes an American constitution. Such jealousy is a human quality, found even in America, and we must never forget that in dealing with the Filipinos we deal with children. And so our government must be simple and strong. Simple and strong! The meaning of those two words must be written in every line of Philippine legislation, realized in every act of Philippine administration.

A Philippine office in our Department of State; an American governor-general in Manila, with power to meet daily emergencies; possibly an advisory council with no power except that of discussing measures with the governor-general, which council would be the germ for future legislatures, a school in practical government; an American lieutenant-governor in each province, with a like council about him; if possible, an American resident in each district and a like council grouped about him; frequent and unannounced visits of provincial governors to the districts of their province; periodical reports to the governor-general; an American board of visitation to make semi-annual trips to the archipelago without power of suggestion or of interference with officials or people, but only to report and recommend to the Philippine office of our State Department; a Philippine civil service, with promotion for efficiency; a reform of local taxation on a just and scientific basis; the minting of abundant money for Philippine and Oriental use; the granting of franchises and concessions upon the theory of developing the resources of the archipelago, and therefore not by sale, but upon participation in the profits of the enterprise; a system of public schools with compulsory attendance rigidly enforced; the establishment of the English language throughout the islands, teaching it exclusively in the schools and using it, through interpreters, exclusively in the courts; a simple civil code and a still simpler criminal code, and both common to all the islands except Sulu, Mindanao, and Paluan; American judges for all but smallest offenses; gradual, slow, and careful introduction of the best Filipinos into the working machinery of the government; no promise whatever of the franchise until the people have been prepared for it; all the legislation backed by the necessary force to execute it; this outline of government the situation demands as soon as tranquillity is established. Until then military government is advisable.

We cannot adopt the Dutch method in Java, nor the English method in the Malay states, because both of these systems rest on and operate through the existing governments of hereditary princes, with Dutch or English residents as advisers. But in the Philippines there are no such hereditary rulers, no such established governments. There is no native machinery of administration except that of the villages. The people have been deprived of the advantages of hereditary native princes, and yet not instructed in any form of regular, just, and orderly government.

Neither is a protectorate practicable. If a protectorate leaves the natives to their own methods more than would our direct administration of their government, it would permit the very evils which it is our duty to prevent. If, on the other hand, under a protectorate, we interfere to prevent those evils, we govern as much as if we directly administer the government, but without system or constructive purpose. In either alternative we incur all the responsibility of directly governing them ourselves, without any of the benefits to us, to them, or to the archipelago, which our direct administration of government throughout the Islands would secure.

Even the elemental plan I have outlined will fail in the hands of any but admirable administrators. Spain did not fail in devising. Many of her plans were excellent. She failed in administering. Her officials as a class were corrupt, indolent, cruel, immoral. They were selected to please a faction in Spain, to placate members of the Cortes, to bribe those whom the Government feared. They were seldom selected for their fitness. They were the spawn of Government favor and Government fear, and therefore of Government iniquity.

The men we send to administer civilized government in the Philippines must be themselves the highest examples of our civilization. I use the word examples, for examples they must be in that word's most absolute sense. They must be men of the world and of affairs, students of their fellow men, not theorists nor dreamers. They must be brave men, physically as well as morally. They must be men whom no force can frighten, no influence coerce, no money buy. Such men come high, even here in America. But they must be had.

Better pure military occupation for years than government by any other quality of administration. Better abandon this priceless possession, admit ourselves incompetent to do our part in the world-redeeming work of our imperial race; *better now haul down the flag than to apply academic notions of self-government to these children or attempt their government by any but the most perfect administrators our country can produce.* I assert that such administrators can be found....

Mr. President, self-government and internal development have been the dominant notes of our first century; administration and the development of other lands will be the dominant notes of our second century. And administration is as high and holy a function as self-government, just as the care of a trust estate is as sacred an obligation as the management of our own concerns.

Administration of good government is not denial of liberty. For what is liberty? The liberty of a people means law. First of all, it is a common rule of action, applying equally to all within its limits. Liberty means protection of property and life without price, free speech without intimidation, justice without purchase or delay, government without favor or favorites. What will best give all this to the people of the Philippines—American administration, developing them gradually toward self-government, or self-government by a people before they know what self-government means?

The Declaration of Independence does not forbid us to do our part in the regeneration of the world....

The Opposition is stopped from denying our constitutional power to govern the Philippines as circumstances may demand, for such power is admitted in the case of Florida, Louisiana, Alaska. How, then, is it denied in the Philippines? Is there a geographical interpretation to the Constitution? Do degrees of longitude fix constitutional limitations? Does a thousand miles of ocean diminish constitutional power more than a thousand miles of land?

The ocean does not separate us from the field of our duty and endeavor—it joins us, an established highway needing no repair, and landing us at any point desired. The seas do not separate the Philippine Islands from us or from each other. The seas are highways through the archipelago, which would cost hundreds of millions of dollars to construct if they were land instead of water. Land may separate men from their desire, the ocean never. Russia has been centuries crossing Siberian wastes; the Puritans crossed the Atlantic in brief and flying weeks.

If the Boers must have traveled by land, they would never have reached the Transvaal; but they sailed on liberty's ocean; they walked on civilization's untaxed highway, the welcoming sea. Our ships habitually sailed round the Cape and anchored in California's harbors before a single trail had lined the desert with the whitening bones of those who made it. No! No! The ocean unites us; steam unites us; electricity unites us; all the elements of nature unite us to the region where duty and interest call us.

No; the oceans are not limitations of the power which the Constitution expressly gives Congress to govern all territory the Nation may acquire....

For the archipelago is a base for the commerce of the East. It is a base for military and naval operations against the only powers with whom conflict is possible; a fortress thrown up in the Pacific, defending our western coast, commanding the waters of the Orient, and giving us a point from which we can instantly strike and seize the possessions of any possible foe....

...Mr. President, this question is deeper than any question of party politics; deeper than any question of the isolated policy of our country; deeper than any question of constitutional power. It is elemental. It is racial. God has not been preparing the English-speaking and Teutonic peoples for a thousand years for nothing but vain and idle self-contemplation and self-admiration. No! He has made us the master organizers of the world to establish system where chaos reigns. He has given us the spirit of progress to overwhelm the forces of reaction throughout the earth. He has made us adepts in government that we may administer government among savage and senile peoples.

Were it not for such a force as this the world would relapse into barbarism and night. And of all our race He has marked the American people as His chosen Nation finally to lead in the regeneration of the world. This is the divine mission of America, and it holds for us all profit, glory, happiness possible to man. We are trustees of the world's progress, guardians of its righteous peace. The judgment of the Master is upon us: "Ye have been faithful over a few things; I will make you ruler over many things."...

...We shall renew our youth at the fountain of new and glorious deeds. We shall exalt our reverence for the flag by carrying it to a noble future as well as by remembering' its ineffable past. Its immortality will not pass, because everywhere and always we shall acknowledge and discharge the solemn responsibilities our sacred flag, in its deepest meaning, puts upon us. And so, Senators, with reverent hearts, where dwells the fear of God, the American people move forward to the future of their hope and the doing of His work.

KAISER WILHELM II
Address to the German People
("The sword must decide")
August 6, 1914

Kaiser Wilhelm II (1859–1941), who abdicated the throne in 1918, was the last of the German Kaisers. His encouragement of Austro-Hungary's revenge on Serbia for the assassination of the Archduke Ferdinand in June of 1914 helped instigate the First World War. In this speech, he prepares his country for that war.

To the German People:

Since the founding of the Empire, during a period of forty-three years, it has been my zealous endeavor and the endeavor of my ancestors to preserve peace to the world and in peace to promote our vigorous development. But our enemies envy us the success of our toil. All professed and secret hostility from East and West and from beyond the sea, we have till now borne in the consciousness of our responsibility and power. Now, however, our opponents desire to humble us. They demand that we look on with folded arms while our enemies gird themselves for treacherous attack. They will not tolerate that we support our ally with unshaken loyalty, who fights for its prestige as a great power, and with whose abasement our power and honor are likewise lost. Therefore the sword must decide.

In the midst of peace the world attacks us.

Therefore up! To arms! All hesitation, all delay were treachery to the Fatherland. It is a question of the existence or non-existence of the Empire which our fathers founded anew. It is the question of the existence or the non-existence of German might and German culture. We shall defend ourselves to the last breath of man and beast. And we shall survive this fight, even though it were against a world of enemies. Never yet was Germany conquered when she was united.

Then forward march with God! He will be with us as He was with our fathers.

VLADIMIR LENIN

On the Dissolution of the Constituent Assembly

Delivered to the All-Russia Central Executive Committee

("The Soviet revolutionary republic will triumph, no matter what the cost")

Moscow, U.S.S.R.

January 6, 1918

The leader of the Russian Revolution was a consistent advocate for terror. After his death in 1924, Josef Stalin, who then spread the terror much further and wider, would carry out Lenin's policies. Lenin's speeches, when not analytical and static, often encouraged a ruthless and violent reprisal against political and intellectual critics of his policies. Robert V. Daniels, in his A Documentary History of Communism in Russia, *quotes, for instance, Lenin's telegraphic orders for suppressing well-off peasants (kulaks) "to set an example."[1] In this speech, he reminds his followers and warns his opponents that ". . . nothing in the world will make us give up Soviet power!"*

---

[1] "Lenin's response to a peasant uprising in Penza Province in August 1918 came to light among the party documents in 1991," writes Robert V. Daniels in *A Documentary History of Communism in Russia.* (Hanover, New Hampshire: University Press of New England. 1993.) "Comrades! The revolt by the five kulak volosts [townships] must be suppressed without mercy. The interest of the *entire* revolution demands this, because *we have* now before us our final decisive battle 'with the kulaks.' We need to set an example.

1) You need to hang (hang without fail, so that the *public sees*) *at least* 100 notorious kulaks, the rich, and the bloodsuckers.

2) Publish their names.

3) Take away *all* of their grain.

4) Execute the hostages—in accordance with yesterday's telegram.

Comrades, the clash between Soviet power and the Constituent Assembly results from the entire course of the Russian revolution, which was confronted by the unprecedented task of reconstructing society on socialist lines. After the events of 1905 there could be no doubt that tsarism's day was over and that it had scrambled out of the pit only because of the backwardness and ignorance of the rural population. The Revolution of 1917 was marked on the one hand by the transformation of the bourgeois imperialist party into a republican party under the pressure of events, and on the other hand, by the emergence of democratic organisations, the Soviets, that had been formed in 1905; even then the socialists had realised that the organisation of these Soviets was creating something great, something new and unprecedented in the history of world revolution. The Soviets, created solely by the initiative of the people, are a form of democracy without parallel in any other country of the world.

The revolution produced two forces—the union of the masses for the purpose of overthrowing tsarism, and the organisations of the working people. When I hear the enemies of the October Revolution exclaim that the ideas of socialism are unfeasible and utopian, I usually put to them a plain and simple question. What in their opinion, I ask, are the Soviets? What gave rise to these organisations of the people, which have no precedent in the history of the development of world revolution? Not one of them has been able to give a precise answer to this question. Defending the bourgeois system by inertia, they oppose these powerful organisations, the formation of which has never before been witnessed in any revolution in the world. All who are fighting the landowners are joining forces with the Soviets of Peasants' Deputies. The Soviets embrace all who do not wish to stand idle and are devoting themselves to creative work. They have spread their network over the whole country, and the denser this network of Soviets of the people, the less will it be possible to exploit the working people. For the existence of the Soviets is incompatible with a prosperous bourgeois system. That is

---

"This needs to be accomplished in such a way that people for hundreds of miles around will see, tremble, know and scream out: *let's choke* and strangle those bloodsucking kulaks.

"Telegraph us acknowledging receipt and execution of this.

"Yours, Lenin

"P.S. Use your *toughest* people for this."

Daniels cites: Lenin, telegram to Penza Communists, August 11, 1918 (Central Party Archive, file 2, dossier 1, document #6898; English translation by the Library of Congress).

the source of all the contradictions among the bourgeoisie, who are fighting our Soviets solely in their own interests.

The transition from capitalism to a socialist system entails a long and bitter struggle. Having overthrown tsarism, the Russian revolution was bound to go farther; it could not stop at the victory of the bourgeois revolution; for the war, and the untold sufferings it caused the exhausted peoples, created a soil favourable for the outbreak of the social revolution. Nothing, therefore, is more ludicrous than the assertion that the subsequent development of the revolution, and the revolt of the masses that followed, were caused by a party, by an individual, or, as they vociferate, by the will of a "dictator." The fire of revolution broke out solely because of the incredible sufferings of Russia, and because of the conditions created by the war, which sternly and inexorably faced the working people with the alternative of taking a bold, desperate and fearless step, or of perishing, of dying from starvation.

And revolutionary fire was manifest in the creation of the Soviets—the mainstay of the workers' revolution. The Russian people have made a gigantic advance, a leap from tsarism to the Soviets. That is a fact, irrefutable and unparalleled. While the bourgeois parliaments of all countries and states, confined within the bounds of capitalism and private property, have never anywhere supported a revolutionary movement, the Soviets, having lit the fire of revolution, imperatively command the people to fight, take everything into their own hands, and organise themselves. In the course of a revolution called forth by the strength of the Soviets there are certain to be all kinds of errors and blunders. But everybody knows that revolutionary movements are always and inevitably accompanied by temporary chaos, destruction and disorder. Bourgeois society is the same war, the same shambles; and it was this circumstance that gave rise to and accentuated the conflict between the Constituent Assembly and the Soviets. Those who point out that we are now "dissolving" the Constituent Assembly although at one time we defended it are not displaying a grain of sense, but are merely uttering pompous and meaningless phrases. At one time, we considered the Constituent Assembly to be better than tsarism and the republic of Kerensky with their famous organs of power; but as the Soviets emerged, they, being revolutionary organisations of the whole people, naturally became incomparably superior to any parliament in the world, a fact that I emphasised as far back as last April. By completely smashing bourgeois and landed property and by facilitating the final upheaval which is sweeping away all traces of the bourgeois system, the Soviets impelled us on to the path that has led the people to organise their own lives. We have taken up this great work of organisation, and it is well that we have done so. Of course, the socialist revolution cannot be immediately presented to the people in a clean, neat and impeccable form; it will inevitably be accompanied by civil war, sabotage and resistance. Those who assert the contrary are either liars or cowards.

The events of April 20, when the people, without any directions from "dictators" or parties, came out independently and solidly against the government of compromisers, showed even then that the bourgeoisie were weak and had no solid support. The masses sensed their power, and to placate them the famous game of ministerial leapfrog began, the object of which was to fool the people. But the people very soon saw through the game, particularly after Kerensky, both his pockets stuffed with predatory secret treaties with the imperialists, began to move the armies for an offensive. Gradually the activities of the compromisers became obvious to the deceived people, whose patience began to be exhausted. The result was the October Revolution. The people learned by experience, having suffered torture, executions and wholesale shootings and it is nonsense for the butchers to assert that the Bolsheviks, or certain "dictators," are responsible for the revolt of the working people. They are given the lie by the split that is occurring among the people themselves at congresses, meetings, conferences, and so forth. The people have not yet fully understood the October Revolution. This revolution has shown in practice how the people must take into their own hands, the hands of the workers' and peasants' state, the land, the natural resources, and the means of transport and production.

Our cry was, "All power to the Soviets!" It is for this we are fighting. The people wanted the Constituent Assembly summoned, and we summoned it. But they sensed immediately what this famous Constituent Assembly really was. And now we have carried out the will of the people, which is *"All power to the Soviets."* As for the saboteurs, we shall crush them. When I came from Smolny, that fount of life and vigor, to the Tauride Palace, I felt as though I were in the company of corpses and lifeless mummies. They drew on all their available resources in order to fight socialism, they resorted to violence and sabotage, they even turned knowledge—the great pride of humanity—into a means of exploiting the working people. But although they managed to hinder somewhat the advance towards the socialist revolution, they could not stop it and will never be able to. Indeed the Soviets that have begun to smash the old, outworn foundations of the bourgeois system, not in gentlemanly, but in a blunt proletarian and peasant fashion, are much too strong.

To hand over power to the Constituent Assembly would again be compromising with the malignant bourgeoisie. The Russian Soviets place the interests of the working people far above the interests of a treacherous policy of compromise disguised in a new garb. The speeches of those outdated politicians, Chernov and Tsereteli, who continue whining tediously for the cessation of civil war, give off the stale and musty odour of antiquity. But as long as Kaledin exists, and as long as the slogan "All power to the Constituent Assembly" conceals the slogan "Down with Soviet power," civil war is inevitable. For nothing in the world will make us give up Soviet power!

And when the Constituent Assembly again revealed its readiness to postpone all the painfully urgent problems and tasks that were placed before it by the Soviets, we told the Constituent Assembly that they must not be postponed for one single moment. And by the will of Soviet power the Constituent Assembly, which has refused to recognise the power of the people, is being dissolved. The Byabushinskys have lost their stakes; their attempts at resistance will only accentuate and provoke a new outbreak of civil war.

The Constituent Assembly is dissolved. The Soviet revolutionary republic will triumph, no matter what the cost.

WILLIAM JENNINGS BRYAN
The Scopes "Monkey Trial"
("The parents have a right to say that no teacher paid by their money shall rob their children of faith in God")

Dayton, Tennessee
July 16, 1925

<blockquote>
In these excerpts from the fifth day's proceedings of the Scopes trial, the most famous American trial of the first half of the twentieth century, the lawyer William Jennings Bryan, former Secretary of State under Woodrow Wilson and three-time presidential candidate, defends the State of Tennessee's right to have made and to enforce laws banning the teaching of evolution in its public schools. He discusses not only the pervasive Christian belief of the state's citizens but the unwelcome interest and participation of outsiders at this trial. The debate he highlights between the teaching of science versus religious beliefs continues today: "The people of this state passed this law, the people of this state knew what they were doing when they passed the law, and they knew the dangers of the doctrine—that they did not want it taught to their children, and my friends." Bryan died only a few days after the trial ended.
</blockquote>

If the court please we are now approaching the end of the first week of this trial and I haven't thought it proper until this time to take part in the discussions that have been dealing with phases of this question, or case, where the state laws and the state rules of practice were under discussion and I feel that those who are versed in the law of the state and who are used to the customs of the court might better take the burden of the case, but today we come to the discussion of a very important part of this case, a question so important that upon its decision will determine the length of this trial. If the court holds, as we believe the court should hold, that the testimony that the defense is now offering is not competent and not proper testimony, then I assume we are near the end of this trial and because the question involved is not confined to local questions, but is the broadest that will possibly arise, I have felt justified in submitting my views on the case for the consideration of the court. I have been tempted to speak at former times, but I have been able to withstand the temptation. I have been drawn into the case by, I think nearly all the lawyers on the other side. The principal attorney has often suggested that I am the arch-conspirator and that I am responsible for the presence of this case and I have almost been credited with leadership of the ignorance and bigotry which he thinks he could alone inspire a law like this. Then Mr. Malone has seen fit to honor me by quoting my opinion on religious liberty. I assume he means that that is the most important opinion on religious liberty that he has been able to find in this country and I feel complimented that I should be picked out from all the men living and dead as the one whose expressions are most vital to the welfare of our country. And this morning I was credited with being the cause of the presence of these so-called experts.

Mr. Hays says that before he got here he read that I said this was to be a duel to the death, between science—was it?—and revealed religion. I don't know who the other duelist was, but I was representing one of them and because of that they went to the trouble and the expense of several thousand dollars to bring down their witnesses. Well, my friend, if you said that this was important enough to be regarded as a duel between two great ideas or groups I certainly will be given credit for foreseeing what I could not then know and that is that this question is so important between religion and irreligion that even the invoking of the divine blessing upon it might seem partisan and partial. I think when we come to consider the importance of this question, that all of us who are interested as lawyers on either side, could claim what we—what your honor so graciously grants—a hearing. I have got down here for fear I might forget them, certain points that I desire to present for your honor's consideration.

In the first place, the statute—our position is that the statute is sufficient. The statute defines exactly what the people of Tennessee desired and intended and did declare unlawful and it needs no interpretation. The caption speaks of the evolutionary theory and the statute specifically states that teachers are forbidden to teach in the schools supported by taxation in this state, any theory of creation of man that denies the divine record of man's creation as found in the Bible, and that there might be no difference of opinion—there might be no ambiguity—that there might be no such confusion of thought as our learned friends attempt to inject into it, the legislature was careful to define what it meant by the first part of the statute. It says to teach that man is a descendant of any lower form of life—if that had not been there—if the first sentence had been the only sentence in the statute, then these gentlemen might come and ask to define what that meant or to explain whether the thing that was taught was contrary to the language of the statute in the first sentence, but the second sentence removes all doubt, as has been stated by my colleague. The second sentence points out specifically what is meant, and that is the teaching that man is the descendant of any lower form of life, and if the defendant taught that as we have proven by the textbook that he used and as we have proven by the students that went to hear him—if he taught that man is a descendant of any lower form of life, he violated that statute, and more than that we have his own confession that he knew he was violating the statute. We have the testimony here of Mr. White, the superintendent of schools, who says that Mr. Scopes told him he could not teach that book without violating the law. We have the testimony of Mr. Robertson—Robinson—the head of the Board of Education, who talked with Mr. Scopes just at the time the schools closed, or a day or two afterward, and Mr. Scopes told him that he had reviewed that book just before the school closed, and that he could not teach it without teaching evolution and without violating the law, and we have Mr. Robinson's statement that Mr. Scopes told him that he and one of the teachers, Mr. Ferguson, had talked it over after the law was passed and had decided that they could not teach it without the violation of the law, and yet while Mr. Scopes knew what the law was, and knew that it violated the law, he proceeded to violate the law.

That is the evidence before this court, and we do not need any expert to tell us what that law means. An expert cannot be permitted to come in here and try to defeat the enforcement of a law by testifying that it isn't a bad law and it isn't—I mean a bad doctrine—no matter how these people phrase the doctrine—no matter how they eulogize it. This is not the place to try to prove that the law ought never to have been passed. The place to prove that, or teach that, was to the legislature. If these people were so anxious to keep the state of Tennessee from disgracing itself, if they were so afraid that by this action taken by the legislature, the state would put itself before the people of the nation as ignorant people and bigoted people—if they had half the affection for Tennessee that you would think they had as they come here to testify, they would have come at a time when their testimony would have been valuable and not at this time to ask you to refuse to enforce a law because they did not think the law ought to have been passed.

And, my friends, if the people of Tennessee were to go into a state like New York—the one from which this impulse comes to resist this law, or go into any state—if they went into any state and tried to convince the people that a law they had passed ought not to be enforced, just because the people who went there didn't think it ought to have been passed, don't you think it would be resented as an impertinence?... The people of this state passed this law, the people of this state knew what they were doing when they passed the law, and they knew the dangers of the doctrine—that they did not want it taught to their children, and my friends. It isn't—Your Honor—it isn't proper to bring experts in here to try to defeat the purpose of the people of this state by trying to show that this thing that they denounce and outlaw is a beautiful thing that everybody ought to believe in.... These people want to come here with experts to make Your Honor believe that the law should never have been passed and because in their opinion it ought not to have been passed, it ought not to be enforced. It isn't a place for expert testimony. We have sufficient proof in the book—doesn't the book state the very thing that is objected to, and outlawed in this state? Who has a copy of that book?

The Court: Do you mean the Bible?

Mr. Bryan: No, sir; the biology. *(Laughter in the courtroom.)*

A Voice: Here it is; Hunter's Biology.

Mr. Bryan: No, not the Bible, you see in this state they cannot teach the Bible. They can only teach things that declare it to be a lie, according to the learned counsel. These people in the state—Christian people—have tied their hands by their constitution. They say we all believe in the Bible, for it is the overwhelming belief in the state, but we will not teach that Bible, which we believe, even to our children through teachers that we pay with our money. No, no, it isn't the teaching of the Bible, and we are not asking it. The question is can a minority in this state come in and compel a teacher to teach that the Bible is not true and make the parents of these children pay the expenses of the teacher to tell their children what these people believe is false and dangerous? Has it come to a time when the minority can take charge of a state like Tennessee and compel the majority to pay their teachers while they take religion out of the heart of the children of the parents who pay the teachers?....

So, my friends, if that were true, if man and monkey were in the same class, called primates, it would mean they did not come up from the same order. It might mean that instead of one being the ancestor of the other they were all cousins. But it does not mean that they did not come up from the lower animals, if this is the only place they could come from, and the Christian believes man came from above, but the evolutionist believes he must have come from below....

Your Honor, I want to show you that we have evidence enough here, we do not need any experts to come in here and tell us about this thing. Here we have Mr. Hunter. Mr. Hunter is the author of this biology and this is the man who wrote the book Mr. Scopes was teaching. And here we have the diagram....

There is that book! There is the book they were teaching your children that man was a mammal and so indistinguishable among the mammals that they leave him there with thirty-four hundred and ninety-nine other mammals....

He tells the children to copy this, copy this diagram. In the notebook, children are to copy this diagram and take it home in their notebooks. To show their parents that you cannot find man. That is the great game to put in the public schools to find man among animals, if you can.

Tell me that the parents of this day have not any right to declare that children are not to be taught this doctrine? Shall not be taken down from the high plane upon which God put man? Shall be detached from the throne of God and be compelled to link their ancestors with the jungle, tell that to these children? Why, my friend, if they believe it, they go back to scoff at the religion of their parents! And the parents have a right to say that no teacher paid by their money shall rob their children of faith in God and send them back to their homes, skeptical, infidels, or agnostics, or atheists....

Your Honor, we first pointed out that we do not need any experts in science. Here is one plain fact, and the statute defines itself, and it tells the kind of evolution it does not want taught, and the evidence says that this is the kind of evolution that was taught, and no number of scientists could come in here, my friends, and override that statute or take from the jury its right to decide this question, so that all the experts that they could bring would mean nothing. And, when it comes to Bible experts, every member of the jury is as good an expert on the Bible as any man that they could bring, or that we could bring.... We have a book here that shows everything that is needed to make one understand evolution, and to show that the man violated the law. Then why should we prolong this case? We can bring our experts here for the Christians; for every one they can bring who does not believe in Christianity, we can bring more than one who believes in the Bible and rejects evolution, and our witnesses will be just as good experts as theirs on a question of that kind. We could have a thousand or a million witnesses, but this case as to whether evolution is true or not, is not going to be tried here, within this city; if it is carried to the state's courts, it will not be tried there, and if it is taken to the great court at Washington, it will not be tried there. No, my friends, no court or the law, and no jury, great or small, is going to destroy the issue between the believer and the unbeliever.

The Bible is the Word of God; the Bible is the only expression of man's hope of salvation.... That Bible is not going to be driven out of this court by experts who come hundreds of miles to testify that they can reconcile evolution, with its ancestor in the jungle, with man made by God in His image, and put here for purposes as a part of the divine plan.... Your court is an office of this state, and we who represent the state as counsel are officers of the state, and we cannot humiliate the great state of Tennessee by admitting for a moment that people can come from anywhere and protest against the enforcement of this state's laws on the ground that it does not conform with their ideas, or because it banishes from our schools a thing that they believe in and think ought to be taught in spite of the protest of those who employ the teacher and pay him his salary.

The facts are simple, the case is plain, and if those gentlemen want to enter upon a larger field of educational work on the subject of evolution, let us get through with this case and then convene a mock court, for it will deserve the title of mock court if its purpose is to banish from the hearts of the people the Word of God as revealed.

JOSEPH GOEBBELS

"Our Hitler"

The Birthday Speech

("For those who do not know Hitler, it seems a miracle
that millions of people love and support him")

Berlin, Germany

April 20, 1933

*Goebbels (1897–1945) was a "doctor" by virtue of his Ph.D. in romantic
literature. As impressed by Hitler's rhetorical gifts as Hitler was by Goebbels'
insidious writing, Goebbels left the National Socialists group he belonged to,
which actually advocated socialism, and joined Hitler's Nazis in 1926. In
1933 he became Chancellor Hitler's Nazi party propaganda minister, and
shortly after delivered this, the first of several "Happy Birthday, Hitler"
speeches. Goebbels retained his position as minister of propaganda until May
1, 1945, when, with the war all but over, he had his six children murdered
and then committed suicide with his wife.*

The newspapers today are filled with congratulations for Reich
Chancellor Adolf Hitler. The nuances vary, depending on the tone,
character, and attitude of the newspaper. All, however, agree on one
thing: Hitler is a man of stature who has already accomplished his-
torically important deeds and faces still greater challenges. He is the
kind of statesman found only rarely in Germany. During his lifetime, he has the good fortune not only to be appreciated and loved
by the overwhelming majority of the German people, but even
more importantly to be understood by them. He is the only German
politician of the post-war period who understood the situation and
drew the necessary hard and firm conclusions. All the newspapers
agree on this. It no longer needs to be said that he has taken up
Bismarck's work and intends to complete it. There is enough proof
of this even for those who do not believe, or who think ill of him.
I therefore do not think it necessary for me to discuss the historical significance and still unknown impact of this man on the eve
of the day on which, far from the bustle of the Reich capital, Adolf
Hitler completes his forty-fourth year. I feel a much deeper need to
personally express my esteem for him, and in doing so I believe that
I am speaking for many hundreds of thousands of National Socialists throughout the country. We shall leave it to those who were

our enemies only a few months ago and who then slandered then to praise him today with awkward words and embarrassing pathos. We know how little Adolf Hitler appreciates such attempts, and how much more the devoted loyalty and lasting support of his friends and fellow fighters correspond to his nature.

The mysterious magic that he exerts on all who come in contact with him cannot alone explain his historic personality. There is more that makes us love and esteem him. Through all the ups and downs of Adolf Hitler's career, from the beginning of his political activity to the crowning of his career as he seized power, he has always remained the same: a person among people, a friend to his comrades, an eager supporter of every ability and talent. He is a pathfinder for those who devoted themselves to his idea, a man who conquered the hearts of his comrades in the midst of battle and never released them.

It seems to me that one thing has to be said in the midst of the profusion of feelings. Only a few know Hitler well. Most of the millions who look to him with faithful trust do so from a distance. He has become to them a symbol of their faith in the future. Normally the great men that we admire from a distance lose their magic when one knows them well. With Hitler the opposite is true. The longer one knows him, the more one admires him, and the more one is ready to give oneself fully to his cause.

We will let others blow the trumpets. His friends and comrades gather round him to shake his hand and thank him for everything that he is to us, and that he has given to us. Let me say it once more: We love this man, and we know that he has earned all of our love and support. Never was a man more unjustly accused by the hate and slanders of his ill wishers of other parties. Remember what they said about him! A mishmash of contradictory accusations! They did not fail to accuse him of every sin, to deny him every virtue. When he nonetheless overcame in the end the flood of lies, triumphing over his enemies and raising the National Socialist flag over Germany, fate showed its favor toward him to the entire world. It raised him from the mass of people and put him in the place he deserved because of his brilliant gifts and his pure and flawless humanity.

I remember the years when—just released from prison—he began to rebuild his party. We passed a few wonderful vacation days with him on his beloved Obersalzburg high above Berchtesgaden. Below us was the quiet cemetery where his unforgettable friend Dietrich Eckart is buried. We walked through the mountains, discussed plans for the future, and talked about theories that today have long since become reality. He then sent me to Berlin. He gave me a difficult and challenging task, and I still thank him today that he gave me the job.

A few months later we sat in a room in a small Berlin hotel. The party had just been banned by the Marxist-Jewish police department. Heavy blows were falling on it. The party was full of discouragement, bickering and quarreling. Everyone was complaining about everyone else. The whole organization seemed to have given up.

Hitler, however, did not lose courage, but immediately began to organize a defense, and helped out where he was needed. Although he had his own personal and political difficulties, he found the time and strength to deal with the problems and support his friends in the Reich capital.

One of his fine and noble traits is that he never gives up on someone who has won his confidence. The more his political opponents attack such a person, the more loyal is Adolf Hitler's support. He is not the kind of person who is afraid of strong associates. The harder and tougher a man is, the more Hitler likes him. If things fall apart, his capable hands put them together again. Who would have thought it possible that a mass organization that includes literally everything could be build in this nation of individualists? Doing that is Hitler's great accomplishment. His principles are firm and unshakable, but he is generous and understanding toward human weaknesses. He is a pitiless enemy of his opponents, but a good and warm-hearted friend to his comrades. That is Hitler.

We saw him at the party's two large Nuremberg rallies, surrounded by the masses who saw in him Germany's hope. In the evenings, we sat with him in his hotel room. He was dressed in a simple brown shirt, the same as always, as if nothing had happened. Someone once said that the great is simple, and the simple is great. If that is true, it surely applies to Hitler. His nature and his whole philosophy is a brilliant simplification of the spiritual need and fragmentation that engulfed the German people after the war. He found the lowest common denominator. That is why his idea won: he modeled it, and through him the average man in the street saw its depth and significance.

One has to have seen him in defeat as well as victory to understand what sort of man he is. He never broke. He never lost courage or faith. Hundreds came to him seeking new hope, and no one left without receiving renewed strength.

On the day before 13 August 1932, we met in a small farmhouse outside Potsdam. We talked deep into the night, but not about our prospects for the next day, but rather about music, philosophy, and worldview issues. Then came the experiences one can only have with him. He spoke of the difficult years of his youth in Vienna and Munich, of his war experiences, of the first years of the party. Few know how hard and bitterly he had to fight. Today he is surrounded by praise and thanks. Only fifteen years ago he was a lonely individual among millions. The only difference between him and they was his burning faith and his fanatic resolve to transform that faith into action.

Those who believed that Hitler was finished after the party's defeat in November 1932 failed to understand him. Only someone who did not know him at all could make such a mistake. Hitler is one of those persons who rises from his defeats. Friedrich Nietzsche's phrase fits him well: "That which does not destroy me only makes me stronger."

This man, suffering under financial and party problems for years, assailed by the flood of lies from his enemies, wounded in the depths of his heart by the disloyalty of false friends, still found the limitless faith to lift his party from desperation to new victories.

How many thousands of kilometers have I sat behind him in cars or airplanes on election campaigns. How often did I see the thankful look of a man on the street, or a mother lifting her child to show him, and how often have I seen joy and happiness when people recognized him.

He kept his pockets filled with packages of cigarettes, each with a one- or two-mark coin. Every working lad he met got one. He had a friendly word for every mother and a warm handshake for every child.

Not without reason does the German youth admire him. They know that this man is young at heart, and that their cause is in his good hands. Last Easter Monday we sat with him in his small house on the Obersalzberg. A group of young hikers from Braunau, where he was born, came by for a visit. How surprised these lads were when they got not only a friendly greeting, but all fifteen lads were invited in. They got a hurriedly prepared lunch, and had to tell him about his hometown of Braunau.

The people have a fine sense for the truly great. Nothing impresses the people as deeply as when a person truly belongs to his people. Of whom but Hitler could this be true: As he returned from Berchtesgaden to Munich, people waved in every village. The children shouted Heil and threw bouquets of flowers into the car. The S.A. had closed the road in Traunstein. There was no moving either forward or back. Confidently and matter-of-factly, the S.A. Führer walked up to the car and said: "My Führer, an old party member is dying in the hospital, and his last wish is to see his Führer."

Mountains of work were waiting in Munich. But Hitler ordered the car to turn around, and sat for half an hour in the hospital at the bedside of his dying party comrade.

The Marxist press claimed he was a tyrant who dominated his satraps. What is he really? He is the best friend of his comrades. He has an open heart for every sorrow and every need, he has human understanding. He knows each of his associates thoroughly, and nothing happens in their public or private lives of which he is not aware. If misfortune happens, he helps them to bear it, and rejoices more than anyone else at their successes.

Never have I seen his two sides in anyone else. We had dinner together on the night of the Reichstag fire. We talked and listened to music. Hitler was a person among people. Twenty minutes later he stood in the smoldering, smoking ruins of the Reichstag building and gave piercing orders that led to the destruction of communism. Later he sat in an editorial office and dictated an article.

For those who do not know Hitler, it seems a miracle that millions of people love and support him. For those who know him, it is only natural. The secret of his success is in the indescribable magic of his personality. Those who know him the best love and honor him the most. One who has sworn allegiance to him is devoted to him body and soul.

I thought it was necessary tonight to say that, and to have it said by someone who really knows him, and who could find the courage to break through the barriers of reserve and speak of Hitler the man.

Today he has left the bustle of the capital. He left the wreaths and hymns of praise in Berlin. He is somewhere in his beloved Bavaria, far from the noise of the streets, to find peace and quiet. Perhaps in a nearby room someone will turn on a loudspeaker. If that should happen, then let me say to him, and to all of Germany: My Führer! Millions and millions of the best Germans send you their best wishes and give you their hearts. And we, your closest associates and friends, are gathered in honor and love. We know how little you like praise. But we must still say this: You have lifted Germany from its deepest disgrace to honor and dignity. You should know that behind you, and if necessary before you, a strong and determined group of fighters stands that is ready at any time to give its all for you and your idea. We wish both for your sake and ours that fate will preserve you for many decades, and that you may always remain our best friend and comrade. This is the wish of your fellow fighters and friends for your birthday. We offer your our hands and ask that you always remain for us what you are today:

Our Hitler!

BENITO MUSSOLINI
Premier of Italy
Radio Broadcast
("We have been patient with Ethiopia for forty years")
October 2, 1935

Benito Mussolini (1883–1945) had been a writer and editor of a socialist newspaper before World War I. After the war, he helped develop the strain of poisonous political philosophy called fascism. After the "March on Rome" by fascists in 1922, Mussolini became the Premier of Italy. By 1925 Mussolini, the so-called "Il Duce," was a dictator of his nationalistic police state. His conquest of Ethiopia in 1935 was one of his attempts to expand his power beyond the borders of Italy; his ruthlessness and use of poison gas there brought him infamy throughout Europe. He aligned himself with Hitler in the Axis Powers, but by 1943 the Allied Forces had taken back Ethiopia, Sicily, and most of Italy. He lost his power in 1943, and in 1945, after attempting a political comeback, he was killed.

Blackshirts of revolution, men and women of all Italy, Italians all over the world, beyond the mountains, beyond the seas, listen. A solemn hour is about to strike in the history of the country. Twenty million Italians are at this moment gathered in the squares of all Italy. It is the greatest demonstration that human history records. Twenty million, one heart alone, one will alone, one decision.

This manifestation signifies that the tie between Italy and fascism is perfect, absolute, unalterable. Only brains softened by puerile illusions, by sheer ignorance, can think differently, because they do not know what exactly is the Fascist Italy of 1935.

For many months the wheel of destiny and of the impulse of our calm determination moves toward the goal. In these last hours the rhythm has increased and nothing can stop it now.

It is not only an army marching towards its goal, but it is forty-four million Italians marching in unity behind this army. Because the blackest of injustices is being attempted against them, that of taking from them their place in the sun. When in 1915 Italy threw in her fate with that of the Allies, how many cries of admiration, how many promises were heard? But after the common victory, which cost Italy six hundred thousand dead, four hundred thousand lost, one million wounded, when peace was being discussed around the table only the crumbs of a rich colonial booty were left for us to pick up. For thirteen years we have been patient while the circle tightened around us at the hands of those who wish to suffocate us.

We have been patient with Ethiopia for forty years. It is enough now.

The League of Nations, instead of recognizing the rights of Italy, dares talk of sanctions, but until there is proof of the contrary, I refuse to believe that the authentic people of France will join in supporting sanctions against Italy. Six hundred thousand dead whose devotion was so heroic that the enemy commander justly admired them—those fallen would now turn in their graves.

And until there is proof to the contrary, I refuse to believe that the authentic people of Britain will want to spill blood and send Europe into a catastrophe for the sake of a barbarian country, unworthy of ranking among civilized nations. Nevertheless, we cannot afford to overlook the possible developments of tomorrow.

To economic sanctions, we shall answer with our discipline, our spirit of sacrifice, our obedience. To military sanctions, we shall answer with military measures. To acts of war, we shall answer with acts of war.

A people worthy of their past and their name cannot and never will take a different stand. Let me repeat, in the most categorical manner, that the sacred pledge which I make at this moment, before all the Italians gathered together today, is that I shall do everything in my power to prevent a colonial conflict from taking on the aspect and weight of a European war.

This conflict may be attractive to certain minds which hope to avenge their disintegrated temples through this new catastrophe. Never, as at this historical hour, have the people of Italy revealed such force of character, and it is against this people to which mankind owes its greatest conquest, this people of heroes, of poets and saints, of navigators, of colonizers, that the world dares threaten sanctions.

Italy! Italy! Entirely and universally Fascist! The Italy of the blackshirt revolution, rise to your feet; let the cry of your determination rise to the skies and reach our soldiers in East Africa. Let it be a comfort to those who are about to fight. Let it be an encouragement to our friends and a warning to our enemies. It is the cry of Italy which goes beyond the mountains and the seas out into the great world. It is the cry of justice and of victory.

JOSEF STALIN

"Defects in Party Work and Measures for Liquidating Trotskyite and Other Double Dealers"

Address to the Plenum of the Central Committee

("Contemporary Trotskyism is not a political tendency in the working class, but an unprincipled band of wreckers")

Moscow, U.S.S.R.

March 3, 1937

Josef Stalin (1878–1953), born Iosif Vissarionovich Dzhugashvili, was a would-be theology student who made himself into a writer, poet, and criminal in his native Georgia. He was jailed several times for robbery and was suspected of terrorism. As a Marxist revolutionary, he eventually found his way to Vladimir Lenin's Bolshevik Central Committee in 1917. His intelligence and cynicism kept him moving up the ranks, until by the time of Lenin's death in 1924, he was a leading contender for the top spot in the Communist Party. He ousted his rivals, including Leon Trotsky, and eventually murdered or exiled them all. He did not set up the Gulag system of prison camps that would result in the deaths of tens of millions of Soviet citizens, but he ensured that the camps would be unforgiving and deadly—and ever supplied with fresh workers for his grandiose building projects. Characteristically suspicious of others, he never ceased targeting groups, regions, and potential political rivals. He was so terrible that, among twentieth-century villains, Hitler is his usual comparison. Here, in a display of paranoia and bullying, he addresses his minions in the Central Committee. This is the complete speech, rarely published in its entirety.

Comrades, from the reports and the discussions on them heard in the plenum, it follows that we have to deal here with the following three basic facts.

First, the wrecking and diversionist–espionage activity of agents of foreign states, among whom a pretty active role was played by the Trotskyists, has affected in one degree or another or nearly all of our organizations—economic, administrative and Party.

Second, agents of foreign countries, including Trotskyites, penetrated not only into subordinate organizations, but also to certain responsible posts.

Third, some of our leading comrades, both in the center and locally, not only failed to discern the real countenance of these wreckers, diversionists, spies, and murderers, but proved so unconcerned, complacent, and naïve, that at times they themselves assisted in promoting agents of the foreign states to one or other responsible posts.

These are the three indisputable facts which naturally arise from the reports and the discussions on them.

I. Political Unconcern

How are we to explain the fact that our leading comrades, having a rich experience in the struggle against anti-Party and anti-Soviet currents of every kind, proved in the present case so naïve and blind that they failed to discern the real countenance of the enemies of the people, failed to recognize the wolves in sheep's clothing, and could not tear away their masks?

Can it be maintained that the wrecking and diversionist-espionage work of the agents of foreign states, acting on the territory of the U.S.S.R., could be for us something unexpected and unprecedented? No, this cannot be maintained. This is demonstrated by the wrecking acts in different branches of the national economy during the last ten years, beginning with the Shakhty period[1], recorded in official documents.

Can it be asserted that in recent times we had no warning signals, no precautionary hints about the wrecking, spying, or terrorist activities of the Trotskyite-Zinovievite agents of fascism? No, this cannot be asserted. There were such signals and Bolsheviks have no right to forget about them.

The foul murder of Comrade Kirov[2] was the first serious warning which indicated that enemies of the people would resort to double-dealing and that they would thus pose as Bolsheviks and Party members in order to gain confidence and access for themselves into our organizations.

The trial of the "Leningrad Center" as well as the trial of "Zinoviev-Kamenev" gave new grounds for the lessons drawn from the fact of the foul murder of Comrade Kirov.

The trial of the "Trotskyite-Zinovievite Bloc" extended the lessons of the preceding trials, having demonstrated before our eyes

---

[1] In 1928, Stalin had engineers from Shakhty, a coal-mining town in the north Caucasus, put on trial for trumped-up charges of "wrecking."

[2] There is evidence that Stalin himself ordered his former protégé and political rival Kirov's "foul" assassination in 1934.

that the Zinovievites and Trotskyites unite around themselves all the hostile bourgeois elements, that they have turned into a spying and diversionist-terrorist agency of the German secret police, that this double-dealing and masquerading are the only means for the Zinovievites and Trotskyites to penetrate into our organizations, that vigilance and political insight are the surest means for the prevention of such penetration and for the liquidation of the Zinovievite-Trotskyite gang.

The Central Committee of the Communist Party of the Soviet Union in its January 18, 1935, on the occasion of the dastardly murder of Comrade Kirov, resolutely warned Party organizations against political complacency and the gaping attitude of the philistine. That confidential letter stated:

> "An end must be put to the opportunistic complacency which arises from the erroneous assumption that, as our forces keep growing, the enemy allegedly becomes ever more tame and more harmless. Such a presumption is fundamentally wrong. It represents a re-echoing of the Right deviation, which assured all and sundry that the enemies would quietly crawl into Socialism, that they would become real Socialists in the long run. Bolsheviks must not rest on their laurels and become open-mouthed. We do not need complacency, but vigilance, genuine Bolshevik, revolutionary vigilance. It must be remembered that the more hopeless the position of the enemies, the more readily will they clutch at extreme measures, as the only measures of the doomed in their struggle against the Soviet power. One must remember this and be vigilant."

In its confidential letter of July 29, 1936, in connection with the espionage-terrorist activity of the Trotskyite-Zinovievite bloc, the Central Committee of the Communist Party of the Soviet Union again appealed to Party organizations for the utmost vigilance, a manifestation of ability to discern the enemies of the people, however well they might be masked. The confidential letter stated:

> "Now, when it has been proved that the Trotskyite-Zinovievite scoundrels unite in the struggle against the Soviet power all the most infuriated and vicious enemies of the toilers of our country—spies, provocateurs, diversionists, White guards, kulaks, and so on; when all boundaries have been obliterated between these elements on the one hand and the Trotskyites and Zinovievites on the other—all of our Party organizations,

all members of the Party must understand that vigilance on the part of Communists is indispensable in any place and under all circumstances. The inalienable quality of every Bolshevik under present conditions must be the ability to recognize the enemy of the Party, however skillfully he may be masked."

Consequently, there were signals and warnings. What did those signals and warnings call for?

They called for an elimination of the weakness of Party organizational work and for turning the Party into an invulnerable fortress into which not a single double-dealer could penetrate.

They called for putting an end to the underestimation of Party-political work and for a decided turn towards the utmost strengthening of such work, towards the strengthening of political vigilance.

And what do we find? The facts have shown that the signals and warnings were but little heeded by our comrades. This was eloquently demonstrated by the well-known facts revealed in the course of the campaign for the verification and exchange of Party documents.

How are we to account for the fact that these warnings and signals did not have their proper effect?

How are we to explain that our Party comrades, despite their experience in the struggle against anti-Soviet elements, despite numerous warning signals and precautionary reminders, proved to be politically shortsighted in the face of the wrecking and spying diversionist activity of the enemies of the people?

Maybe our Party comrades have become worse than they were before, less conscious and less disciplined? No, of course not!

Maybe they have begun to degenerate? This is not true either. Such a presumption would be totally unfounded.

What then is the matter? Whence such a gaping attitude, unconcern, complacency and blindness?

The fact of the matter is that our Party comrades, engrossed in economic campaigns and elated by the colossal successes on the front of economic construction, simply forgot a few extremely important facts which Bolsheviks have no right to forget. They forgot one basic fact connected with the international position of the U.S.S.R. and failed to perceive two highly important facts which have direct bearing on the present-day wreckers, spies, diversionists and murderers who shield themselves behind the Party card and mask themselves as Bolsheviks.

II. Capitalist Encirclement

What facts are these which our Party comrades have forgotten or which they simply have not noticed?

They have forgotten that Soviet power was victorious in only one-sixth of the world, that five-sixths of the world is in the possession of capitalist states. They have forgotten that the Soviet Union finds itself in circumstances of capitalist encirclement. We have the habit of chattering about capitalist encirclement, but many do not want to ponder over what exactly this capitalist encirclement means.

Capitalist encirclement is not an empty phrase, it is a very real and unpleasant phenomenon. Capitalist encirclement means that there is one country, the Soviet Union, which has established at home a Socialist order, and that there are, besides, many countries, bourgeois countries, which continue to carry on the capitalist form of life, and which encircle the Soviet Union, awaiting the opportunity to attack it, to crush it, or, in any case, to undermine its might and weaken it.

This fundamental fact our comrades have forgotten. And surely, it is just this which determines the basis of the mutual relations between the capitalist encirclement and the Soviet Union.

Let us take, for example, the bourgeois states themselves. Naïve people may think that exceptionally good relations exist between them as states of the same type. But only naïve people can think this. In actual fact, the relations between them are very far from being good neighborly relations. It is as proven as surely as twice two are four that bourgeois states send to each other's rear their spies, wreckers, diversionists, and sometimes also murderers, with the task of penetrating into the institutions and enterprises of these states, to create their own network there and "in case of necessity," to disrupt their rear in order to weaken them and undermine their power.

This is how the matter stands at the present time. This is how the matter stood in the past as well. Let us take, for example, the states in Europe at the time of Napoleon I. France was then swarming with spies and diversionists from the camps of the Russians, Germans, Austrians, and British. And, on the other hand, England, the German states, Austria, Russia then had in their rear a no less number of spies and diversionists from the French camp. The agents of England twice made an attempt on the life of Napoleon and several times roused the Vendee peasants in France against the government of Napoleon. And what did the Napoleonic government represent? A bourgeois government which stifled the French Revolution and retained only those results of the revolution which were advantageous to the big bourgeoisie. Needless to say, the Napoleonic

government did not remain in debt to its neighbors and also under-
took its diversive measures.

Thus it was in the past, 130 years ago. Thus the matter stands
today, 130 years after Napoleon I. France and England are now
swarming with German spies and diversionists and, on the other
hand, Anglo-French spies and diversionists are active in turn in
Germany. America is swarming with Japanese spies and diversionists, and Japan with American.

Such is the law of the mutual relations between bourgeois states.

The question arises, why should bourgeois states be milder and
more neighborly towards the Soviet Socialist State than towards
bourgeois states of their own type? Why should they send to the
rear of the Soviet Union fewer spies, wreckers, diversionists, and
murderers than they send to the rear of the bourgeois states akin to
them? Whence this assumption? Would it not be more true, from
the point of view of Marxism, to assume that the bourgeois states
would send to the rear of the Soviet Union two and three times as
many wreckers, spies, diversionists, and murderers than to the rear
of any bourgeois state?

Is it not clear that so long as we have a capitalist encirclement,
we shall have in our own country wreckers, spies, diversionists, and
murderers sent to our rear by agents of foreign states?

All this our Party comrades had forgotten, and, having forgotten
this, they were taken by surprise.

That is why the espionage-diversionist work of the Trotskyite
agents of the Japanese-German secret police was a complete surprise
to some of our comrades.

III. Contemporary Trotskyism

Further. In waging the struggle with Trotskyist agents, our Party
comrades did not notice, overlooked, that present-day Trotskyism is
no longer what it was, let us say, seven or eight years ago; that Trotskyism and the Trotskyites have, during that time, undergone a serious
evolution which has fundamentally altered the face of Trotskyism;
that for this reason the struggle against Trotskyism and the methods
of struggle against it likewise must be fundamentally altered.

Our Party comrades have not noticed that Trotskyism has ceased
to be a political tendency in the working class, that from the political tendency in the working class that it was seven or eight years
ago, Trotskyism has become a frenzied and unprincipled band of
wreckers, diversionists, spies, and murderers, acting on instructions
from intelligence service organs of foreign states.

What is a political tendency within the working class? A political tendency in the working class is a group or party which has its definite political physiognomy, platform, program; which does not hide and cannot hide its views from the working class, but, on the contrary, propagates its views openly and honestly before the eyes of the working class; which does not fear to reveal its political countenance to the working class, and is not afraid to demonstrate its real aims and tasks before the working class, but, on the contrary, with opened visor, goes to the working class in order to convince it of the correctness of its views. Trotskyism in the past, seven or eight years ago, was one of such political tendencies within the working class; true, anti-Leninist and hence profoundly erroneous, but nevertheless a political tendency.

Can it be said that present-day Trotskyism, the Trotskyism, let us say, of the year 1936, is a political tendency in the working class? No, this cannot be said. Why? Because the contemporary Trotskyists are afraid to show the working class their real countenance, are afraid to reveal to it their real aims and tasks, assiduously conceal their political physiognomy from the working class, fearing that if the working class finds out their real intentions it will condemn them as people alien to the workers, and drive them away.

This in substance explains why the basic method of Trotskyite work is not now an open and honest propaganda of their views among the working class, but a masking of their views, servile and toadying praise of the views of their opponents, pharisaic and false trampling in the mud of their own views.

At the trial in 1936, if you remember, Kamenev and Zinoviev[3] categorically denied that they had any kind of political platform. They had full opportunity to unfold their political platform at the trial. Nevertheless, they did not do so, declaring that they had no political platform whatsoever. There can be no doubt that they both lied in denying that they had a platform. Now, even the blind can see that they had their own political platform. But why did they deny the existence of any political platform? Because they were afraid to disclose their true political countenance, they feared to demonstrate their real political platform—the restoration of capitalism in the U.S.S.R.—they feared that such a platform would arouse the aversion of the working class.

---

[3] Two of the former heroes of the Russian Revolution, Lev Kamenev and Grigory Zinoviev were put on trial during one of Stalin's purges and soon after shot.

At the 1937 trial, Pyatakov, Radek, and Sokolnikov[4] took a different course. They did not deny the existence of a political platform of the Trotskyites and Zinovievites. They admitted they had a definite political platform, admitted it and expounded it in their testimony. But expounded it not in order to rally the working class, or rally the people in support of the Trotskyist platform, but in order to revile and stigmatize it as a platform against the people and against the proletariat.

The restoration of capitalism, the liquidation of the collective and state farms, the re-establishment of a system of exploitation; an alliance with the fascist forces in Germany and Japan to bring nearer a war with the Soviet Union; a struggle for war and against the policy of peace; the territorial dismemberment of the Soviet Union, handing the Ukraine to the Germans and the Maritime Province to the Japanese; the scheming for the military defeat of the Soviet Union in the event of her being attacked by hostile states, and, as a means of achieving these aims, wrecking, diversion, individual terror against the leaders of the Soviet power, espionage in favor of Japanese-German fascist forces—such was the political platform of contemporary Trotskyism as unfolded by Pyatakov, Radek, and Sokolnikov.

It is clear that the Trotskyites could not but conceal such a platform from the people, from the working class. And they concealed it not only from the working class, but from the Trotskyite rank and file as well, and not only from the Trotskyite rank and file, but even from the upper Trotskyite leadership, composed of a small handful of thirty or forty people. When Radek and Pyatakov demanded permission from Trotsky to convene a small conference of thirty or forty Trotskyites to furnish information on the nature of this platform, Trotsky forbade them to do so, saying that it was inexpedient to speak of the true nature of the platform even to a small handful of Trotskyites, since such an "operation" might lead to a split.

"Political figures" concealing their platform, not only from the working class but also from the Trotskyite rank and file, and not only from the Trotskyist rank and file but also from the upper Trotskyite leadership—such is the physiognomy of contemporary Trotskyism.

But from this it follows that contemporary Trotskyism can no longer be called a political tendency in the working class.

Contemporary Trotskyism is not a political tendency in the

---

[4] These men were also former revolutionaries who had recently fallen out of favor with Stalin. All three "confessed" at the show trial; Pyatakov was executed in January 1937; Radek and Sokolnikov served time in prison before being murdered.

working class, but an unprincipled band of wreckers devoid of ideas, diversionists, intelligence agents, spies, murderers, a band of sworn enemies of the working class in the hire of the intelligence service organs of foreign states.

Such is the indisputable result of the evolution of Trotskyism within the past seven or eight years.

Such is the difference between Trotskyism in the past and Trotskyism in the present.

The mistake of our Party comrades lies in the fact they did not notice this profound difference between Trotskyism in the past and the Trotskyism of the present day. They did not perceive that the Trotskyites have long since ceased to be people of ideas, that the Trotskyites have long since degenerated into highway robbers capable of any villainy, capable of all that is base down to espionage and direct treason to their fatherland in order to injure the Soviet state and the Soviet power. They did not discern this and were therefore unable to reorganize themselves in time to wage a struggle against the Trotskyites along new lines, more decisively.

That is why the abominations of the Trotskyites in recent years have come as an utter surprise to some of our Party comrades.

Further. Finally, our Party comrades did not perceive that there is a substantial difference on the one hand between the present-day wreckers and diversionists, among whom the Trotskyite agents of fascism play a fairly active role, and the wreckers and diversionists of the time of the Shakhty period, on the other.

In the first place, the Shakhty and industrial Party people were people openly hostile to us. They were for the most part former owners of enterprises, former managers under the former owners, former shareholders of old stock companies, or simply old bourgeois specialists openly hostile to us politically. None of our people doubted the genuineness of the political countenance of these gentlemen. Moreover, the Shakhty people themselves did not conceal their inimical attitude to the Soviet system.

The same cannot be said about the present-day wreckers and diversionists, about the Trotskyites. The present-day wreckers and diversionists, the Trotskyites, are mostly Party people, with Party membership cards in their pockets—hence, people who are formally not alien to us. While the old wreckers went against our people, the new wreckers, on the contrary, fawn upon our people, praise our people, flatter them in order to worm their way into confidence. As you see, the difference is essential.

Secondly. The strength of the Shakhty people and Industrial Party people lay in the fact that they possessed to a greater or lesser degree the necessary technical knowledge at a time when our people, lacking such knowledge, were compelled to learn from them. This circumstance gave the wreckers of the Shakhty period great advantage; gave them the opportunity to wreck freely and unhindered; gave them the opportunity to deceive our people in *technical* matters. Not so the present-day wreckers, the Trotskyites.

The present-day wreckers have no technical advantage over our people whatsoever. On the contrary, technically our people are better trained than the wreckers of today, the Trotskyites. From the time of the Shakhty period up to our days, tens of thousands of real Bolshevik cadres well versed in technical matters have grown up among us. It is possible to name thousands and tens of thousands of Bolshevik leaders mature in technical matters, in comparison with whom all these Pyatakovs and Livshitzes, Shestovs and Boguslavskys, Muralovs and Drobnises are mere chatterboxes and schoolboys from the standpoint of technical training.

Wherein then lies the strength of the contemporary wreckers, the Trotskyites? Their strength lies in their Party membership card, in their possession of the Party membership card. Their strength lies in the fact that the Party membership card gains for them political confidence and opens all our institutions and organizations to them. Their advantage lay in the fact that, possessing Party membership cards and pretending to be friends of the Soviet power, they have deceived our people *politically*, abused confidence, wrecked on the sly, and revealed our state secrets to the enemies of the Soviet Union. A doubtful "advantage" in its political and moral value, but nevertheless an "advantage." This "advantage" explains, in substance, why the Trotskyite wreckers, as people with Party membership cards having access everywhere, to all our institutions and organizations, proved to be a real find for the intelligence service organs of foreign states.

The mistake made by some of our Party comrades was that they did not perceive, did not understand this difference between the old and new wreckers, between the Shakhty people and Trotskyite wreckers, and not perceiving this, were not able to reorganize themselves to wage a struggle against the new wreckers along new lines.

IV. Dark Sides of Our Economic Successes

Such are the basic facts connected with our international and internal situation which were forgotten or unnoticed by many of our Party comrades. That is why our people were caught unawares by the events of recent years in regard to wrecking and diversion.

It may be asked: why did our people fail to perceive all this, why did they forget about all this? Whence came all this forgetfulness, blindness, unconcern, and complacency?

Is not this an organic defect in the work of our people? No, it is not an organic defect. It is a temporary phenomenon which can be rapidly eliminated by the exertion of some effort on the part of our people.

What then is the matter?

The fact of the matter is that our Party comrades in recent years have been entirely absorbed in economic work, they were extremely elated over the economic successes, and in their excitement about all these things they forgot about everything else, neglected all the rest.

The fact of the matter is that in their excitement over the economic successes they began to see in the latter the beginning and end of everything, while to such matters as the international position of the Soviet Union, the capitalist encirclement, the strengthening of the political work of the Party, the struggle against wrecking and so on, they simply stopped paying attention, assuming that all these questions were of second-rate or even third-rate importance.

Of course, successes and achievements are a very great thing. Our successes in the domain of Socialist construction are tremendous indeed. Nevertheless, successes, as everything else in this world, also have their dark sides. In the case of people little versed in politics, big successes and big achievements lead at times to unconcern, complacency, self-contentment, excessive self-confidence, conceit and boastfulness. You cannot deny that lately we have had an abundant crop of boasters. No wonder that in this atmosphere of great and substantial successes in Socialist construction there arises a disposition to boastfulness, a disposition to parade our successes, there arises a disposition to underestimate the forces of our enemies, a disposition to overestimate our own forces, and as the result of all this, political blindness ensues.

Here I must say a few words on the dangers associated with successes, on the dangers associated with achievements. As to dangers associated with difficulties, this we know from experience. We have already been waging a struggle against dangers of this kind for several years, and it must be said, not without success. The dangers associated with difficulties beget at times in unstable people moods of despondency, of mistrust in their own forces, moods of pessimism. On the other hand, in the struggle to overcome dangers arising from difficulties people become tempered in the process and emerge from it really stalwart Bolsheviks. Such is the nature of the dangers associated with difficulties. Such are the results of surmounting difficulties.

But there are dangers of a different kind—dangers associated with successes, dangers associated with achievements. Yes, yes, comrades, dangers associated with successes, with achievements. These dangers consist in this that people who are little versed in politics, who have had little experience of the atmosphere of success—success after success, achievement after achievement, over-fulfillment of plan after over-fulfillment—are apt to fall into a disposition of unconcern and self-satisfaction; an atmosphere is created of ceremonial parades and mutual congratulations which stultify the sense of proportion and blunt the political sense, puffing up people and impelling them to rest on their laurels.

No wonder that, in this stupefying atmosphere of conceit and self-satisfaction, the atmosphere of parades and noisy self-praise, people forget certain essential facts which are of paramount importance to the destinies of our country; people begin to overlook such unpleasant facts as the capitalist encirclement, the new forms of wrecking, the dangers associated with our successes and so on.

Capitalist encirclement? Why, this is nonsense! What does such a thing as capitalist encirclement matter, if we fulfill and over-fulfill our economic plans? New forms of wrecking, the struggle against Trotskyism? All these are trifles! What can such trifles signify, if we fulfill and over-fulfill our economic plans? Party rules, election of Party organs, accountability of Party leaders before the membership? Is there any need of all this? Is it worthwhile generally to bother about these trifles, if our economy is growing, while the material conditions of the workers and peasants are improving more and more? All this is a trifling matter! We are over-fulfilling the plans, our Party is not a bad one, the Central Committee of the Party is not bad either—what more do we need? Strange people sit in Moscow, in the Central Committee of the Party; they invent various questions, talk about some sort of wrecking, do not sleep themselves, and do not let other people sleep....

Here you have a glaring example of how easily and "simply" some of our inexperienced comrades become infected with political blindness as a result of having their heads turned by economic successes.

Such are the dangers associated with successes, with achievements. Such are the reasons why our Party comrades, elated with economic successes, have forgotten about facts of an international and internal character which are of essential importance for the Soviet Union, and overlooked a great number of dangers which surround our country.

Such are the roots of our unconcern, forgetfulness, complacency and political blindness. Such are the roots of the defects of our economic and Party work.

V. Our Tasks

How can these defects in our work be eliminated? What has to be done?

The following measures must be carried out:

(1) It is necessary above all to turn the attention of our Party comrades, absorbed in "current questions" in one institution or another, towards big political questions of an international and internal character.

(2) It is necessary to raise the political work of our Party to the proper level, placing in the foreground the task of political education and the Bolshevik tempering of Party, Soviet and industrial cadres.

(3) It is necessary to explain to our Party comrades that economic successes—the importance of which is undoubtedly very great and for which we will continue to strive from day to day, from year to year—nevertheless do not exhaust the whole work of our Socialist construction.

To explain that the dark sides linked up with economic successes and expressed in self-satisfaction, unconcern, in the blunting of political feeling, can be eliminated only if economic successes are combined with successes of Party structure and with the widely developed political work of our Party.

To explain that economic successes themselves, their stability and endurance entirely and fully depend upon the successes of Party-organizational and Party-political work, that without this condition the economic successes may find themselves built on sand.

(4) It is necessary to remember and never to forget that capitalist encirclement is the basic fact determining the international position of the Soviet Union. To remember and never to forget that so long as there is capitalist encirclement there will also be wreckers, diversionists, spies, terrorists, sent to the rear of the Soviet Union by the organs of the intelligence service of foreign States; to remember this, and to wage a struggle with those comrades who underestimate the importance of the fact of the capitalist encirclement, who underestimate the power and significance of wrecking.

To explain to our Party comrades that no economic successes, however great they may be, can eliminate the fact of the capitalist encirclement and the results arising therefrom.

To take the necessary measures in order that our comrades, Party and non-Party Bolsheviks, have the opportunity of learning the aims and tasks, the practice and technique of the wrecking-diversionist and espionage work of foreign intelligence service organs.

(5) It is necessary to explain to our Party comrades that the Trotsky-ites, representing the active elements of the diversionist-wrecking and espionage activity of the foreign intelligence service organs, have long ago ceased to be a political current in the working class, that they have long ago ceased to serve any kind of idea compatible with the interests of the working class, that they have become an unprincipled band of wreckers devoid of ideas, diversionists, spies, murderers hired by foreign intelligence service organs.

To explain that in the struggle with contemporary Trotskyism, not the old methods are now needed, not methods of discussion, but new methods, methods of uprooting and destroying.

(6) It is necessary to explain to our Party comrades the difference between contemporary wreckers and the wreckers of the Shakhty period, to explain that whilst the wreckers of the Shakhty period deceived our people in technique, taking advantage of the technical backwardness of the latter, the contemporary wreckers, possessing Party membership cards, deceive our people's political confidence in them, as members of the Party, taking advantage of the political unconcern of our people.

It is necessary to supplement the old slogan of mastering technique, corresponding with the period of the Shakhty days, by a new slogan—the political education of cadres, the mastering of Bolshevism and the abolition of our political credulity, that is, by a slogan fully in accordance with the period through which we are now passing.

It may be asked: Was it really not possible ten years ago, in the days of the Shakhty period, to have proclaimed both slogans at once, both the first slogan for mastering technique, and the second slogan for the political education of cadres? No, it was not possible. Things are not done in this way in the Bolshevik Party. At turning points of the revolutionary movement some one main slogan, as the central one, is always brought forward so that in grasping it the whole chain may be pulled along. Lenin thus taught us: Find the main link in the chain of our work, grasp it, pull it so that the whole chain is drawn along, and thus go forward.

The history of the revolutionary movement shows that these tactics are the only correct tactics. In the Shakhty period the weak-ness of our people consisted in their technical backwardness. Not political, but technical questions then constituted our weak spot. As regards our political relations with the wreckers of that time, they were perfectly clear as relations with the wreckers of that time, they were perfectly clear as relations of Bolsheviks to politically alien people. This technical weakness of ours we eliminated by issuing the slogan of mastering technique. We educated during the past period tens and hundreds of thousands of technically versed Bolshevik cadres.

It is another thing now, when we already have technically versed Bolshevik cadres, and when in the role of wreckers there appear people not openly alien to us, not having any technical advantages compared with our people, but people possessing Party membership cards and utilizing all the rights of members of the Party. At present the weakness of our people does not lie in technical backwardness, but in political unconcern, in blind confidence in people accidentally receiving Party membership cards; in the lack of verification of people, not by their political declarations, but by the results of their work.

The central question for us now is, not the abolition of the technical backwardness of our cadres, for in the main it has already been abolished, but in the abolition of political unconcern and political credulity toward wreckers who have accidentally received Party membership cards.

Such is the fundamental difference between the central question in the matter of the struggle for cadres in the Shakhty period, and the central question of the present period.

That is why we could not and should not have issued ten years ago both slogans simultaneously, both the slogan of mastering technique and the slogan of the political education of cadres.

That is why the old slogan of mastering technique must now be supplemented with the new slogan of mastering Bolshevism, of the political education of our cadres and elimination of our political unconcern.

(7) It is necessary to shatter and discard the rotten theory to the effect that with every step of progress which we make the class struggle here is bound to die down more and more, that in proportion to the growth of our successes the class enemy becomes more and more tamed.

This is not only a rotten theory, but also a dangerous theory, for it lulls our people to sleep, it leads them into a snare, while allowing the class enemy the possibility of rallying for the struggle against the Soviet power.

On the contrary, the greater our progress, the greater our successes, the more embittered the remnants of the smashed exploiting classes will become, the more quickly they will resort to sharper forms of struggle, the more they will do damage to the Soviet state, the more they will clutch at the most desperate means of struggle as the last resort of the doomed.

We must bear in mind that the remnants of the routed classes in the U.S.S.R. are not alone. They have direct support from our enemies beyond the borders of the U.S.S.R. It would be a mistake to assume that the sphere of the class struggle is bounded by the frontiers of the U.S.S.R. While one end of the class struggle operates within the U.S.S.R., its other end extends into the bourgeois states around us. The remnants of the routed classes cannot be unaware of this. And just because they are aware of it, they will go on with their desperate sallies.

This is what history teaches us. This is what Leninism teaches us. We must remember all this and be on guard.

(8) It is necessary to shatter and discard another rotten theory which alleges that he who is not always engaged in wrecking, and who at least sometimes shows success in his work, cannot be a wrecker.

This strange theory betrays the naïveté of its authors. No wrecker will go on wrecking all the time, if he does not wish to be exposed very rapidly. On the contrary, the real wrecker will show success in his work from time to time, for this is the only means of staying on the job, of worming himself into confidence and continuing his wrecking activity.

I believe this question is clear and needs no further elucidation.

(9) It is necessary to shatter and discard a third rotten theory, the meaning of which is that systematic fulfillment of the economic plans allegedly sets at nought wrecking and the results of wrecking.

Such a theory can pursue but one aim: to tickle the departmental vanity of our workers, to reassure them, and to relax their struggle against wrecking. What is meant by "systematic fulfillment of our economic plans?"

Firstly, it has been demonstrated that all our economic plans put too low, for they do not take into consideration the huge reserves and possibilities latent within our national economy.

Secondly, summary fulfillment of economic plans by People's Commissariats on the whole does not yet signify that the plans are also being fulfilled in some very important branches. On the contrary, the facts go to show that a number of People's Commissariats which fulfilled or even over-fulfilled their annual economic plans are systematically failing to fulfill the plans in some very important branches of the national economy.

Thirdly, there can be no doubt that had the wreckers not been exposed and thrown out matters would have been far worse as regards the fulfillment of economic plans, and this is what the shortsighted authors of the theory with which we are dealing should bear in mind.

Fourthly, the wreckers usually time their major wrecking work not for the period of peacetime but for the period on the eve of war or of war itself. Let us assume that we permitted ourselves to be lulled by the rotten theory of "systematic fulfillment of the economic plans" and did not molest the wreckers. Can the authors of this rotten theory imagine what colossal harm would have been done to our state by the wreckers in the event of war, had we allowed them to stay within our national economy under the wing of the rotten theory of "systematic fulfillment of economic plans?" Is it not clear that the theory of "systematic fulfillment of economic plans" is a theory which suits the wreckers?

(10) It is necessary to shatter and discard a fourth rotten theory which alleges that the Stakhanov movement is the basic means of doing away with wrecking. The theory was invented in order to sidetrack the blow from the wreckers by the noisy prattle on Stakhanovites and the Stakhanov movement.

Comrade Molotov in his report cited a number of facts which tell us how the Trotskyite and non-Trotskyite wreckers in the Kuzbas and the Donbas, abusing the confidence of our politically unconcerned comrades, systematically led the Stakhanovites by the nose, put spokes in the wheels, artificially created a series of obstacles to their successful work and eventually succeeded in disrupting their work. What could the Stakhanovites alone do if the wrecking management of capital construction, say, in the Donbas, caused a discrepancy between the preparatory work for the mining of coal and all other operations?

Is it not clear that the Stakhanov movement itself needs a real assistance on our part against all and sundry machinations of the wreckers in order to forge ahead and carry out its great mission? Is it not clear that the struggle against wrecking, the struggle for the elimination of wrecking, the curbing of wrecking, is the indispensable condition for the Stakhanov movement to develop to its full breadth? I think that this question is equally clear and needs no further elucidation.

(11) It is necessary to shatter and discard a fifth rotten theory which alleges that the Trotskyite wreckers have no more reserves, which alleges that they are rallying their last cadres.

This is not true, comrades. This theory could be invented only by naïve people. For the Trotskyite wreckers have their reserves. They consist above all of the remnants of the routed exploiting classes in the U.S.S.R. They consist of a number of groups and organizations beyond the borders of the U.S.S.R. that are hostile to the Soviet Union.

Take, for instance, the Trotskyite counter-revolutionary Fourth International which is two-thirds composed of spies and diversionists. Are these not reserves? Is it not clear that this spy international will furnish cadres for the spying and wrecking activity of the Trotskyites?[5]

Or take, for example, the group of the rascal Sheflo in Norway, who provided a haven for the arch-spy Trotsky and helped him to do harm to the Soviet Union.

Isn't this group a reserve? Who can deny that this counter-revolutionary group will continue in the future to render services to the Trotskyite spies and wreckers?

Or take, for example, the Souvarine group in France, a group of rascals like Sheflo. Isn't this a reserve? Can it be denied that this group of scoundrels will also help the Trotskyites in their espionage and wrecking work against the Soviet Union?

All these ladies and gentlemen from Germany, all the Ruth Fischers, Maslovs and Urbans who have sold themselves body and soul to the fascists—aren't they reserves for the espionage and wrecking work of the Trotskyites?

Or take, for example, the well-known gang of American writers headed by the notorious racketeer Eastman, all these gangsters of the pen who live by slandering the working class of the Soviet Union—aren't they reserves for Trotskyism?

No, it is necessary to cast away the rotten theory that the Trotskyites are rallying their last cadres.

(12) Finally, it is necessary to smash and cast off one more rotten theory to the effect that since there are many of us Bolsheviks, and few of the wreckers, since we Bolsheviks are supported by tens of millions of people while the Trotskyite wreckers are merely individuals and dozens, therefore we Bolsheviks can afford not to pay any attention to some handful of wreckers.

This is incorrect, comrades. This more than strange theory has been invented in order to console some of our leading comrades who have failed in their work owing to their inability to combat wrecking, and to lull their vigilance and let them sleep in peace.

That the Trotskyite wreckers are supported by individuals and the Bolsheviks by tens of millions of people is, of course, true. But from this it by no means follows that the wreckers cannot wreak very serious harm to our estate. To injure and harm by no means requires a large number of people. To build the Dneiprostroi requires tens of thousands of workers, but to blow it up requires perhaps a few score people, no more. In order to win a battle during a war it might require several

---

[5] The next five paragraphs, deleted by Coates, are quoted from the website "From Marx to Mao": http://www.marx2mao.com/Stalin/MB37.html#s6.

corps of Red Army men. But to secure the defeat of this gain on the front, it is sufficient for a few spies somewhere in the army staff or even in the division staff to steal the plan of operations and hand it to the enemy. To build a big railroad bridge thousands of people are required. But in order to blow it up, only a few people are sufficient. Scores and hundreds of such examples might be given.

Hence, we must not console ourselves with the fact that we are many and they, the Trotskyite wreckers, are few.

We must see to it that there shall be none of these Trotskyite wreckers in our ranks.

Such is the position regarding the question of how to liquidate the defects in our work, common to all our organizations, both economic and Soviet, administrative and party.

Such are the measures necessary in order to eradicate these shortcomings.

As regards the party organizations in particular, and the defects in their work, the measures for the eradication of these defects are dealt with in sufficient detail in the draft resolution submitted for your consideration. I think therefore that there is no necessity to elaborate here on this aspect of the matter.

I should merely like to say a few words on the question of the political training and perfecting of our Party cadres.

I believe that if we were able, if it were possible for our party cadres, from top to bottom, to be trained ideologically and tempered politically in such a way as to enable them to orientate themselves readily in the internal and international situation; if we could make of them fully mature Leninists, Marxists, capable of solving, without serious mistakes, questions concerning the leadership of the country then we would have solved nine-tenths of all our tasks.

How do we stand with regard to the leading section of our party? In the composition of our party, if we have in view its leading stratum, there are nearly 3,000 to 4,000 higher leaders. This is, I would say, the general staff of our party. Then follow 30,000–40,000 middle-leaders. These are our party officers. Then come nearly 100,000–150,000 of the lower party commanding staff. These are, so to speak, the non-commissioned officers of our party.

To raise the ideological level and political tempering of these commanding cadres, to augment these cadres with fresh forces ready for promotion and thus broaden the composition of the leading cadres—this is the task.

What is required for this?

First of all it is necessary to suggest to our party leaders, from cell secretaries to the secretaries of province and republic party organizations, to select, within a certain period, two people in each case, two party workers capable of beign their real substitutes. It may be said: and where are we to find two substitutes each, we have no such persons, we have no suitable workers. This is not true, comrades. There are tens of thousands of capable people, talented people among us. It is necessary only to know them and to promote them in time so that they may not get stale in their old posts and begin to decay. Seek and thou shalt find.

Further. For the party instruction and re-training of cell secretaries it is necessary to set up in each province center four-month "Party Courses." Secretaries of all primary party organizations (cells) should be sent to these courses, and later after graduating from these courses and upon their return to their posts—their substitutes and the more capable members of the primary party organizations should be sent to these courses.

Further. For the political re-training of first secretaries of district organizations it is necessary throughout the U.S.S.R., let us say, in ten of the most important centers, to set up eight-month "Leninist Courses." To these courses should be sent the first secretaries of district and regional party organizations, and later upon their graduation and return to their posts—their substitutes and the more capable members of the district and regional organizations should be sent to these courses.

Further. For the ideological re-training and political perfecting of the secretaries of city organizations it is necessary to set up, under the auspices of the Central Committee of the Communist Party of the Soviet Union, six-month "Courses on the History and Policy of the Party." To these courses should be sent the first and second secretaries of city organizations, and later, upon their graduation and return to their posts—the more capable members of the city organizations.

Finally, it is necessary to set up under the auspices of the Central Committee of the C.P.S.U. a six-month "Conference on Questions of Internal and International Policy." Hither should be sent the first secretaries of prince and territory organizations and central committees of the national Communist Parties. These comrades must provide not one, but several alternates, capable of being substitutes for the leaders of the Central Committee of our party. This is necessary and this must be done.

I am concluding, comrades.

We have thus set forth the basic shortcomings in our work, both those which are common to all of our organizations, economic, administrative, party, as well as those which are peculiar only to special party organizations, defects utilized by the enemies of the working class for their diversionist-wrecking and espionage-terrorist work.

We have outlined, further, the basic measures necessary in order to eradicate these deficiencies and to render harmless the diversionist-wrecking and espionage-terrorist sallies of the Trotskyite-fascist agents of foreign intelligence service departments.

It may be asked, can we carry out all these measures, do we possess all the necessary means? Certainly we can. We can, because we have at our disposal all the means necessary to carry out these measures.

What, then, do we lack?

We lack only one thing: the readiness to eliminate our own unconcern, our own complacency, our own political shortsightedness.

Here is the rub.

But is it possible that we shall not be able to cope with this absurd and idiotic disease—we, who have overthrown capitalism, built the fundamentals of socialism, and raised the great banner of world communism?

We have no grounds for doubting that we shall certainly be able to cope with it, if, of course, we wish to do so. We shall cope with it not simply, but in Bolshevik fashion, properly.

And when we shall have done with this idiotic disease we shall be able to say with complete conviction that we fear no enemies, either internal or external; we do not fear their dirty work for we shall crush them in the future just as we are crushing them in the present, as we have crushed them in the past.

NEVILLE CHAMBERLAIN
Prime Minister of the United Kingdom
"The Munich Agreement"
House of Commons Debate

("After everything that has been said about the
German Chancellor [Hitler] today and in the past,
I do feel that the House ought to recognise
the difficulty for a man in that position")

London, England

October 3, 1938

Neville Chamberlain (1869–1940) became Prime Minister in 1937. After Hitler began taking over various parts of Europe, Chamberlain trusted Hitler's assurances that the Reich's aggressive policies were complete. Chamberlain's appeasement opened him to criticism, which he here anticipates: "I know I shall have plenty of critics who will say I have been guilty of facile optimism and that the better plan would have been to disbelieve every word by rulers of other great states of Europe." As critics speak up immediately, Chamberlain answers them: "I believe there are many who will feel with me that such a declaration, signed by the German Chancellor and myself, is something more than a pious expression of opinion. In our relations with other countries everything depends upon there being sincerity and goodwill on both sides. I believe that there is sincerity and good will on both sides in this declaration." Hitler's cynical betrayal of the naïve prime minister led to Chamberlain's ouster in 1940 (he was replaced by Winston Churchill, whom Hitler loathed). Chamberlain died shortly after.

Before I come to describe the Agreement which was signed at Munich in the small hours of Friday morning last, I would like to remind the House of two things which I think it very essential not to forget when those terms are being considered. The first is this: We did not go there to decide whether the predominantly German areas in the Sudetenland should be passed over to the German Reich. That had been decided already. Czechoslovakia had accepted the Anglo-French proposals. What we had to consider was the method, the conditions and the time of the transfer of the territory. The second point to remember is that time was one of the essential factors. All the elements were present on the spot for the outbreak of a conflict which might have precipitated the catastrophe. We had populations inflamed to a high degree; we had extremists on both sides ready to work up and provoke incidents; we had considerable quantities of arms which were by no means confined to regularly organised forces. Therefore, it was essential that we should quickly reach a conclusion, so that this painful and difficult operation of transfer might be carried out at the earliest possible moment and concluded as soon as was consistent, with orderly procedure, in order that we might avoid the possibility of something that might have rendered all our attempts at peaceful solution useless....

...To those who dislike an ultimatum, but who were anxious for a reasonable and orderly procedure, every one of [the] modifications [of the Godesberg Memorandum by the Munich Agreement] is a step in the right direction. It is no longer an ultimatum, but is a method which is carried out largely under the supervision of an international body.

Before giving a verdict upon this arrangement, we should do well to avoid describing it as a personal or a national triumph for anyone. The real triumph is that it has shown that representatives of four great Powers can find it possible to agree on a way of carrying out a difficult and delicate operation by discussion instead of by force of arms, and thereby they have averted a catastrophe which would have ended civilisation as we have known it. The relief that our escape from this great peril of war has, I think, everywhere been mingled in this country with a profound feeling of sympathy.

HONORABLE MEMBERS: Shame.

CHAMBERLAIN: I have nothing to be ashamed of. Let those who have, hang their heads. We must feel profound sympathy for a small and gallant nation in the hour of their national grief and loss.

FREDERICK BELLENGER: It is an insult to say it.

CHAMBERLAIN: I say in the name of this House and of the people of this country that Czechoslovakia has earned our admiration and respect for her restraint, for her dignity, for her magnificent discipline in face of such a trial as few nations have ever been called upon to meet.

The army, whose courage no man has ever questioned, has obeyed the order of their president, as they would equally have obeyed him if he had told them to march into the trenches. It is my hope and my belief, that under the new system of guarantees, the new Czechoslovakia will find a greater security than she has ever enjoyed in the past....

I pass from that subject, and I would like to say a few words in respect of the various other participants, besides ourselves, in the Munich Agreement. After everything that has been said about the German Chancellor today and in the past, I do feel that the House ought to recognise the difficulty for a man in that position to take back such emphatic declarations as he had already made amidst the enthusiastic cheers of his supporters, and to recognise that in consenting, even though it were only at the last moment, to discuss with the representatives of other Powers those things which he had declared he had already decided once for all, was a real and a substantial contribution on his part. With regard to Signor Mussolini, his contribution was certainly notable and perhaps decisive. It was on his suggestion that the final stages of mobilisation were postponed for 24 hours to give us an opportunity of discussing the situation, and I wish to say that at the Conference itself both he and the Italian Foreign Secretary, Count Ciano, were most helpful in the discussions. It was they who, very early in the proceedings, produced the Memorandum which M. Daladier and I were able to accept as a basis of discussion. I think that Europe and the world have reason to be grateful to the head of the Italian Government for his work in contributing to a peaceful solution....

In my view the strongest force of all, one which grew and took fresh shapes and forms every day war, the force not of any one individual, but was that unmistakable sense of unanimity among the peoples of the world that war must somehow be averted. The peoples of the British Empire were at one with those of Germany, of France and of Italy, and their anxiety, their intense desire for peace, pervaded the whole atmosphere of the conference, and I believe that that, and not threats, made possible the concessions that were made. I know the House will want to hear what I am sure it does not doubt, that throughout these discussions the Dominions, the Governments of the Dominions, have been kept in the closest touch with the march of events by telegraph and by personal contact, and I would like to say how greatly I was encouraged on each of the journeys I made to Germany by the knowledge that I went with the good wishes of the Governments of the Dominions. They shared all our anxieties and all our hopes. They rejoiced with us that peace was preserved, and with us they look forward to further efforts to consolidate what has been done.

Ever since I assumed my present office my main purpose has been to work for the pacification of Europe, for the removal of those suspicions and those animosities which have so long poisoned the air. The path which leads to appeasement is long and bristles with obstacles. The question of Czechoslovakia is the latest and perhaps the most dangerous. Now that we have got past it, I feel that it may be possible to make further progress along the road to sanity.

My right honorable friend has alluded in somewhat bitter terms to my conversation last Friday morning with Herr Hitler. I do not know why that conversation should give rise to suspicion, still less to criticism. I entered into no pact. I made no new commitments. There is no secret understanding. Our conversation was hostile to no other nation. The objects of that conversation, for which I asked, was to try to extend a little further the personal contact which I had established with Herr Hitler and which I believe to be essential in modern diplomacy. We had a friendly and entirely non-committal conversation, carried on, on my part, largely with a view to seeing whether there could be points in common between the head of a democratic Government and the ruler of a totalitarian State. We see the result in the declaration which has been published, in which my right Honorable Friend finds so much ground for suspicion. What does it say?

There are three paragraphs. The first says that we agree, "in recognising that the question of Anglo-German relations is of the first importance for the two countries and for Europe." Does anyone deny that? The second is an expression of opinion only. It says that: "We regard the agreement signed last night and the Anglo-German Naval Agreement as symbolic of the desire of the two peoples never to go to war with one another again." Once more I ask, does anyone doubt that that is the desire of the two peoples? What is the last paragraph? "We are resolved that the method of consultation shall be the method adopted to deal with any other questions that may concern our two countries, and we are determined to continue our efforts to remove possible sources of difference and thus to contribute to assure the peace of Europe." Who will stand up and condemn that sentence?

I believe there are many who will feel with me that such a declaration, signed by the German Chancellor and myself, is something more than a pious expression of opinion. In our relations with other countries everything depends upon there being sincerity and good will on both sides. I believe that there is sincerity and good will on both sides in this declaration. That is why to me its significance goes far beyond its actual words. If there is one lesson which we should learn from the events of these last weeks it is this, that lasting peace is not to be obtained by sitting still and waiting for it to come. It requires active, positive efforts to achieve it. No doubt I shall have plenty of critics who will say that I am guilty of facile optimism, and that I should disbelieve every word that is uttered by rulers of other great States in Europe. I am too much of a realist to believe that we are going to achieve our paradise in a day. We have only laid the foundations of peace. The superstructure is not even begun.

For a long period now we have been engaged in this country in a great programme of rearmament, which is daily increasing in pace and in volume. Let no one think that because we have signed this agreement between these four Powers at Munich we can afford to relax our efforts in regard to that programme at this moment. Disarmament on the part of this country can never be unilateral again. We have tried that once, and we very nearly brought ourselves to disaster. If disarmament is to come it must come by steps, and it must come by the agreement and the active cooperation of other countries. Until we know that we have obtained that cooperation and until we have agreed upon the actual steps to be taken, we here must remain on guard.

When, only a little while ago, we had to call upon the people of this country to begin to take those steps which would be necessary if the emergency should come upon us, we saw the magnificent spirit that was displayed. The Naval Reservists, the Territorial Army, the

Auxiliary Air Force, the Observers' Corps, obeyed the summons to mobilise very readily. We must remember that most of these men gave up their peacetime work at a moment's notice to serve their country. We should like to thank them. We should like to thank also the employers who accepted the inevitable inconvenience of mobilisation. I know that they will show the same spirit of patriotic cooperation in taking back all their former employees when they are demobilised. I know that, although the crisis has passed, they will feel proud that they are employing men upon whom the State can rely if a crisis should return.

While we must renew our determination to fill up the deficiencies that yet remain in our armaments and in our defensive precautions, so that we may be ready to defend ourselves and make our diplomacy effective—[*Interruption*]—yes I am a realist—nevertheless I say with an equal sense of reality that I do see fresh opportunities of approaching this subject of disarmament opening up before us, and I believe that they are at least as hopeful today as they have been at any previous time. It is to such tasks—the winning back of confidence, the gradual removal of hostility between nations until they feel that they can safely discard their weapons, one by one, that I would wish to devote what energy and time may be left to me before I hand over my office to younger men.

VYACHESLAV MIKHAILOVICH MOLOTOV

U.S.S.R. People's Commissar for Foreign Affairs

"The Meaning of the Soviet-German Non-Aggression Pact"

Address to the Supreme Soviet

("Only yesterday the German fascists were pursuing a foreign policy hostile to us")

Moscow, U.S.S.R.

August 31, 1939

Molotov (1890–1986) was one of Stalin's favorites, and wielded enormous power until after Stalin's death. Stalin assigned him to negotiate a non-aggression pact in Moscow with Nazi Germany's foreign minister Joachim von Ribbentrop. A week after the pact between the two warring

titans of repression was signed, Molotov argued the benefits of the shock-
ing arrangement: "...the day the Soviet-German Non-Aggression Pact
was signed, is to be regarded as a date of great historical importance." After
Germany and the U.S.S.R. invaded their agreed-upon portions of Poland,
the Nazis, not a bit surprisingly in retrospect, broke the treaty, invading the
U.S.S.R. in June 1941, and thereby set the Soviets against them for the
rest of World War II.

Comrades:

Since the third session of the Supreme Soviet the international
situation has shown no change for the better. On the contrary, it has
become even more tense. The steps taken by various governments to
put an end to this state of tension have obviously proved inadequate.
They met with no success. This is true of Europe.

Nor has there been any change for the better in East Asia. Japanese
troops continue to occupy the principal cities and a considerable part
of the territory of China. Nor is Japan refraining from hostile acts
against the U.S.S.R. Here, too, the situation has changed in the
direction of further aggravation.

In view of this state of affairs, the conclusion of a pact of non-
aggression between the U.S.S.R. and Germany is of tremendous
positive value, eliminating the danger of war between Germany and
the Soviet Union. In order more fully to define the significance of
this pact, I must first dwell on the negotiations which have taken
place in recent months in Moscow with representatives of Great
Britain and France. As you know, Anglo-French–Soviet negotiations for conclusion of a pact of mutual assistance against aggression
in Europe began as far back as April.

True, the initial proposals of the British Government were, as
you know, entirely unacceptable. They ignored the prime requisites
for such negotiations—they ignored the principle of reciprocity and
equality of obligations. In spite of this, the Soviet Government did
not reject the negotiations and in turn put forward its own proposals. We were mindful of the fact that it was difficult for the Governments of Great Britain and France to make an abrupt change in their
policy from an unfriendly attitude towards the Soviet Union which
had existed quite recently to serious negotiations with the U.S.S.R.
based on the condition of equality of obligations.

However, the subsequent negotiations were not justified by their
results. The Anglo-French–Soviet negotiations lasted four months.
They helped to elucidate a number of questions. At the same
time they made it clear to the representatives of Great Britain and
France that the Soviet Union has to be seriously reckoned with in

international affairs. But these negotiations encountered insuperable obstacles. The trouble, of course, did not lie in individual "formulations" or in particular clauses in the draft of the pact. No, the trouble was much more serious.

The conclusion of a pact of mutual assistance against aggression would have been of value only if Great Britain, France and the Soviet Union had arrived at agreement as to definite military measures against the attack of an aggressor. Accordingly, for a certain period not only political but also military negotiations were conducted in Moscow with representatives of the British and French armies. However, nothing came of the military negotiations.

They encountered the difficulty that Poland, which was to be jointly guaranteed by Great Britain, France and the U.S.S.R., rejected military assistance on the part of the Soviet Union. Attempts to overcome the objections of Poland met with no success. More, the negotiations showed that Great Britain was not anxious to overcome these objections of Poland, but on the contrary encouraged them. It is clear that, such being the attitude of the Polish Government and its principal ally towards military assistance on the part of the Soviet Union in the event of aggression, the Anglo-French-Soviet negotiations could not bear fruit. After this it became clear to us that the Anglo-French-Soviet negotiations were doomed to failure.

What have the negotiations with Great Britain and France shown? The Anglo-French-Soviet negotiations have shown that the position of Great Britain and France is marked by howling contradictions throughout. Judge for yourselves. On the one hand, Great Britain and France demanded that the U.S.S.R. should give military assistance to Poland in case of aggression. The U.S.S.R., as you know, was willing to meet this demand, provided that the U.S.S.R. itself received like assistance from Great Britain and France. On the other hand, precisely Great Britain and France brought Poland on the scene, who resolutely declined military assistance on the part of the U.S.S.R. Just try under such circumstances to reach an agreement regarding mutual assistance, when assistance on the part of the U.S.S.R. is declared beforehand to be unnecessary.

Further, on the one hand, Great Britain and France offered to guarantee the Soviet Union military assistance against aggression in return for like assistance on the part of the U.S.S.R. On the other hand, they hedged round their assistance with such reservations regarding indirect aggression as could convert this assistance into a myth and provide them with formal legal excuse to evade giving assistance and place the U.S.S.R. in a position of isolation in the face of the aggressor. Just try to distinguish between such a "pact of mutual assistance" and a pact of more or less camouflaged chicanery.

Further, on the one hand Great Britain and France stressed the importance and gravity of negotiations for a pact of mutual assignee and demanded that the U.S.S.R. should treat the matter most seriously and settle very rapidly all questions relating to the pact. On the other hand they themselves displayed extreme dilatoriness and an absolutely light-minded attitude towards the negotiations, entrusting them to individuals of secondary importance who were not invested with adequate powers.

It is enough to mention that the British and French military missions came to Moscow without any definite powers and without the right to conclude any military convention.

More, the British military mission arrived in Moscow without any mandate at all, and it was only on the demand of our military mission that on the very eve of the breakdown of the negotiations they presented written credentials. But even these credentials were of the vaguest kind, that is, credentials without proper weight. Just try to distinguish between this light-minded attitude towards the negotiations on the part of Great Britain and France and frivolous make-believe at negotiations designed to discredit the whole business of negotiations.

Such are the intrinsic contradictions in the attitude of Great Britain and France towards the negotiations with the U.S.S.R. which led to their breakdown.

What is the root of these contradictions in the position of Great Britain and France? In a few words, it can be put as follows: On the one hand, the British and French Governments fear aggression, and for that reason they would like to have a pact of mutual assistance with the Soviet Union provided it helped strengthen them, Great Britain and France.

But, on the other hand, the British and French Governments are afraid that the conclusion of a real pact of mutual assistance with the U.S.S.R. may strengthen our country, the Soviet Union, which, it appears, does not answer their purpose. It must be admitted that these fears of theirs outweighed other considerations. Only in this way can we understand the position of Poland, who acts on the instructions of Great Britain and France.

I shall now pass to the Soviet-German Non-Aggression Pact.

The decision to conclude a non-aggression pact between the U.S.S.R. and Germany was adopted after military negotiations with France and Great Britain had reached an impasse owing to the insuperable differences I have mentioned. As the negotiations had shown that the conclusion of a pact of mutual assistance could not be expected, we could not but explore other possibilities of ensuring peace and eliminating the danger of war between Germany and the U.S.S.R. If the British and French governments refused to reckon with this, that is their affair. It is our duty to think of the interests of the Soviet people, the interests of the Union of Soviet Socialist Republics. All the more since we are firmly convinced that the interests of the U.S.S.R. coincide with the fundamental interests of the peoples of other countries. But that is only one side of the matter.

Another circumstance was required before the Soviet-German Non-Aggression Pact could come into existence. It was necessary that in her foreign policy Germany should make a turn towards good-neighborly relations with the Soviet Union.

Only when this second condition was fulfilled, only when it became clear to us that the German government desired to change its foreign policy so as to secure an improvement of relations with the U.S.S.R., was the basis found for the conclusion of a Soviet-German Non-Aggression Pact. Everybody knows that during the last six years, ever since the National-Socialists [Nazis] came into power, political relations between Germany and the U.S.S.R. have been strained. Everybody also knows that despite the differences of outlook and political systems, the Soviet Government endeavored to maintain normal business and political relations with Germany. There is no need now to revert to individual incidents of these relations during recent years, which are well known to you.

I must, however, recall the explanation of our foreign policy given several months ago at the Eighteenth Party Congress. Speaking of our tasks in the realm of foreign policy, Stalin defined our attitude to other countries as follows:

"1. To continue the policy of peace and of strengthening business relations with all countries;
"2. To be cautious and not to allow our country to be drawn into conflicts by warmongers who are accustomed to have others pull the chestnuts out of the fire for them."[1]

As you see, Stalin hit the nail on the head when he exposed the machinations of the Western European politicians who were trying to set Germany and the Soviet Union at loggerheads.

It must be confessed that there were some shortsighted people even

---

[1] The translator cites Joseph Stalin's *From Socialism to Communism in the Soviet Union* (New York: International Publishers. 1939).

in our own country who, carried away by oversimplified anti-fascist propaganda, forgot about this provocative work of our enemies. Mindful of this, Stalin even then suggested the possibility of other, unhostile, good-neighborly relations between Germany and the U.S.S.R. It can now be seen that on the whole Germany correctly understood these statements of Stalin and drew practical conclusions from them. The conclusion of the Soviet-German Non-Aggression Pact shows that Stalin's historic prevision has been brilliantly confirmed.

In the spring of this year the German Government made a proposal to resume commercial and credit negotiations. Soon after, the negotiations were resumed. By making mutual concessions, we succeeded in reaching an agreement. As you know, this agreement was signed on August 19. This was not the first commercial and credit agreement concluded with Germany under her present government.

But this agreement differs favorably not only from the 1935 agreement but from all previous agreements, not to mention the fact that we had no economic agreement equally advantageous with Great Britain, France or any other country. The agreement is advantageous to us because its credit conditions (a seven-year credit) enables us to order a considerable additional quantity of such equipment as we need. By this agreement, the U.S.S.R. undertakes to sell to Germany a definite quantity of our surplus raw materials for her industry, which fully answers to the interests of the U.S.S.R.

Why should we reject such advantageous economic agreement? Surely not to please those who are generally averse to the Soviet Union having advantageous economic agreements with other countries? And it is clear that the commercial and credit agreement with Germany is fully in accord with the economic interests and defense needs of the Soviet Union. This agreement is fully in accord with the decision of the Eighteenth Congress of our Party, which approved Stalin's statement as to the need for "strengthening business relations with all countries."

When, however, the German government expressed the desire to improve political relations as well, the Soviet government had no grounds for refusing. This gave rise to the question of concluding a non-aggression pact.

Voices are now being heard testifying to the lack of understanding of the most simple reasons for the improvement of political relations between the Soviet Union and Germany which has begun. For example, people ask with an air of innocence how the Soviet Union could consent to improve political relations with a state of a fascist type. "Is that possible?" they ask. But they forget that this is not a question of our attitude towards the internal regime of another country but of the foreign relations between the two states. They forget that we hold the position of not interfering in the internal affairs of other countries and, correspondingly, of not tolerating interference in our own internal affairs. Furthermore, they forget the important principle or our foreign policy which was formulated by Stalin at the Eighteenth Party Congress as follows:

> "We stand for peace and the strengthening of business relations with all countries. That is our position; and we shall adhere to this position as long as these countries maintain like relations with the Soviet Union, and as long as they make no attempt to trespass on the interests of our country."[2]

The meaning of these words is quite clear: the Soviet Union strives to maintain good-neighborly relations with all non-Soviet countries provided that these countries maintain a like altitude towards the Soviet Union. In our foreign policy towards non-Soviet countries, we have always been guided by Lenin's well-known principle of the peaceful coexistence of the Soviet state and of capitalist countries. A large number of examples might be cited to show how this principle has been carried out in practice. But I will confine myself to only a few.

We have, for instance, a non-aggression and neutrality treaty with fascist Italy ever since 1933. It has never occurred to anybody as yet to object to this treaty. And that is natural. Inasmuch as this pact meets the interests of the U.S.S.R., it is in accord with our principle of the peaceful coexistence of the U.S.S.R. and the capitalist countries. We have non-aggression pacts also with Poland and certain other countries whose semi-fascist system is known to all. These pacts have not given rise to any misgivings either. Perhaps it would not be superfluous to mention the fact that we have not even treaties of this kind with certain other non-fascist bourgeois-democratic countries, with Great Britain herself, for instance. But that is not our fault.

Since 1926, the political basis of our relations with Germany has been the treaty of neutrality which was already extended by the present German government in 1933. This treaty of neutrality remains in force to this day. The Soviet government considered it desirable even before this to take a further step towards improving political relations with Germany, but the circumstances have been such that this has become possible only now.

It is true that it is not a pact of mutual assistance that is in ques-

---

[2] Ibid.

tion, as in the case of the Anglo-French-Soviet negotiations, but only of a non-aggression pact. Nevertheless, conditions being what they are, it is difficult to overestimate the international importance of the Soviet-German pact. That is why we favored the visit of Von Ribbentrop, the German Minister for Foreign Affairs, to Moscow.

August 23, 1939, the day the Soviet-German Non-Aggression Pact was signed, is to be regarded as a date of great historical importance. The Non-Aggression Pact between the U.S.S.R. and Germany marks a turning point in the history of Europe and not only of Europe. Only yesterday the German fascists were pursuing a foreign policy hostile to us. Yes, only yesterday we were enemies in the sphere of foreign relations. Today, however, the situation has changed and we are enemies no longer.

The art of politics in the sphere of foreign relations does not consist in increasing the number of enemies for one's country. On the contrary, the art of politics in this sphere is to reduce the number of such enemies and to make the enemies of yesterday good neighbors, maintaining peaceable relations with one another.

History has shown that enmity and wars between our country and Germany have been to the detriment of our country, not to their benefit. Russia and Germany suffered most of all countries in the war of 1914–1918. Therefore the interest of the peoples of the Soviet Union and Germany stand in need of peaceable relations. The Soviet-German Non-Aggression Pact puts an end to enmity between Germany and the U.S.S.R. and this is in the interests of both countries. The fact that our outlooks and political systems differ must not and cannot be obstacles to the establishment of good political relations between both states, just as like differences are not impediments to good political relations which the U.S.S.R. maintains with other non-Soviet capitalist countries. Only enemies of Germany and the U.S.S.R. can strive to create and foment enmity between the peoples of these countries. We have always stood for amity between the peoples of the U.S.S.R. and Germany, for the growth and development of friendship between the peoples of the Soviet Union and the German people.

The chief importance of the Soviet-German Non-Aggression Pact lies in the fact that the two largest states of Europe have agreed to put an end to the enmity between them, to eliminate the menace of war and live at peace one with the other, making narrower thereby the zone of possible military conflicts in Europe. Even if military conflicts in Europe should prove unavoidable, the scope of hostilities will now be restricted. Only the instigators of a general European war can be displeased by this state of affairs, those who under the mask of pacifism would like to ignite a general conflagration in Europe.

The Soviet-German Pact has been the object of numerous attacks in the English, French and American press. Conspicuous in these efforts are certain "Socialist" newspapers, diligent servitors of "their" national capitalism, servitors of gentlemen who pay them decently. It is clear that the real truth cannot be expected from gentry of this calibre. Attempts are being made to spread the fiction that the signing of the Soviet-German Pact disrupted the negotiations with England and France on a mutual assistance pact. This lie has already been nailed in the interview given by Voroshilov.

In reality, as you know, the very reverse is true. The Soviet Union signed the Non-Aggression Pact with Germany, for one thing, in view of the fact that the negotiations with France and England had run into insuperable differences and ended in failure through the fault of the ruling classes of England and France.

Further, they go so far as to blame us because the pact, if you please, contains no clause providing for its denunciation in case one of the signatories is drawn into war under conditions which might give someone an external pretext to qualify this particular country as an aggressor. But they forget for some reason that such a clause and such a reservation is not to be found either in the Polish-German non-aggression pact signed in 1934 and annulled by Germany in 1939 against the wishes of Poland, or in the Anglo-German declaration on non-aggression signed only a few months ago. The question arises: Why cannot the U.S.S.R. allow itself the same privilege as Poland and England allowed themselves long ago?

Finally there are wiseacres who construe from the pact more than is written in it. For this purpose, all kinds of conjectures and hints are mooted in order to cast doubt on the pact in one or another country. But all this merely speaks for the hopeless impotence of the enemies of the pact who are exposing themselves more and more as enemies of both the Soviet Union and Germany, striving to provoke war between these countries.

In all this, we find fresh corroboration of Stalin's warning that we must be particularly cautious with warmongers who are accustomed to have others pull the chestnuts out of the fire for them. We must be on guard against those who see an advantage to themselves in bad relations between the U.S.S.R. and Germany, in enmity between them, and who do not want peace and good neighborly relations between Germany and the Soviet Union.

We can understand why this policy is being pursued by out-and-out imperialists. But we cannot ignore such facts as the especial zeal with which some leaders of the Socialist Parties of Great Britain and France have recently distinguished themselves in this matter. And these gentlemen have really gone the whole hog, and no mistake. These people positively demand the U.S.S.R. get itself involved in war against Germany on the side of Great Britain. Have not these rabid warmongers taken leave of their senses? Is it really difficult for these gentlemen to understand the purpose of the Soviet-German Non-Aggression Pact, on the strength of which the U.S.S.R. is not obliged to involve itself in war either on the side of Great Britain against Germany or on the side of Germany against Great Britain? Is it really difficult to understand that the U.S.S.R. is pursuing and will continue to pursue its own independent policy, based on the interests of the peoples of the U.S.S.R. and only their interests?

If these gentlemen have such an uncontrollable desire to fight, let them do their own fighting without the Soviet Union. We could see what fighting stuff they are made of.

In our eyes, in the eyes of the entire Soviet people, these are just as much enemies of peace as all other instigators of war in Europe. Only those who desire a grand new slaughter, a new holocaust of nations, only they want to set the Soviet Union and Germany at loggerheads, they are the only people who want to destroy the incipient restoration of good-neighborly relations between the peoples of the U.S.S.R. and Germany.

The Soviet Union signed a pact with Germany, fully assured that peace between the peoples of the U.S.S.R. and Germany is in the interests of all peoples, in the interests of universal peace. Every sincere supporter of peace will realize the truth of this. This pact corresponds to the fundamental interests of the working people of the Soviet Union and cannot weaken our vigilance in defense of these interests. This pact is backed by firm confidence in our real forces, in their complete preparedness to meet any aggression against the U.S.S.R.

This pact, like the unsuccessful Anglo-French-Soviet negotiations, proves that no important questions of international relations, and questions of Eastern Europe even less, can be settled without the active participation of the Soviet Union, that any attempts to shut out the Soviet Union and decide such questions behind its back are doomed to failure.

The Soviet-German Non-Aggression Pact spells a new turn in the development of Europe, a turn towards improvement of relations between the two largest states of Europe. This pact not only eliminates the menace of war with Germany, narrows down the zone of possible hostilities in Europe, and serves thereby the cause of universal peace: it must open to us new possibilities of increasing our strength, of further consolidation of our positions, of further growth of the influence of the Soviet Union on international developments.

There is no need to dwell here on the separate clauses of the pact. The Council of People's Commissars has reason to hope that the pact will meet with your approval as a document of cardinal importance to the U.S.S.R.

The Council of People's Commissars submits the Soviet-German Non-Aggression Pact to the Supreme Soviet and proposes that it be ratified.

On the conclusion of Molotov's statement, the joint sitting of the Council of the Union and the Council of Nationalities of the Supreme Soviet of the U.S.S.R., on a motion of Deputy Shcherbakov, unanimously adopted the following resolution:

"Having heard the statement of Comrade V. M. Molotov, the Chairman of the Council of People's Commissars and People's Commissar for Foreign Affairs, on the ratification of the Non-Aggression Pact between the U.S.S.R. and Germany, the Supreme Soviet of the U.S.S.R. resolves:

"1. To approve the foreign policy of the Government.
"2. To ratify the Non-Aggression Pact between the U.S.S.R. and Germany, concluded in Moscow, August 23, 1939."

CHARLES A. LINDBERGH
"America First"
("The leaders of both the British and the Jewish races,...for reasons which are not American, wish to involve us in the war")

Des Moines, Iowa

September 11, 1941

The famous American aviator (1902–1974) was criticized for accepting awards and recognition from the Nazis for his accomplishments as a pilot and flight engineer. As a well-known member of the America First organization, he led rallies against the United States' preparations for involvement in World War II.

It is now two years since this latest European war began. From that day in September 1939, until the present moment, there has been an over-increasing effort to force the United States into the conflict.

That effort has been carried on by foreign interests, and by a small minority of our own people; but it has been so successful that, today, our country stands on the verge of war.

At this time, as the war is about to enter its third winter, it seems appropriate to review the circumstances that have led us to our present position. Why are we on the verge of war? Was it necessary for us to become so deeply involved? Who is responsible for changing our national policy from one of neutrality and independence to one of entanglement in European affairs?

Personally, I believe there is no better argument against our intervention than a study of the causes and developments of the present war. I have often said that if the true facts and issues were placed before the American people, there would be no danger of our involvement.

Here, I would like to point out to you a fundamental difference between the groups who advocate foreign war, and those who believe in an independent destiny for America.

If you will look back over the record, you will find that those of us who oppose intervention have constantly tried to clarify facts and issues; while the interventionists have tried to hide facts and confuse issues.

We ask you to read what we said last month, last year, and even before the war began. Our record is open and clear, and we are proud of it.

We have not led you on by subterfuge and propaganda. We have not resorted to steps short of anything, in order to take the American people where they did not want to go.

What we said before the elections, we say [illegible] and again, and again today. And we will not tell you tomorrow that it was just campaign oratory. Have you ever heard an interventionist, or a British agent, or a member of the administration in Washington ask you to go back and study a record of what they have said since the war started? Are their self-styled defenders of democracy willing to put the issue of war to a vote of our people? Do you find these crusaders for foreign freedom of speech, or the removal of censorship here in our own country?

The subterfuge and propaganda that exists in our country is obvious on every side. Tonight, I shall try to pierce through a portion of it, to the naked facts which lie beneath.

When this war started in Europe, it was clear that the American people were solidly opposed to entering it. Why shouldn't we be? We had the best defensive position in the world; we had a tradition of independence from Europe; and the one time we did take part in a European war left European problems unsolved, and debts to America unpaid.

National polls showed that when England and France declared war on Germany, in 1939, less than 10 percent of our population favored a similar course for America. But there were various groups of people, here and abroad, whose interests and beliefs necessitated the involvement of the United States in the war. I shall point out some of these groups tonight, and outline their methods of procedure. In doing this, I must speak with the utmost frankness, for in order to counteract their efforts, we must know exactly who they are.

The three most important groups who have been pressing this country toward war are the British, the Jewish and the Roosevelt administration.

Behind these groups, but of lesser importance, are a number of capitalists, Anglophiles, and intellectuals who believe that the future of mankind depends upon the domination of the British Empire. Add to these the Communistic groups who were opposed to intervention until a few weeks ago, and I believe I have named the major war agitators in this country.

I am speaking here only of war agitators, not of those sincere but misguided men and women who, confused by misinformation and frightened by propaganda, follow the lead of the war agitators.

As I have said, these war agitators comprise only a small minority of our people; but they control a tremendous influence. Against the determination of the American people to stay out of war, they have marshaled the power of their propaganda, their money, their patronage.

Let us consider these groups, one at a time.

First, the British: It is obvious and perfectly understandable that Great Britain wants the United States in the war on her side. England is now in a desperate position. Her population is not large enough and her armies are not strong enough to invade the continent of Europe and win the war she declared against Germany.

Her geographical position is such that she cannot win the war by the use of aviation alone, regardless of how many planes we send her. Even if America entered the war, it is improbable that the Allied armies could invade Europe and overwhelm the Axis powers. But one thing is certain. If England can draw this country into the war, she can shift to our shoulders a large portion of the responsibility for waging it and for paying its cost.

As you all know, we were left with the debts of the last European war; and unless we are more cautious in the future than we have been in the past, we will be left with the debts of the present case. If it were not for her hope that she can make us responsible for the war financially, as well as militarily, I believe England would have negotiated a peace in Europe many months ago, and be better off for doing so.

England has devoted, and will continue to devote every effort to get us into the war. We know that she spent huge sums of money in this country during the last war in order to involve us. Englishmen have written books about the cleverness of its use.

We know that England is spending great sums of money for propaganda in America during the present war. If we were Englishmen, we would do the same. But our interest is first in America; and as Americans, it is essential for us to realize the effort that British interests are making to draw us into their war.

The second major group I mentioned is the Jewish.

It is not difficult to understand why Jewish people desire the overthrow of Nazi Germany. The persecution they suffered in Germany would be sufficient to make bitter enemies of any race.

No person with a sense of the dignity of mankind can condone the persecution of the Jewish race in Germany. But no person of honesty and vision can look on their pro-war policy here today without seeing the dangers involved in such a policy both for us and for them. Instead of agitating for war, the Jewish groups in this country should be opposing it in every possible way for they will be among the first to feel its consequences.

Tolerance is a virtue that depends upon peace and strength. History shows that it cannot survive war and devastations. A few far-sighted Jewish people realize this and stand opposed to intervention. But the majority still do not.

Their greatest danger to this country lies in their large ownership and influence in our motion pictures, our press, our radio and our government.

I am not attacking either the Jewish or the British people. Both races, I admire. But I am saying that the leaders of both the British and the Jewish races, for reasons which are as understandable from their viewpoint as they are inadvisable from ours, for reasons which are not American, wish to involve us in the war.

We cannot blame them for looking out for what they believe to be their own interests, but we also must look out for ours. We cannot allow the natural passions and prejudices of other peoples to lead our country to destruction.

The Roosevelt administration is the third powerful group which has been carrying this country toward war. Its members have used the war emergency to obtain a third presidential term for the first time in American history. They have used the war to add unlimited billions to a debt which was already the highest we have ever known. And they have just used the war to justify the restriction of congressional power, and the assumption of dictatorial procedures on the part of the president and his appointees.

The power of the Roosevelt administration depends upon the maintenance of a wartime emergency. The prestige of the Roosevelt administration depends upon the success of Great Britain to whom the president attached his political future at a time when most people thought that England and France would easily win the war. The danger of the Roosevelt administration lies in its subterfuge. While its members have promised us peace, they have led us to war heedless of the platform upon which they were elected.

In selecting these three groups as the major agitators for war, I have included only those whose support is essential to the war party. If any one of these groups—the British, the Jewish, or the administration—stops agitating for war, I believe there will be little danger of our involvement.

I do not believe that any two of them are powerful enough to carry this country to war without the support of the third. And to these three, as I have said, all other war groups are of secondary importance.

When hostilities commenced in Europe, in 1939, it was realized by these groups that the American people had no intention of entering the war. They knew it would be worse than useless to ask us for a declaration of war at that time. But they believed that this country could be entered into the war in very much the same way we were entered into the last one.

They planned: first, to prepare the United States for foreign war under the guise of American defense; second, to involve us in the war, step by step, without our realization; third, to create a series of incidents which would force us into the actual conflict. These plans were of course, to be covered and assisted by the full power of their propaganda.

Our theaters soon became filled with plays portraying the glory of war. Newsreels lost all semblance of objectivity. Newspapers and magazines began to lose advertising if they carried anti-war articles. A smear campaign was instituted against individuals who opposed intervention. The terms "fifth columnist," "traitor," "Nazi," "anti-Semitic" were thrown ceaselessly at any one who dared to suggest that it was not to the best interests of the United States to enter the war. Men lost their jobs if they were frankly anti-war. Many others dared no longer speak.

Before long, lecture halls that were open to the advocates of war were closed to speakers who opposed it. A fear campaign was inaugurated. We were told that aviation, which has held the British fleet off the continent of Europe, made America more vulnerable than ever before to invasion. Propaganda was in full swing.

There was no difficulty in obtaining billions of dollars for arms under the guise of defending America. Our people stood united on a program of defense. Congress passed appropriation after appropriation for guns and planes and battleships, with the approval of the overwhelming majority of our citizens. That a large portion of these appropriations was to be used to build arms for Europe, we did not learn until later. That was another step.

To use a specific example; in 1939, we were told that we should increase our air corps to a total of 5,000 planes. Congress passed the necessary legislation. A few months later, the administration told us that the United States should have at least 50,000 planes for our national safety. But almost as fast as fighting planes were turned out from our factories, they were sent abroad, although our own air corps was in the utmost need of new equipment; so that today, two years after the start of war, the American army has a few hundred thoroughly modern bombers and fighters—less in fact, than Germany is able to produce in a single month.

Ever since its inception, our arms program has been laid out for the purpose of carrying on the war in Europe, far more than for the purpose of building an adequate defense for America.

Now at the same time we were being prepared for a foreign war, it was necessary, as I have said, to involve us in the war. This was accomplished under that now famous phrase "steps short of war."

England and France would win if the United States would only repeal its arms embargo and sell munitions for cash, we were told. And then [illegible] began, a refrain that marked every step we took toward war for many months—"the best way to defend America and keep out of war." we were told, was "by aiding the Allies."

First, we agreed to sell arms to Europe; next, we agreed to loan arms to Europe; then we agreed to patrol the ocean for Europe; then we occupied a European island in the war zone. Now, we have reached the verge of war.

The war groups have succeeded in the first two of their three major steps into war. The greatest armament program in our history is under way.

We have become involved in the war from practically every standpoint except actual shooting. Only the creation of sufficient "incidents" yet remains; and you see the first of these already taking place, according to plan [illegible]...a plan that was never laid before the American people for their approval.

Men and women of Iowa; only one thing holds this country from war today. That is the rising opposition of the American people. Our system of democracy and representative government is on test today as it has never been before. We are on the verge of a war in which the only victor would be chaos and prostration.

We are on the verge of a war for which we are still unprepared, and for which no one has offered a feasible plan for victory—a war which cannot be won without sending our soldiers across the ocean to force a landing on a hostile coast against armies stronger than our own.

We are on the verge of war, but it is not yet too late to stay out. It is not too late to show that no amount of money, or propaganda, or patronage can force a free and independent people into war against its will. It is not yet too late to retrieve and to maintain the independent American destiny that our forefathers established in this new world.

The entire future rests upon our shoulders. It depends upon our action, our courage, and our intelligence. If you oppose our intervention in the war, now is the time to make your voice heard.

Help us to organize these meetings; and write to your representatives in Washington. I tell you that the last stronghold of democracy and representative government in this country is in our house of representatives and our senate.

There, we can still make our will known. And if we, the American people, do that, independence and freedom will continue to live among us, and there will be no foreign war.

ADOLPH HITLER
Chancellor of the Third Reich
"Nothing is Impossible for the German Soldier"
Address to the Reichstag

("For what does [Churchill] care for the lives of others? What does he care for culture or for architecture?")

Berlin, Germany

May 4, 1941

The Austrian painter and vegetarian (1889–1945) found his medium in hatred and murder, leading the National Socialist Party to power in Germany. As the chancellor of the Third Reich from 1933, he militarized

Germany and began invading its neighbors. After England resisted his takeover of Europe, he implemented his long desired "Final Solution," the Holocaust, wherein by his orders more than six million people were murdered. He killed himself in April of 1945.

Deputies/Men of the German Reichstag:

At a time when only deeds count and words are of little importance, it is not my intention to appear before you, the elected representatives of the German people, more often than absolutely necessary. The first time I spoke to you was at the outbreak of the war when, thanks to the Anglo-French conspiracy against peace, every attempt at an understanding with Poland, which otherwise would have been possible, had been frustrated.

The most unscrupulous men of the present time had, as they admit today, decided as early as 1936 to involve the Reich, which in its peaceful work of reconstruction was becoming too powerful for them, in a new and bloody war and, if possible, to destroy it. They had finally succeeded in finding a State that was prepared for their interests and aims, and that State was Poland.

All my endeavors to come to an understanding with Britain were wrecked by the determination of a small clique which, whether from motives of hate or for the sake of material gain, rejected every German proposal for an understanding due to their resolve, which they never concealed, to resort to war, whatever happened.

The man behind this fanatical and diabolical plan to bring about war at whatever cost was Mr. Churchill. His associates were the men who now form the British Government.

These endeavors received most powerful support, both openly and secretly, from the so-called great democracies on both sides of the Atlantic. At a time when the people were more and more dissatisfied with their deficient statesmanship, the responsible men over there believed that a successful war would be the most likely means of solving problems that otherwise would be beyond their power to solve.

Behind these men there stood the great international Jewish financial interests that control the banks and the Stock Exchange as well as the armament industry. And now, just as before, they scented the opportunity of doing their unsavory business. And so, just as before, there was no scruple about sacrificing the blood of the peoples. That was the beginning of this war. A few weeks later the State that was the third country in Europe, Poland, but had been reckless enough to allow herself to be used for the financial interests of these warmongers, was annihilated and destroyed.

In these circumstances I considered that I owed it to our German people and countless men and women in the opposite camps, who as individuals were as decent as they were innocent of blame, to make yet another appeal to the common sense and the conscience of these statesmen. On October 6, 1939, I therefore once more publicly stated that Germany had neither demanded nor intended to demand anything either from Britain or from France, that it was madness to continue the war and, above all, that the scourge of modern weapons of warfare, once they were brought into action, would inevitably ravage vast territories.

But just as the appeal I made on September 1, 1939, proved to be in vain, this renewed appeal met with indignant rejection. The British and their Jewish capitalist backers could find no other explanation for this appeal, which I had made on humanitarian grounds, than the assumption of weakness on the part of Germany.

They assured the people of Britain and France that Germany dreaded the clash to be expected in the spring of 1940 and was eager to make peace for fear of the annihilation that would then inevitably result.

Already at that time the Norwegian Government, misled by the stubborn insistence of Mr. Churchill's false prophecies, began to toy with the idea of a British landing on their soil, thereby contributing to the destruction of Germany by permitting their harbors and Swedish iron ore fields to be seized.

So sure were Mr. Churchill and Paul Reynaud of the success of their new scheme that finally, whether from sheer recklessness or perhaps under the influence of drink, they deemed it no longer necessary to make a secret of their intentions.

It was thanks to these two gentlemen's tendency to gossip that the German Government at that time gained cognizance of the plans being made against the Reich. A few weeks later this danger to Germany was eliminated. One of the boldest deeds of arms in the whole history of warfare frustrated the attack of the British and French armies against the right flank of our line of defense.

Immediately after the failure of these plans, increased pressure was exerted by the British warmongers upon Belgium and Holland. Now that the attack upon our sources for the supply of iron ore had proved unsuccessful, they aimed to advance the front to the Rhine by involving the Belgian and Dutch States and thus to threaten and paralyze our production centers for iron and steel.

On May 10 of last year perhaps the most memorable struggle in all German history commenced. The enemy front was broken up in a few days and the stage was then set for the operation that culminated in the greatest battle of annihilation in the history of the world. Thus France collapsed, Belgium and Holland were already occupied, and the battered remnants of the British expeditionary force were driven from the European continent, leaving their arms behind.

On July 19, 1940, I then convened the German Reichstag for the third time in order to render that great account which you all still remember. The meeting provided me with the opportunity of expressing the thanks of the nation to its soldiers in a form suited to the uniqueness of the event. Once again I seized the opportunity of urging the world to make peace. And what I foresaw and prophesied at that time happened. My offer of peace was misconstrued as a symptom of fear and cowardice.

The European and American warmongers succeeded once again in befogging the sound common sense of the masses, who can never hope to profit from this war, by conjuring up false pictures of new hope. Thus, finally, under pressure of public opinion, as formed by their press, they once more managed to induce the nation to continue this struggle.

Even my warnings against night bombings of the civilian population, as advocated by Mr. Churchill, were interpreted as a sign of German impotence. He, the most bloodthirsty or amateurish strategist that history has ever known, actually saw fit to believe that the reserve displayed for months by the German Air Force could be looked upon only as proof of their incapacity to fly by night.

So this man for months ordered his paid scribblers to deceive the British people into believing that the Royal Air Force alone—and no others—was in a position to wage war in this way, and that thus, ways and means had been found to force the Reich to its knees by the ruthless onslaught of the British Air Force on the German civilian population in conjunction with the starvation blockade.

Again and again I uttered these warnings against this specific type of aerial warfare, and I did so for over three and a half months. That these warnings failed to impress Mr. Churchill does not surprise me in the least. For what does this man care for the lives of others? What does he care for culture or for architecture? When war broke out he stated clearly that he wanted to have his war, even though the cities of England might be reduced to ruins. So now he has got his war.

My assurances that from a given moment every one of his bombs would be returned if necessary a hundredfold failed to induce this man to consider even for an instant the criminal nature of his action. He professes not to be in the least depressed and he even assures us that the British people, too, after such bombing raids, greeted him with a joyous serenity, causing him to return to London refreshed by his visits to the stricken areas.

It is possible that this sight strengthened Mr. Churchill in his firm determination to continue the war in this way, and we are no less determined to continue to retaliate, if necessary, a hundred bombs for every one of his and to go on doing so until the British nation at last gets rid of this criminal and his methods.

The appeal to forsake me, made to the German nation by this fool and his satellites on May Day, of all days, are only to be explained either as symptomatic of a paralytic disease or of a drunkard's ravings. His abnormal state of mind also gave birth to a decision to transform the Balkans into a theater of war.

For over five years this man has been chasing around Europe like a madman in search of something that he could set on fire. Unfortunately, he again and again finds hirelings who open the gates of their country to this international incendiary.

After he had succeeded in the course of the past winter in persuading the British people by a wave of false assertions and pretensions that the German Reich, exhausted by the campaign in the preceding months, was completely spent, he saw himself obliged, in order to prevent an awakening of the truth, to create a fresh conflagration in Europe.

In so doing he returned to the project that had been in his mind as early as the autumn of 1939 and the spring of 1940. It was thought possible at the time to mobilize about 100 divisions in Britain's interest.

The sudden collapse which we witnessed in May and June of the past year forced these plans to be abandoned for the moment. But by the autumn of last year Mr. Churchill began to tackle this problem once again.

In the meantime, however, certain difficulties had arisen. As a result, Rumania, owing to internal changes, dropped out of England's political scheme.

In dealing with these conditions, I shall begin by giving you a brief outline of the aims of Germany's policy in the Balkans. As in the past, the Reich never pursued any territorial or any other selfish political interest in the Balkans. In other words, the Reich has never taken the slightest interest in territorial problems and internal conditions in these States for any selfish reason whatsoever.

On the other hand, the Reich has always endeavored to build up and to strengthen close economic ties with these States in particular. This, however, not only served the interests of the Reich but equally the interests of these countries themselves.

If any two national economic systems ever effectively comple- mented one another, that is especially the case regarding the Balkan States and Germany. Germany is an industrial country and requires foodstuffs and raw materials. The Balkan States are agrarian coun- tries and are short of these raw materials. At the same time, they require industrial products.

It was therefore hardly surprising when Germany thus became the main business partner of the Balkan States. Nor was this in Germany's interest alone, but also in that of the Balkan peoples themselves.

And none but our Jew-ridden democracies, which can think only in terms of capitalism, can maintain that if one state delivers machinery to another state it thereby dominates that other state. In actual fact such domination, if it occurs, can be only a reciprocal domination.

It is presumably easier to be without machinery than without food and raw materials. Consequently, the partner in need of raw material and foodstuffs would appear to be more tied down than the recipient of industrial products. *In this transaction there was neither conqueror nor conquered. There were only partners.*

The German Reich of the National Socialist revolution has prided itself on being a fair and decent partner, offering in exchange high-quality products instead of worthless democratic paper money. For these reasons the Reich was interested in only one thing if, indeed, there was any question of political interest, namely, in see- ing that internally the business partner was firmly established on a sound and healthy basis.

The application of this idea led in fact not only to increasing prosper- ity in these countries but also to the beginning of mutual confidence. All the greater, however, became the endeavor of that world incendi- ary, Churchill, to put an end to this peaceful development and by shamelessly imposing upon these States utterly worthless British guarantees and promises of assistance to introduce into this peace- able European territory elements of unrest, uncertainty, distrust and, finally, conflict.

Originally, Rumania was first won over by these guarantees and later, of course, Greece. It has, meanwhile, probably been suf- ficiently demonstrated that he had absolutely no power of any kind to provide real help and that these guarantees were merely intended to rope these States in to follow the dangerous trend of filthy Brit- ish politics.

Rumania has had to pay bitterly for the guarantees, which were calculated to estrange her from the Axis powers.

Greece, which least of all required such a guarantee, was offered her share to link her destiny to that of the country that provided her King with cash and orders.

Even today I feel that I must, as I believe in the interest of historical accuracy, distinguish between the Greek people and that thin top layer of corrupt leaders who, inspired by a king who had no eyes for the duty of true leadership, preferred instead to further the aims of British war politics. To me this is a subject of profound regret.

Germany, with the faint hope of still being able to contribute in some way to a solution of the problem, had not severed relations with Greece. But even then I was bound in duty to point out before the whole world that we would not tacitly allow a revival of the old Salonika scheme of the Great War.

Unfortunately, my warning was not taken seriously enough. That we were determined, if the British tried to gain another foothold in Europe, to drive them back into the sea was not taken seriously enough.

The result was that the British began in an increasing degree to establish bases for the formation of a new Salonika army. They began by laying out airdromes and by establishing the necessary ground organization in the firm conviction that the occupation of the airdromes themselves could afterward be carried out very speedily.

Finally a continuous stream of transports brought equipment for an army which, according to Mr. Churchill's idea and plans, was to be landed in Greece. As I have said, already we were aware of this. For months we watched this entire strange procedure with attention, if with restraint.

The reverses suffered by the Italian Army in North Africa, owing to a certain material inferiority of their tanks and anti-tank guns, finally led Mr. Churchill to believe that the time was ripe to transfer the theater of war from Libya to Greece. He ordered the transport of the remaining tanks and of the infantry division, composed mainly of Anzacs, and was convinced that he could now complete his scheme, which was to set the Balkans aflame.

Thus did Mr. Churchill commit one of the greatest strategic blunders of this war. As soon as there could be no further doubt regarding Britain's intentions of gaining a foothold in the Balkans, I took the necessary steps.

Germany, by keeping pace with these moves, assembled the necessary forces for the purpose of counteracting any possible tricks of that gentleman. In this connection I must state categorically that this action was not directed against Greece.

The Duce did not even request me to place one single German

division at his disposal for this purpose. He was convinced that with the advent of good weather his stand against Greece would have been brought to a successful conclusion. I was of the same opinion.

The concentration of German forces was therefore not made for the purpose of assisting the Italians against Greece. It was a precautionary measure against the British attempt under cover of the clamor caused by the Italo-Greek war to entrench themselves secretly in the Balkans in order to force the issue from that quarter on the model of the Salonika army during the World War, and, above all, to draw other elements into the whirlpool.

This hope was founded principally on two States, namely, Turkey and Yugoslavia. But with these very States I have striven during the years since I came into power to establish close co-operation.

The World War actually started from Belgrade. Nevertheless, the German people, who are by nature so ready to forgive and forget, felt no animosity toward that country. Turkey was our ally in the World War. The unfortunate outcome of that struggle weighed upon that country just as heavily as it did upon us.

The great genius who created the new Turkey was the first to set a wonderful example of recovery to our allies whom fortune had at that time deserted and whom fate had dealt so terrible a blow. Whereas Turkey, thanks to the practical attitude of her leaders, preserved her independence in carrying out her own resolutions, Yugoslavia fell a victim to British intrigue.

Most of you, especially my old Party comrades among you, know what efforts I have made to establish a straightforward understanding and indeed friendly relations between Germany and Yugoslavia. In pursuance of this aim Herr von Ribbentrop, our Minister of Foreign Affairs, submitted to the Yugoslav Government proposals that were so outstanding and so fair that at least even the Yugoslav State of that time seemed to become increasingly eager for such close co-operation.

Germany had no intention of starting a war in the Balkans. On the contrary, it was our honest intention as far as possible to contribute to a settlement of the conflict with Greece by means that would be tolerable to the legitimate wishes of Italy.

The Duce not only consented to, but lent his full support to our efforts to bring Yugoslavia into a close community of interests with our peace aims. Thus it finally became possible to induce the Yugoslav Government to join the Threepower Pact, which made no demands whatever on Yugoslavia but only offered that country advantages.

Thus on March 26 of this year a pact was signed in Vienna that offered the Yugoslav State the greatest future conceivable and could have assured peace for the Balkans. Believe me, gentlemen, on that day I left the beautiful city of the Danube truly happy not only because it seemed as though almost eight years of foreign policies had received their reward but also because I believed that perhaps at the last moment German intervention in the Balkans might not be necessary.

We were all stunned by the news of that coup, carried through by a handful of bribed conspirators who had brought about the event that caused the British Prime Minister to declare in joyous words that at last he had something good to report.

You will surely understand, gentlemen, that when I heard this I at once gave orders to attack Yugoslavia. To treat the German Reich in this way is impossible. One cannot spent years in concluding a treaty that is in the interest of the other party merely to discover that this treaty has not only been broken overnight but also that it has been answered by the insulting of the representative of the German Reich, by the threatening of his military attaché, by the injuring of the aide de camp of this attaché, by the maltreating of numerous other Germans, by demolishing property, by laying waste the homes of German citizens and by terrorizing.

God knows that I wanted peace. But I can do nothing but protect the interests of the Reich with those means which, thank God, are at our disposal. I made my decision at that moment all the more calmly because I knew that I was in accord with Bulgaria, who had always remained unshaken in her loyalty to the German Reich, and with the equally justified indignation of Hungary.

Both of our old allies in the World War were bound to regard this action as a provocation emanating from the State that once before had set the whole of Europe on fire and had been guilty of the indescribable sufferings that befell Germany, Hungary, and Bulgaria in consequence.

The general directions of operations issued by me through the Supreme Command of the German forces on March 27 confronted the Army and the Air Force with a formidable task. By a mere turn of the hand an additional campaign had to be prepared. Units that had already arrived had to be moved about. Supplies of armaments had to be assured and the air force had to take over numerous improvised airports part of which were still under water.

Without the sympathetic assistance of Hungary and the extremely loyal attitude of Rumania it would have been very difficult to carry out my orders in the short time envisaged.

I fixed April 6 as the day on which the attack was to begin. The main plan of operation was: First, to proceed with an army coming from Bulgaria against Thrace in Greece in the direction of the Aegean Sea.

The main striking strength of this army lay in its right wing, which was to force a passage through to Salonika by using mountain divisions and a division of tanks; second, to thrust forward with a second army with the object of establishing connection as speedily as possible with the Italian forces advancing from Albania. These two operations were to begin on April 6.

Third, a further operation, beginning on the eighth, provided for the break-through of an army from Bulgaria with the object of reaching the neighborhood of Belgrade. In conjunction with this, a German army corps was to occupy the Banat on the tenth.

In connection with these operations general agreement had been made with our allies, Italy and Hungary. Agreements as to co-operation had also been reached between the two air forces. The command of the German Armies operating against Macedonia and Greece was placed in the hands of Field Marshal von List, who had already particularly distinguished himself in the previous campaigns. Once more and under the most exacting conditions he carried out the task confronting him in truly superior fashion.

The forces advancing against Yugoslavia from the southwest and from Hungary were commanded by Col. Gen. von Weick. He, too, in a very short time with the forces under his command reached his objective.

The Army and SS detachments operating under Field Marshal von Brauchitsch, as Commander in Chief, and the Chief of the General Staff, Col. Gen. Halder, forced the Greek Army in Thrace to capitulate after only five days, established contact with the Italian forces advancing from Albania, occupied Salonika, and thus generally prepared the way for the difficult and glorious break-through via Larissa to Athens.

These operations were crowned by the occupation of the Peloponnesus and numerous Greek islands. A detailed appreciation of the achievements will be given by the German High Command.

The Air Force under the personal command of Reich Marshal Goering was divided into two main groups, commanded by Col. Gen. Loehr and General von Richthofen. It was their task, first, to shatter the enemy air force and to smash its ground organization; second, to attack every important military objective in the conspirators' headquarters at Belgrade, thus eliminating it from the very outset; third, by every manner of active co-operation everywhere with the fighting German troops to break the enemy's resistance, to impede the enemy's flight, to prevent as far as possible his embarkation.

The German armed forces have truly surpassed themselves in this campaign. There is only one way of characterizing that campaign:

Nothing is impossible for the German soldier. Historical justice, however, obliges me to say that of the opponents that have taken up arms against us, *most particularly the Greek soldiers, have fought with the greatest bravery and contempt of death.* They only capitulated when further resistance became impossible and therefore useless.

But I am now compelled to speak of the enemy who is the main cause of this conflict. As a German and as a soldier I consider it unworthy ever to revile a fallen enemy. But it seems to me to be necessary to defend the truth from the wild exaggerations of a man who as a soldier is a bad politician and as a politician is an equally bad soldier.

Mr. Churchill, who started this struggle, is endeavoring, as with regard to Norway or Dunkerque, to say something that sooner or later might perhaps be twisted around to resemble success. I do not consider that honorable but in his case it is understandable.

The gift Mr. Churchill possesses is the gift to lie with a pious expression on his face and to distort the truth until finally glorious victories are made out of the most terrible defeats.

A British Army of 60,000 to 70,000 men landed in Greece. Before the catastrophe the same man maintained, moreover, that it consisted of 240,000 men. The object of this army was to attack Germany from the south, inflict a defeat upon her, and from this point as in 1918 turn the tide of the war.

I prophesied more correctly than Mr. Churchill in my last speech, in which I announced that wherever the British might set foot on the Continent they would be attacked by us and driven into the sea.

Now, with his brazen effrontery, he asserts that this war has cost us 75,000 lives. He causes his presumably not over-intelligent fellow-countrymen to be informed by one of his paid creatures that the British, after having slain enormous masses of Germans, finally turned away from sheer abhorrence of the slaughter and, strictly speaking, withdrew for this reason alone.

I will now present to you the results of this campaign in a few short figures. In the course of the operations against Yugoslavia there were the following numbers of purely Serbian prisoners, leaving out soldiers of German origin and some other groups: 6,198 officers, 313,864 men.

The number of Greek prisoners, 8,000 officers and 210,000 men, has not the same significance. The number of Englishmen, New

Zealanders and Australians taken prisoner exceeds 9,000 officers and men.

The German share of the booty alone, according to the estimates at present available, amounts to more than half a million rifles, far more than 1,000 guns, many thousand machine-guns and anti-aircraft machine-guns, vehicles, and large amounts of ammunition....

The losses of the German Army and the German Air Force as well as those of the SS troops in this campaign are the smallest that we have ever suffered so far. The German armed forces have in fighting against Yugoslavia and Greece as well as against the British in Greece lost:

Army and SS Troops: Fifty-seven officers and 1,042 noncommissioned officers and men killed, 181 officers and 3,571 noncommissioned officers and men wounded, and 13 officers and 372 noncommissioned officers and men missing.

Air Force: Ten officers and 42 noncommissioned officers and men killed, and 36 officers and 104 noncommissioned officers and men missing.

Once more I can only repeat that we feel the hardship of the sacrifice borne by the families concerned. The entire German nation expresses to them its heartfelt gratitude.

Taking the measures as a whole, however, the losses suffered are so small that they constitute supreme justification, first, for the planning and timing of this campaign; second for the conduct of operations; third, for the manner in which they were carried through.

The training of our officers is excellent beyond comparison The high standard of efficiency of our soldiers, the superiority of our equipment, the quality of our munitions and the indomitable courage of all ranks have combined to lead at such small sacrifice to a success of truly decisive historical importance.

Churchill, one of the most hopeless dabblers in strategy, thus managed to lose two theaters of war at one single blow. The fact that this man, who in any other country would be court-martialed, gained fresh admiration as Prime Minister cannot be construed as an expression of magnanimity such as was accorded by Roman senators to generals honorably defeated in battle. It is merely proof of that perpetual blindness with which the gods afflict those whom they are about to destroy.

The consequences of this campaign are extraordinary. In view of the fact that a small set of conspirators in Belgrade again were able to foment trouble in the service of extra continental interests, the radical elimination of this danger means the removal of an element of tension for the whole of Europe.

The Danube as an important waterway is thus safeguarded against any further act of sabotage. Traffic has been resumed in full.

Apart from the modest correction of its frontiers, which were infringed as a result of the outcome of the World War, the Reich has no special territorial interests in these parts. As far as politics are concerned we are merely interested in safeguarding peace in this region, while in the realm of economics we wish to see an order that will allow the production of goods to be developed and the exchange of products to be resumed in the interests of all.

It is, however, only in accordance with supreme justice if those interests are also taken into account that are founded upon ethnographical, historical, or economic conditions.

I can assure you that I look into the future with perfect tranquillity and great confidence. The German Reich and its allies represent power, military, economic and, above all, in moral respects, which is superior to any possible coalition in the world. The German armed forces will always do their part whenever it may be necessary. The confidence of the German people will always accompany their soldiers.

EZRA POUND

Radio Speech #6 from Fascist Italy

("The United States has been led down the garden path, and may be down under the daisies")

January 29, 1942

The American poet Ezra Pound (1885–1972) was probably the most important figure in English-language literature in the twentieth century. As an expatriate writing and editing in Europe from 1908, he lost the portion of his non-literary mind in the 1920s to economic theory, which led him by the end of the 1920s into senseless anti-Semitism and cagey support for Mussolini's fascism. The man who helped foster some of the masterworks of American and British poetry promoted with all his customary wit and irascible personality some of the ugliest political ideas. From Italy, during World War II, he gave many broadcast speeches on the radio promoting Mussolini's Italy and attacking America. After the war, he was arrested and convicted by the United States for treason; judged to be insane, however, he was confined for a dozen years in a Washington, D.C. mental hospital. Upon his release in 1958, he moved back to Italy. (Note: The odd punctuation and capitalizations as well as the fanciful spellings are all part of Pound's deliberate style.)

On Arbour Day, Pearl Arbour Day, at 12 o'clock noon I retired from the capital of the old Roman Empire to Rapallo to seek wisdom from the ancients.

I wanted to figure things out. I had a perfectly good alibi, if I wanted to play things safe. I was and am officially occupied with a new translation of the Ta S'eu of Confucius. I have in Rapallo the text of Confucius, and of Mencius, the text of the world's finest anthology, namely that which Confucius compiled from earlier authors, and I have in reach the text of a book which bears on its front page the title Li Ki (which the head of the Chinese Department in our Congressional Library tells me proper minded Chi Sinologues now think is pronounced Lee Gee). And I have six volumes of the late Dr. Morrison's Dictionary, not the most up to date dictionary of Chinese Ideograms, but nevertheless good enough.

That is, I have WORK thaaar for some years, if I don't die before I git to the middle.

The Odes are to me very difficult. They are of extreme beauty. Thousands of poets have looked at those odes and despaired. There are points at which some simple ideogram (that is, Chinese picture word) is so used as to be eternal, insofar as our human sense of eternity can reach. There is one of the sunrise that I despair of ever getting translated.

There was to face this, the SITUATION. That is to say the United States had been for months ILLEGALLY at war, through what I considered to be the criminal acts of a President whose mental condition was NOT, as far as I could see, all that could or should be desired of a man in so responsible a position or office.

He had, so far as evidence available to me showed, broken his promises to the electorate; he had to my mind violated his oath of office. He had to my mind violated the oath of allegiance to the United States Constitution which even the ordinary American citizen is expected to take every time he gets a new passport.

It was obviously a mere question of hours, between that day and hour, and the time when the United States of America would be legally at war with the Axis.

I spent a month tryin' to figure things out, well did I, perhaps I concluded sooner. At any rate I had a month clear to make up my mind about some things. I had Confucius and Mencius, both of whom had been up against similar problems. Both of whom had seen empires fallin'. Both of whom had seen deeper into the causes of human confusion than most men even think of lookin'.

Then there was my old dad in bed with a broken hip; Lord knows who is going to mend it or whether it will mend. So—I read him a few pages of Aristotle in the Loeb Classical Library, English version, to take his mind off it. Also to keep my own work in progress.

Because for some time I have had in mind the need of comparing the terminology of Chinese and Greek philosophy, and also comparing that with the terminology of mediaeval Catholic theology.

No. For a man cut off from all his NORMAL contacts with the non-European world, I can't say I was destitute—mentally—there was plenty lyin' there for me to be busy about, if I had wanted to "contract OUT." If I had wanted to go into a funk hole, I had a nice sizeable funk hole. About as good as an endowed professorship in one of our otiose or veiled, shall we say veiled universities, or even Oxford or Cambridge. Plenty of muckers down there settin' pretty, and drawin' 5000 dollars or ten thousand a year for not tellin'. I reckon it is Mencius who thought that "the true sage seeks not repose."

It is not a claustral motto. I began figurin' out that a COMPLETE severance of communication between the calm and sentient men is not to be desired.

I have before now pointed out that England was CUT off from the current of European thought during and BY the Napoleonic Wars, and that she never got ketched up again, not during all the damned nasty and 19th century. Always laggin' behind. Perhaps she allus WAS laggin' behind. I have pointed out the difference of up-to-dateness between Voltaire and Mr. Samuel Johnson.

At any rate it is NO GOOD.

The United States has been MISinformed. The United States has been led down the garden path, and may be down under the daisies. All thru shuttin' out news.

There is no end to the amount of shuttin' out news that the sons of Blood who started this war, and wanted this war, and monkeyed round to git a war started and monkeyed round to keep the war goin', and spreadin'. There is NO end to the shuttin' out and perversions of news that these blighters ain't up to, and that they haven't, and aren't still trying to com pass. Whatever happens it is NOT going to do the United States any good to be as cut off from all news, and all NEWS of CONTEMPORARY thought like the damn fools and utterly decadent Britons have got themselves cut off from.

As you can HEAR from the British Blurb Corporation any Monday and Tuesday evening, and any Wednesday, Thursday, Friday, Saturday and Sunday evening that you choose to listen in to their phenomenal hogwash.

That's where they've got to. And for their bein' there neither I nor any man I shake hands with, is to blame in any way whatsoever.

Every English friend I got in the world, has done his damnest to keep England from makin' such a thunderin' and abysmal ass of herself.

As for my American friends, Senator Borah is dead, not that I knew him much save by letter; but I can still feel his hand on my shoulder as just before he was getting into an elevator in the Senate building, and I can still hear him sayin':

"Well, I'm sure I don't know what a man like you would find to DO here."

That was a few days sooner, mebbe the first time I met him. Neither he, nor William J. Bryan lived to hear Senator Wallace tellin' the world there would be no peace till the nations of the world knocked under and bowed down to the GOLD standard. Bowed down like drunken and abject fools and said, let gold rule humanity, let all human exchange of goods be bottle necked and ask permission from a few bloodthirsty kikes who OWN gold. Bow down and say monopoly is God over all men; and this from a man, said to be, or to HAVE BEEN, interested in farmers, and farmer's welfare. This after all the lies from the London gold ring, this after 20 years of evasion, this in fact after 20 years' attempt to conceal from the English people that they were being asked to go out and DIE for gold, for the monopoly of the owners and brokers; owners of gold mines, brokers, and owners of gold.

Back in December I had never expected such a confession from anyone as high in office.

Yaaas, I knew that was what the war was about: gold, usury and monopoly. I had said as much when I was last in America. I had then said: IF a war is pushed onto us. So now we have got pushed out of Guam, and Wake, and I suppose out of the Philippines, and a 30 years war is in process? Is it? Is a 30 years war what the American citizen thinks will do most good to the United States of America?

Or has someone been MiSinformed? And IF so, who misinformed him? Accordin' to the reports of the American press now available to the aver age European, someone in charge of American destiny miscalculated somethin' or other.

An "inquiry" is in progress, at least as they print here. It bein' my private belief that I could have avoided a war with Japan, if anybody had had the unlikely idea of sending me out there, with any sort of official powers.

The Japanese have a past. Of course when I talk to 'em now, they are apt to remind me that they have ALSO a present.

They have not mentioned the future in our conversations.

The last American journalist I saw, and that was the night before Arbour Day, told me the Japs would never etc., etc.

A nation evolves by process of history. Japan to me consists in part of what I learned from a sort of half trunk full of the late Ernest Fenollosa's papers. Anybody who has read the plays entitled Kumasaka and Kagekiyo, would have AVOIDED the sort of bilge printed in Time and the American press, and the sort of fetid imbecility I heard a few nights ago from the British Broadcasting Company.

There are certain depths of ignorance that can be fatal to a man or a nation. When these are conjoined with malice and baseness of spirit, it seems almost useless to mention them.

A BBC commentator somewhere about January 8 was telling his presumably music hall audience that the Japs were jackals, and that they had just recently, I think he said, within living men's lifetime, emerged from barbarism. I don't know what patriotic end you think, or he thinks, or the British authorities think (if that is the verb), is served by such fetid ignorance.

A glance at Japanese sword guards, a glance at Jimmy Whistler's remarks about Hokusai, or, as I indicated a minute ago, a familiarity with the Awoi no Uye, Kumasaka, Nishikigi, or Funa-Benkei. These are Japanese classical plays, and would convince any man with more sense than a pea hen, of the degree of Japanese civilization; let alone what they conserved when China was, as Fenollosa tells us, incapable of preserving her own cultural heritage.

China lettin' Confucius go OUT of the schools, for example.

And you needn't sniff, the Bostonians kulturbund needn't sniff and say the British Broadcasting Company, the Bloody Boobs Corporation, is over in vulgar London, such things couldn't happen in Boston.

Almost equal imbecility was attained by Time weekly magazine in November of 1941.

Someone had apparently blundered, as Lord Tennyson wrote of the charge at Balaclava. And blundered, we think, considerably worse. Waaal now who blundered. A commission has been appointed—possibly to white wash who blundered. I don't know that it is in the citizen's duty to white wash who blundered.

I think the United States and even her British Allies might do well to keep more in touch with continental opinion.

I don't think anybody is going to whitewash who blundered into the alliance with Russia.

I think there are some crimes that nothing will whitewash.

I don't think an alliance with Stalin's Russia is lucky. I don't think the crime of even going thru the motions of invitin' Russia into slaughter and kill all eastern Europe is a NECESSARY part of the program; program of defense, program of offense. I don't think this horror was NECESSARY.

I don't think it is the function, even of the Commander-in-Chief of the United States American Army, to dictate the citizens' politics;

NOT to the point of invitin' Bolshevik Russia to kill off the whole east half of Europe!

I don't think it is a lucky move. EVEN if Eden hopes to double-cross Russia, which nothing indicates that he does hope.

The day Hitler went into Russia, England had her chance to pull out. She had her chance to say, let bygones be bygones. If you can stop the Moscovite horror, we will let bygones be bygones. We will try to see at least HALF of your argument.

Instead of which Hank Wallace comes out—no peace till the world accepts the gold standard.

Quem Deus vult perdere.

Does look like there was a weakness of mind in some quarters. Whom God would destroy, he first sends to the bug house.

JOSEPH R. McCARTHY
U.S. Senator from Wisconsin
"Enemies from Within"

Address to the Republican Women's Club

("I have here in my hand a list of 205—a list of names that were made known to the Secretary of State as being members of the Communist Party")

Wheeling, West Virginia

February 9, 1950

Joseph R. McCarthy (1908–1957), a Wisconsin Senator from 1946 to 1957, made himself notorious by indulging in America's paranoia about communists. He bullied and intimidated the government and its representatives for several years, until the blindness of his accusations and the relentlessness of his persecutions proved for the most part only his own disreputableness. He never produced the "list of 205" Communist Party members, but for the next four years menaced or threatened to menace thousands of innocent Americans.

Ladies and gentlemen, tonight as we celebrate the one hundred forty-first birthday of one of the greatest men in American history, I would like to be able to talk about what a glorious day today is in the history of the world. As we celebrate the birth of this man who with his whole heart and soul hated war, I would like to be able to speak of peace in our time—of war being outlawed—and of world-wide disarmament. These would be truly appropriate things to be able to mention as we celebrate the birthday of Abraham Lincoln.

Five years after a world war has been won, men's hearts should anticipate a long peace—and men's minds should be free from the heavy weight that comes with war. But this is not such a period—for this is not a period of peace. This is a time of "the cold war." This is a time when all the world is split into two vast, increasingly hostile, armed camps—a time of a great armament race.

Today we can almost physically hear the mutterings and rumblings of an invigorated god of war. You can see it, feel it, and hear it all the way from the Indochina hills, from the shores of Formosa, right over into the very heart of Europe itself.

The one encouraging thing is that the "mad moment" has not yet arrived for the firing of the gun or the exploding of the bomb which will set civilization about the final task of destroying itself. There is still a hope for peace if we finally decide that no longer can we safely blind our eyes and close our ears to those facts which are shaping up more and more clearly—and that is that we are now engaged in a show-down fight—not the usual war between nations for land areas or other material gains, but a war between two diametrically opposed ideologies.

The great difference between our western Christian world and the atheistic Communist world is not political, gentlemen, it is moral. For instance, the Marxian idea of confiscating the land and factories and running the entire economy as a single enterprise is momentous. Likewise, Lenin's invention of the one-party police state as a way to make Marx's idea work is hardly less momentous.

Stalin's resolute putting across of these two ideas, of course, did much to divide the world. With only these differences, however, the east and the west could most certainly still live in peace.

The real, basic difference, however, lies in the religion of immoralism—invented by Marx, preached feverishly by Lenin, and carried to unimaginable extremes by Stalin. This religion of immoralism, if the Red half of the world triumphs—and well it may, gentlemen—this religion of immoralism will more deeply wound and damage mankind than any conceivable economic or political system.

Karl Marx dismissed God as a hoax, and Lenin and Stalin have added in clear-cut, unmistakable language their resolve that no nation, no people who believe in a god, can exist side by side with their communistic state.

Karl Marx, for example, expelled people from his Communist

Party for mentioning such things as love, justice, humanity or morality. He called this "soulful ravings" and "sloppy sentimentality."

While Lincoln was a relatively young man in his late thirties, Karl Marx boasted that the Communist specter was haunting Europe. Since that time, hundreds of millions of people and vast areas of the world have come under Communist domination. Today, less than 100 years after Lincoln's death, Stalin brags that this Communist specter is not only haunting the world, but is about to completely subjugate it.

Today we are engaged in a final, all-out battle between communistic atheism and Christianity. The modern champions of communism have selected this as the time, and ladies and gentlemen, the chips are down—they are truly down.

Lest there be any doubt that the time has been chosen, let us go directly to the leader of communism today—Joseph Stalin. Here is what he said—not back in 1928, not before the war, not during the war—but 2 years after the last war was ended: "To think that the Communist revolution can be carried out peacefully, within the framework of a Christian democracy, means one has either gone out of one's mind and lost all normal understanding, or has grossly and openly repudiated the Communist revolution."

This is what was said by Lenin in 1919—and quoted with approval by Stalin in 1947:

"We are living," says Lenin, "not merely in a state, but in a system of states, and the existence of the Soviet Republic side by side with Christian states for a long time is unthinkable. One or the other must triumph in the end. And before that end supervenes, a series of frightful collisions between the Soviet Republic and the bourgeois states will be inevitable."

Ladies and gentlemen, can there be anyone tonight who is so blind as to say that the war is not on? Can there be anyone who fails to realize that the Communist world has said the time is now?—that this is the time for the showdown between the democratic Christian world and the communistic atheistic world?

Unless we face this fact, we shall pay the price that must be paid by those who wait too long.

Six years ago, at the time of the first conference to map out the peace, there was within the Soviet orbit, 180,000,000 people. Lined up on the anti-totalitarian side there were in the world at that time, roughly 1,625,000,000 people. Today, only 6 years later, there are 80,000,000,000 people under the absolute domination of Soviet Russia—an increase of over 400 percent. On our side, the figure has shrunk to around 500,000. In other words, in less than 6 years, the odds have changed from 9 to 1 in our favor to 8 to 1 against us.

This indicates the swiftness of the tempo of Communist victories and American defeats in the cold war. As one of our outstanding historical figures once said, "When a great democracy is destroyed, it will not be from enemies from without, but rather because of enemies from within."

The truth of this statement is becoming terrifyingly clear as we see this country each day losing on every front.

At war's end we were physically the strongest nation on earth and at least potentially the most powerful intellectually and morally. Ours could have been the honor of being a beacon in the desert of destruction—shining proof that civilization was not yet ready to destroy itself. Unfortunately, we have failed miserably and tragically to arise to the opportunity.

The reason why we find ourselves in a position of impotency is not because our only powerful potential enemy has sent men to invade our shores—but rather because of the traitorous actions of those who have been treated so well by this Nation. It has not been the less fortunate, or members of minority groups who have been traitorous to this Nation—but rather those who have had all the benefits that the wealthiest Nation on earth has had to offer— the finest homes, the finest college education and the finest jobs in government we can give.

This is glaringly true in the State Department. There the bright young men who are born with silver spoons in their mouths are the ones who have been most traitorous.

Now I know it is very easy for anyone to condemn a particular bureau or department in general terms. Therefore, I would like to cite some specific cases.

When Chiang Kai-shek was fighting our war, the State Department had in China a young man named John Service. His task, obviously, was not to work for communization of China. However, strangely, he sent official reports back to the State Department urging that we torpedo our ally Chiang Kai-shek—and stating in unqualified terms (and I quote) that "communism was the only hope of China."

Later, this man—John Service—and please remember that name, ladies and gentlemen, was picked up by the Federal Bureau of Investigation for turning over to the Communists secret State Department information. Strangely, however, he was never prosecuted. However, John Grew, the Under Secretary of State, who insisted on his prosecution, was forced to resign. Two days after, his successor, Dean Acheson, took over as Under Secretary of State. This man, John Service, who had been picked up by the FBI and who had previously urged that communism was the only hope of China, was not only reinstated in the State Department, but promoted—and finally, under Acheson, placed in charge of all placements and promotions. Today, ladies and gentlemen, this man Service is on his way to represent the State Department and Acheson in Calcutta, by far and away the most important listening post in the Far East.

That's one case. Let's go to another—Gustavo Duran, who was labeled as (I quote) "a notorious international Communist," was made assistant to the Assistant Secretary of State in charge of Latin American affairs. He was taken into the State Department from his job as a lieutenant colonel in the Communist International Brigade. Finally, after intense congressional pressure and criticism, he resigned in 1946 from the State Department. And, ladies and gentlemen, where do you think he is now? He took over a high-salaried job, as Chief of Cultural Activities Section in the office of the Assistant Secretary General of the United Nations.

Then there was a Mrs. Mary Jane Kenney, from the Board of Economic Warfare in the State Department, who was named in a FBI report and in a House committee report as a courier for the Communist Party while working for the Government. And where do you think Mrs. Mary Jane is—she is now an editor in the United Nations Document Bureau.

Then there was Julian H. Wadleigh, economist in the Trade Agreements Section of the State Department for 11 years. And who was sent to Turkey and Italy and other countries as United States representative. After the statute of limitations had run so he could not be prosecuted for treason, he openly and brazenly not only admitted but proclaimed that he had been a member of the Communist Party—that while working for the State Department he stole a vast number of secret documents—and furnished these documents to the Russian spy ring of which he was a part.

And, ladies and gentlemen, while I cannot take the time to name all the men in the State Department who have been named as active members of the Communist Party and members of a spy ring, I have here in my hand a list of 205—a list of names that were made known to the Secretary of State as being members of the Communist Party and who nevertheless are still working and shaping policy in that State Department.

One thing to remember in discussing the Communists in our Government is that we are not dealing with spies who get 30 pieces of silver to steal the blueprints of a new weapon. We are dealing with a far more sinister type of activity because it permits the enemy to guide and shape our policy.

In that connection I would like to read to you very briefly from the testimony of Larry E. Kerley, a man who was with the Counterespionage Section of the FBI for 8 years. And keep in mind as I read this to you that at the time he is speaking there was in the State Department Alger Hiss (the convicted traitor), John Service (the man whom the FBI picked up for espionage), Julian Wadleigh (who brazenly admitted he was a spy and wrote newspaper articles in regard thereto).

Here is what the FBI man said: "In accordance with instructions of the State Department to the Federal Bureau of Investigation, the FBI was not even permitted to open an espionage case against any Russian suspect without State Department approval."

And some further questions:

MR. ARENS. "Did the State Department ever withhold from the Justice Department the right to intern suspects?"

KERLEY. "They withheld the right to get out process for them which, in effect, kept them from being arrested, as in the case of Schevchenko and others."

ARENS. "In how many instances did the State Department decline to permit process to be served on Soviet agents?"

KERLEY. "Do you mean how many Soviet agents were affected?"

ARENS. "Yes."

KERLEY. "That would be difficult to say because there were so many people connected in one espionage ring, whether or not they were directly conspiring with the ring."

ARENS. "Was that order applicable to all persons?"

KERLEY. "Yes, all persons in the Soviet espionage organization."

ARENS. "What did you say the order was as you understood it or as it came to you?"

KERLEY. "That no arrests of any suspects in the Russian espionage activities in the United States were to be made without the prior approval of the State Department."

Now the reason for the State Department's opposition to arresting any of this spy ring is made rather clear in the next question and answer.

SENATOR O'CONNOR. "Did you understand that that was to include also American participants?"

KERLEY. "Yes, because if they were arrested that would disclose the whole apparatus, you see."

In other words they could not afford to let the whole ring which extended to the State Department, be shown.

This brings us down to the case of one Algier Hiss who is important not as an individual any more, but rather because he is so representative of a group in the State Department. It is unnecessary to go over the sordid events showing how he sold out the Nation which had given him so much. Those are rather fresh in all of our minds.

However, it should be remembered that the facts in regard to his connection with this international Communist spy ring were made known to the then Under Secretary of State Berle three days after Hitler and Stalin signed the Russo German Alliance Pact. At that time one Wittaker Chambers—who was also part of the spy ring—apparently decided that with Russia on Hitler's side he could no longer betray our Nation. He gave Under Secretary of State Berle—and this is all a matter of record—practically all, if not more, of the facts upon which Hiss' conviction was based.

Under Secretary Berle promptly contacted Dean Acheson and received word in return that Acheson (and I quote) "could vouch for Hiss absolutely"—at which time the matter was dropped. And this, you understand, was at a time when Russia was an ally of Germany. This condition existed while Russia and Germany were invading and dismembering Poland, and while the Communist groups here were screaming "warmonger" at the United States for their support of the Allied nations.

Again in 1943 the FBI had occasion to investigate the facts surrounding Hiss. But even after that FBI report was submitted, nothing was done.

Then late in 1948—on August 5—when the Un-American Activities Committee called Algier Hiss to give an accounting, President Truman and the left-wing press commenced a systematic program of villification of that committee. On the day that Truman labeled the Hiss investigation a "red herring," on that same day (and listen to this, ladies and gentlemen) President Truman also issued a Presidential directive ordering all Government agencies to refuse to turn over any information whatsoever in regard to the Communist activities of any Government employee to a congressional committee.

Incidentally, even after Hiss was convicted it is interesting to note that the President still labeled the exposé of Hiss as a "red herring."

If time permitted, it might be well to go into detail about the fact that Hiss was Roosevelt's chief advisor at Yalta when Roosevelt was admittedly in ill health and tired physically and mentally—

and when, according to the Secretary of State, Hiss and Gromiko drafted the report on the conference.

According to the then Secretary of State, here are some of the things that Hiss helped to decide at Yalta. (1) The establishment of a European High Commission; (2) the treatment of Germany—this you will recall was the conference at which it was decided that we would occupy Berlin with Russia occupying an area completely circling the city, which, as you know, resulted in the Berlin air lift which cost 31 American lives; (3) the Polish question; (4) the relationship between UNRRA and the Soviet; (5) the rights of Americans on control commissions of Rumania, Bulgaria and Hungary: (6) Iran; (7) China—here's where we gave away Manchuria; (8) Turkish Straits question; (9) international trusteeship; (10) Korea.

Of the results of this conference, Arthur Bliss Lane of the State Department had this to say: "As I glanced over the document, I could not believe my eyes. To me, almost every line spoke of a surrender to Stalin."

As you hear this story of high treason, I know that you are saying to yourself—well, why doesn't the Congress do something about it. Actually, ladies and gentlemen, the reason for the graft, the corruption, the dishonesty, the disloyalty, the treason in high government positions—the reason this continues is because of a lack of moral uprising on the part of the 140,000,000 American people. In the light of history, however, this is not hard to explain.

It is the result of an emotional hangover and a temporary moral lapse which follows every war. It is the apathy to evil which people who have been subjected to the tremendous evils of war feel. As the people of the world see mass murder, the destruction of defenseless and innocent people, and all of the crime and lack of morals which go with war, they become numb and apathetic. It has always been thus after war.

However, the morals of our people have not been destroyed. They still exist. This cloak of numbness and apathy has only needed a spark to rekindle them. Happily, this has finally been supplied.

As you know, very recently the Secretary of State proclaimed his loyalty to a man guilty of what has always been considered as the most abominable of all crimes—being a traitor to the people who gave him a position of trust—high treason. The Secretary of State in attempting to justify his continued devotion to the man who sold out the Christian world to the atheistic world, referred to Christ's Sermon on the Mount as a justification and reason therefore.

And the reaction of the American people to this would have made the heart of Abraham Lincoln happy.

Thus this pompous diplomat in striped pants, with a phony British accent, tells the American people that Christ on the Mount endorsed communism, high treason, and betrayal of a sacred trust, this blasphemy was just great enough to awaken the dormant, inherent decency indignation of the American people.

He has lighted the spark which is resulting in a moral uprising and will end only when the whole sorry mess of twisted, warped thinkers are swept from the national scene so that we may have a new birth of honesty and decency in government.

MAO TSE-TUNG

"A Great Leap Forward"

The Second Session of the Eighth Party Congress

("The best outcome may be that only half of the population is left")

Beijing, China

May 17, 1958

Much of this speech by Mao (1893–1976), the premier of China from 1943 until his death, is a recounting of political rhetoric, facts and figures (or supposed facts and figures), and his prediction of the downfall of the capitalist world. Most of those sections have been deleted for this edition. Amid the bombast is the casual dismissal of the "rumors" about the very real starvation of millions in China as a result of Mao's own economic assaults on the peasants, and his equanimical remarks on the possible results of an atomic holocaust.

...Let us discuss the domestic problem. The peasant alliance remains to be the domestic problem. China's revolution has always been the issue of this alliance. Without it, the working class could not have gained liberation; it would not be able to build a powerful nation. Prior to the liberation, China's working class numbered only four million (excluding handicraft). Now there are 12 million, or three times as many. When we include the family members, the number is only around 40 million, while the peasant population reaches over 500 million. Therefore, China's problem has always been the problem of the peasant alliance. Some comrades are not very clear about this, not even after having worked in the rural village for decades.

Why did we make anti-adventurist mistakes in 1956? The major cause rested with the problem of the peasant alliance. The thinking and feelings of the peasants were not thoroughly understood; there-fore, there was no basis and, the moment there was a storm, vacil-lation could easily occur. In 1956 we published a book on the rural socialist high tide, including material from 190 cooperatives in the provinces and regions...

Then, there was the case of a poor cooperative in central Hopeh. All the middle peasants fled, leaving only three poor peasant house-holds, but these three families held on. They pointed out the direc-tion of the 500 million peasants. Each and every province had many cooperatives with production increases. The increases ranged one to several folds. Do you still refuse to believe it? The 40 articles of agriculture will definitely be realized. Can you still refuse to believe it? I feel that they can be realized. In 1955, 1956 and the first half of 1957, the number of disbelievers was considerably big and there were many tide-watchers in all levels including the Central.

At present, XXX are talking about settling accounts after the fall. They look only for the negative elements, not the positive. When a few cadres are overheard to say that the rural village is not so good, three or four individuals would whisper into one another's ears that the cooperative is not so good, the future looks bleak, the peasants do not have enough to eat, there is no output increase nor reserve grain, etc. When the family writes for money, they will always exaggerate, making life sound harder than it is and complaining about the lack of grain, oil and fabric, for otherwise you will not remit. You must analyze all these. Is it true that there is no grain, oil, or fabric?

Comrade K'o Ch'ing-shih told me about the statistics of Kiangsu Province. In 1955, 30 percent of the cadres of the county, district and township levels made loud protests, complained about the "hardships" on behalf of the peasants and objected to the excessive "control" in the "unified" purchasing and selling.

What kind of people were those cadres? They were all well-to-do middle peasants, or formerly poor and lower-middle peasants who had become well-to-do middle peasants. The so-called hardships of the peasants were the hardship of the well-to-do middle peas-ants. The well-to-do middle peasants wanted to hoard their grain instead of surrendering it and they wanted to promote capitalism. Therefore, they squawked about the hardships of the peasants. The lower levels squawked, but did someone in the regional, provincial, or central level complain also? Was there anyone who was not more or less influenced by his family in the home village? The question is the standpoint you take in looking at a problem. Do you take the standpoint of the working class and poor and lower-middle peasants, or do you take that of the well-to-do middle peasants?

Now it is a little better. The rural areas have made a great leap forward. After the rectification, the anti-rightist movement, cadre participation in labor and worker participation in a part of the management, the urban and rural political atmosphere has changed. One can say that the agricultural "pessimism" and "hopelessness," and the lack of confidence in realizing the "40 articles" have been swept clean. However, some of the "tide watchers" and "fall account settlers" have not been swept clean. Therefore, attention must be given to this work. The XXX report suggested guarding against fancy words without substance, surface without depth and generalization without detail. The suggestion was made by Kiangsu. What they mean is to see one's own defects. Among the 10 fingers, nine of them are bright and the remaining one in darkness. "Fancy" means flowery, blooming without bearing fruit. In regard to "generalization without detail," Chang Fei gave attention to the details even though he dealt in generalization. We want to be Chang Fei and give attention to the details. We must not bloom without bearing fruit or give attention to the general while ignoring the details, for otherwise we may not attain our quota in the fall. Comrades of all occupations, professions and units must pay attention, regardless of their type of work, whether industry, agriculture, commerce, culture and education, or writing novels.

The domestic situation is very good and the future looks bright. In the past, thinking was not unified. There was no confidence in achieving greater, faster, better and more economical results. Industry, agriculture and communication are concerned with these results. The basic issue is agriculture, the issue of the 40 articles. Now confidence has increased because of the great leap forward in agricultural production. The agricultural leap forward creates a pressure on industry and causes it to catch up, leaping forward together and motivating the entire work. A proposal was made at the Nan-ning Conference. The provinces should make plans on just how long it would take, five, seven, or so many years, for the value of industrial production to catch up with or surpass that of agricultural production. In only three months after the proposal, industries at the local provincial, county and township levels flourished. Now this is understood by many comrades. In the second half of 1956 some of the Central comrades did not understand it very clearly. After 1956 and the first half of 1957, the problem has been solved. Comrade Chou En-lai's report at the People's Congress in June of last year was very good, declaring war on the bourgeoisie with the posture of the proletarian warrior. That article should be read over again. At that time, the problem was truly solved, but profound understanding did not come until later....

Let us discuss the elimination of the four pests. Is it good to eliminate the four pests? I find it very interesting. According to *Reference News,* the Indians are also interested and they also wish to eliminate pests. They have the pest of monkeys which eat up a lot of grain. No one dares to touch them because they are considered sacred.

We do not propose the slogans "cadres decide everything" or "technology decides everything," or the slogan "communism is the Soviet Union plus electrification." But does it mean we do not want electrification? We want electrification just the same and even more urgently. The first two slogans were Stalin's way and rather one-sided. If "technology decides everything," then what about politics? If "cadres decide everything," then what about the masses? Dialectics is missing here. Stalin sometimes understood dialectics and sometimes not. I mentioned this at the Moscow Conference.

Our slogan is: A little more, a little faster, a little better and a little more economical. I think our slogan is a little more intelligent. We should be more intelligent, because the pupil should be better than the teacher. Green comes from blue, but it excels blue. The latecomer should be on top. I feel our communism may arrive in advance of schedule....

Dialectics should develop in China. We are not concerned about other places; we are concerned about China. What we do are more compatible with dialectics and with Lenin, but not very compatible with Stalin. Stalin said that the socialist society's production relations completely conformed to the development of the production force; he negated contradictions. Before his death, he wrote an article to negate himself. He stated that complete conformity did not indicate the absence of contradictions and that improper handling could develop into antagonistic contradictions. One couldn't say that he lacked dialectics. He had some. While there were superstition and one-sidedness, his method did succeed in building socialism, defeating the enemy, producing 50 million tons of steel, possibly 55 million tons this year and in putting three satellites in orbit. His was one kind of method. Can we find another method? The purpose is to promote socialism and Marxism-Leninism. Take the class struggle as an example. We have adopted Lenin's method, not Stalin's. When discussing the socialist economy, Stalin said the post-revolutionary reform was a peaceful reform proceeding from the top to the bottom levels. He did not undertake the class struggle from the bottom to the top, but introduced peaceful land reform in Eastern Europe and North Korea, without struggling against the landowners or the rightists, only proceeding from the top to the bottom and struggling against the capitalists. We proceed from the top to the bottom, but we also add the class struggle from the bottom to the top, settling the roots and linking together. We struggled against the bourgeoisie in the "five-evils movement." Now we are promoting construction and the mass movement. We require some things from the top to the bottom, such as government directives and orders, regulations and systems, but the masses must undertake a large number of things. We are opposed to favoritism and peaceful land reform. We call the method of Eastern Europe and North Korea favoritism. Peaceful land reform, without class struggle and without struggling against the landowners and capitalists, is of the wrong line and will produce harmful results.

Why is the speed of our construction faster than the Soviet Union? Because our conditions are different. We have 600 million people. We follow the road traveled by the Soviet Union; we have its technical aid. Therefore, we should develop faster than the Soviet Union. We expand the tradition of the October Revolution and the mass line of Lenin and rely on the masses, on the poor peasants in the rural areas, except that Lenin did not say this.

Yesterday a comrade said that one couldn't go wrong if one followed a certain individual. By "a certain individual," he meant me. This statement needs modification. One should follow and yet not follow. An individual is sometimes right and sometimes wrong. Follow him when he is right and do not follow him when he is wrong. One must not follow without discrimination. We follow Marx and Lenin and we follow Stalin in some places. We follow whoever has the truth in his hands. Even if he should be a manure carrier or street sweeper, as long as he has the truth, he should be followed. Our cooperativization is for the poor and lower-middle peasants. We advocate the concept of greater, faster, better and more economical results because it came from the masses. We look for the advanced and the good among the plants, rural villages, stores, schools, troops.... Wherever truth is, we follow. Do not follow any particular individual. It is dangerous to follow an individual without discrimination. One must have independent thinking....

I now wish to discuss the gloomy side of things. We must prepare for major disasters. With thousands of li of bare earth, great droughts and great floods are possible. We must also prepare for major wars. What should we do if the war maniacs drop atom bombs? Let them drop the atom bomb! The possibility is there as long as the warmongers exist. We must also prepare for troubles in the party—splits. There will be no splits if we handle it right, but it is limited to certain situations and one cannot say that splits are impossible. Was there not a split in the Soviet Union?...

Between war and peace, the possibility of peace is greater. Currently the possibility of peace is greater than in the past. The strength of the socialist camp is greater than the past and the possibility of peace is greater than at the time of World War II. The Soviet Union is powerful and the national independence movement is our strong ally. The Western nations are not stable. The working class, a part of the bourgeoisie and the American people do not want war; therefore, the possibility of peace is greater than that of war. Nevertheless, there is also the possibility of war. There are the maniacs and imperialism wants to extricate itself from economic crises. The duration of atomic warfare today will be short, three instead of four years. We must be prepared.

What should be done if war really comes? I want to discuss this problem. If there is war, we will fight. Let imperialism be swept clean and we will start construction again. Thereafter there will not be any more world war. Since a world war is possible, we must prepare for it. We must not spend our time napping. Do not be alarmed either if there should be war. It would merely mean getting people killed and we've seen people killed in war. Eliminating half of the population occurred several times in China's history. The 50 million population in the time of Emperor Wu in the Han Dynasty was reduced to 10 million by the time of the Three Kingdoms, the two Chin Dynasties and the North and South Dynasties. The war lasted for decades and intermittently for several hundred years, from the Three Kingdoms to the North and South Dynasties. The T'ang Dynasty began with a population of 20 million and did not reach 50 million until Emperor Hsuan. And Lu-shan staged a revolt and the country was divided into many states. It was not reunited until the Sung Dynasty, some 100 or 200 years later, with a population of just over 10 million. I once discussed this with XXX. I maintained that modern weapons were not as powerful as the big sword of China's Kuan Yun-Ch'ang, but he did not agree with me. Not very many people were killed in the two World Wars, 10 million in the first and 20 million in the second, but we had 40 million killed in one war. So, how destructive were the big swords!

We have no experience in atomic war. So, how many will be killed cannot be known. The best outcome may be that only half of the population is left and the second best may be only one-third. When 900 million are left out of 2.9 billion, several five-year plans can be developed for the total elimination of capitalism and for permanent peace. It is not a bad thing....

GEORGE C. WALLACE

The Governor of Alabama's Inaugural Address

("I draw the line in the dust and toss the gauntlet before
the feet of tyranny...and I say...segregation today...
segregation tomorrow...segregation forever")

Montgomery, Alabama

January 14, 1963

*The four-term Governor of Alabama was a blunt proponent of racial seg-
regation in the early 1960s. Later, however, after an assassination attempt
in 1972, Wallace (1919–1998) repented of his fight against integration.
In this, his first speech as governor of Alabama, he audaciously argues that
whites, controlling at this time every aspect of political power and big business
in America, Europe, and half of the rest of the world, face persecution: "As
the national racism of Hitler's Germany persecuted a national minority to the
whim of a national majority...so the international racism of the liberals seek
to persecute the international white minority to the whim of the international
colored majority."*

Governor Patterson, Governor Barnette, from one of the greatest states in this nation, Mississippi, Judge Brown, representing
Governor Hollings of South Carolina,...members of the Alabama
Congressional Delegation, members of the Alabama Legislature,
distinguished guests, fellow Alabamians:

Before I begin my talk with you, I want to ask you for a few
minutes patience while I say something that is on my heart: I want
to thank those home folks of my county who first gave an anxious
country boy his opportunity to serve in State politics. I shall always
owe a lot to those who gave me that *first* opportunity to serve.

I will never forget the warm support and close loyalty at the
folks of Suttons, Haigler's Mill, Eufaula, Beat 6 and Beat 14, Rich-
ards Cross Roads and Gammage Beat...at Baker Hill, Beat 8, and
Comer, Spring Hill, Adams Chapel and Mount Andrew...White
Oak, Baxter's Station, Clayton, Louisville and Cunnigham Place;
Horns Crossroads, Texasville and Blue Springs, where the vote was
304 for Wallace and 1 for the opposition...and the dear little lady
whom I heard had made that one vote against me...by mistake...
because she couldn't see too well...and she had pulled the wrong

lever...Bless her heart. At Clio, my birthplace, and Elamville. I shall never forget them. May God bless them.

And I shall forever remember that election day morning as I waited...and suddenly at ten o'clock that morning the first return of a box was flashed over this state: it carried the message...Wallace 15, opposition zero; and it came from the Hamrick Beat at Putman's Mountain where live the great hill people of our state. May God bless the mountain man...his loyalty is unshakeable, he'll do to walk down the road with.

I hope you'll forgive me these few moments of remembering... but I wanted them...and you...to know, that I shall never forget.

And I wish I could shake hands and thank all of you in this state who voted for me...and those of you who did not...for I know you voted your honest convictions...and now, we must stand together and move the great State of Alabama forward.

I would be remiss, this day, if I did not thank my wonderful wife and fine family for their patience, support and loyalty...and there is no man living who does not owe more to his mother than he can ever repay, and I want my mother to know that I realize my debt to her.

This is the day of my Inauguration as Governor of the State of Alabama. And on this day I feel a deep obligation to renew my pledges, my covenants with you...the people of this great state.

General Robert E. Lee said that "duty" is the sublimest word on the English language and I have come, increasingly, to realize what he meant. I SHALL do my duty to you, God helping...to every man, to every woman...yes, to every child in this state. I shall fulfill my duty toward honesty and economy in our State government so that no man shall have a part of his livelihood cheated and no child shall have a bit of his future stolen away.

I have said to you that I would eliminate the liquor agents in this state and that the money saved would be returned to our citizens... I am happy to report to you that I am now filling orders for several hundred one-way tickets and stamped on them are these words... "for liquor agents...destination:...out of Alabama." I am happy to report to you that the big-wheeling cocktail-party boys have gotten the word that their free whiskey and boat rides are over...that the farmer in the field, the worker in the factory, the businessman in his office, the housewife in her home, have decided that the money can be better spent to help our children's education and our older citizens...and they have put a man in office to see that it is done. It shall be done. Let me say one more time....No more liquor drinking in your governor's mansion.

I shall fulfill my duty in working hard to bring industry into our state, not only by maintaining an honest, sober and free-enterprise climate of government in which industry can have confidence... but in going out and getting it...so that our people can have industrial jobs in Alabama and provide a better life for their children.

I shall not forget my duty to our senior citizens...so that their lives can be lived in dignity and enrichment of the golden years, nor to our sick, both mental and physical...and they will know we have not forsaken them. I want the farmer to feel confident that in this State government he has a partner who will work with him in raising his income and increasing his markets. And I want the laboring man to know he has a friend who is sincerely striving to better his field of endeavor.

I want to assure every child that this State government is not afraid to invest in their future through education, so that they will not be handicapped on every threshold of their lives.

Today I have stood, where once Jefferson Davis stood, and took an oath to my people. It is very appropriate then that from this Cradle of the Confederacy, this very Heart of the Great Anglo-Saxon Southland, that today we sound the drum for freedom as have our generations of forebears before us done, time and time again through history. Let us rise to the call of freedom-loving blood that is in us and send our answer to the tyranny that clanks its chains upon the South. In the name of the greatest people that have ever trod this earth, I draw the line in the dust and toss the gauntlet before the feet of tyranny...and I say...segregation today...segregation tomorrow...segregation forever.

The Washington, D.C., school riot report is disgusting and revealing. We will not sacrifice our children to any such type school system—and you can write that down. The federal troops in Mississippi could be better used guarding the safety of the citizens of Washington, D.C., where it is even unsafe to walk or go to a ballgame—and that is the nation's capitol. I was safer in a B-29 bomber over Japan during the war in an air raid, than the people of Washington are walking to the White House neighborhood. A closer example is Atlanta. The city officials fawn for political reasons over school integration and *then* build barricades to stop residential integration—what hypocrisy!

Let us send this message back to Washington by our representatives who are with us today...that from this day we are standing up, and the heel of tyranny does not fit the neck of an upright man...that we intend to take the offensive and carry our fight for freedom across the nation, wielding the balance of power we know we possess in the Southland...that *we*, not the insipid bloc of voters of some sections...will determine in the next election who shall sit in the White House of these United States....That from this day, from this hour...from this minute...we give the word of a race of honor that we will tolerate their boot in our face no longer...and let those certain judges put *that* in their opium pipes of power and smoke it for what it is worth.

Hear me, Southerners! You sons and daughters who have moved north and west throughout this nation...we call on you from your native soil to join with us in national support and vote... and we know...wherever you are...away from the hearths of the Southland...that you will respond, for though you may live in the fartherest reaches of this vast country...your heart has never left Dixieland.

And you native sons and daughters of old New England's rock-ribbed patriotism...and you sturdy natives of the great Mid-West...and you descendants of the far West flaming spirit of pioneer freedom...we invite you to come and be with us...for you are of the Southern spirit...and the Southern philosophy...you are Southerners too and brothers with us in our fight.

What I have said about segregation goes double this day...and what I have said to or about some federal judges goes *triple* this day.

Alabama has been blessed by God as few states in this Union have been blessed. Our state owns ten percent of all the natural resources of all the states in our country. Our inland waterway system is second to none...and has the potential of being the greatest waterway transport system in the entire world. We possess over thirty minerals in usable quantities and our soil is rich and varied, suited to a wide variety of plants. Our native pine and forestry system produces timber faster than we can cut it and yet we have only pricked the surface of the great lumber and pulp potential.

With ample rainfall and rich grasslands our live stock industry is in the infancy of a giant future that can make us a center of the big and growing meat packing and prepared foods marketing. We have the favorable climate, streams, woodlands, beaches, and natural beauty to make us a recreational mecca in the booming tourist and vacation industry. Nestled in the great Tennessee Valley, we possess the rocket center of the world and the keys to the space frontier.

While the trade with a developing Europe built the great port cities of the east coast, our own fast developing port of Mobile faces as a magnetic gateway to the great continent of South America, well over twice as large and hundreds of times richer in resources, even now awakening to the growing probes of enterprising capital with a potential of growth and wealth beyond any present dream for our port development and corresponding results throughout the connecting waterways that thread our state.

And while the manufacturing industries of free enterprise have been coming to our state in increasing numbers, attracted by our bountiful natural resources, our growing numbers of skilled workers and our favorable conditions, their present rate of settlement here can be increased from the trickle they now represent to a stream of enterprise and endeavor, capital and expansion that can join us in our work of development and enrichment of the educational futures of our children, the opportunities of our citizens and the fulfillment of our talents as God has given them to us. To realize our ambitions and to bring to fruition our dreams, we as Alabamians must take cognizance of the world about us. We must re-define our heritage, re-school our thoughts in the lessons our forefathers knew so well, first hand, in order to function and to grow and to prosper. We can no longer hide our head in the sand and tell ourselves that the ideology of our free fathers is not being attacked and is not being threatened by another idea...for it is. We are faced with an idea that if a centralized government assume enough authority, enough power over its people, that it can provide a utopian life...that if given the power to dictate, to forbid, to require, to demand, to distribute, to edict and to judge what is best and enforce that will produce only "good"...and it shall be our father...and our God. It is an idea of government that encourages our fears and destroys our faith...for where there is faith, there is no fear, and where there is fear, there is no faith. In encouraging our fears of economic insecurity it demands we place that economic management and control with government; in encouraging our fear of educational development it demands we place that education and the minds of our children under management and control of government, and even in feeding our fears of physical infirmities and declining years, it offers and demands to father us through it all and even into the grave. It is a government that claims to us that it is bountiful as it buys its power from us with the fruits of its rapaciousness of the wealth that free men before it have produced and builds on crumbling credit without responsibilities to the debtors...our children. It is an ideology of government erected on the encouragement of fear and fails to recognize the basic law of our fathers that governments do not produce wealth... people produce wealth...free people; and those people become less free...as they learn there is little reward for ambition...that it requires faith to risk...and they have none...as the government must restrict and penalize and tax incentive and endeavor and must increase its expenditures of bounties...then this government must assume more and more police powers and we find we are become government-fearing people...not God-fearing people. We find we have replaced faith with fear...and though we may give lip service to the Almighty...in reality, government has become our god. It is, therefore, a basically ungodly government and its appeal to the pseudo-intellectual and the politician is to change their status from servant of the people to master of the people...to play at being God...without faith in God...and without the wisdom of God. It is a system that is the very opposite of Christ for it feeds and encourages everything degenerate and base in our people as it assumes the responsibilities that we ourselves should assume. Its pseudo-liberal spokesmen and some Harvard advocates have never examined the logic of its substitution of what it calls "human rights" for individual rights, for its propaganda play on words has appeal for the unthinking. Its logic is totally material and irresponsible as it runs the full gamut of human desires...including the theory that everyone has voting rights without the spiritual responsibility of preserving freedom. Our founding fathers recognized those rights...but only within the framework of those spiritual responsibilities. But the strong, simple faith and sane reasoning of our founding fathers has long since been forgotten as the so-called "progressives" tell us that our Constitution was written for "horse and buggy" days...so were the Ten Commandments.

Not so long ago men stood in marvel and awe at the cities, the buildings, the schools, the autobahns that the government of Hitler's Germany had built...just as centuries before they stood in wonder of Rome's building...but it could not stand...for the system that built it had rotted the souls of the builders...and in turn...rotted the foundation of what God meant that men should be. Today that same system on an international scale is sweeping the world. It is the "changing world" of which we are told...it is called "new" and "liberal." It is as old as the oldest dictator. It is degenerate and decadent. As the *national* racism of Hitler's Germany persecuted a *national* minority to the whim of a national majority...so the *international* racism of the liberals seek to persecute the *international* white minority to the whim of the *international* colored majority...so that we are footballed about according to the favor of the Afro-Asian bloc. But the Belgian survivors of the Congo cannot present their case to a war crimes commission...nor the Portuguese of Angola...nor the survivors of Castro...nor the citizens of Oxford, Mississippi.

It is this theory of international power politic that led a group of men on the Supreme Court for the first time in American history to issue an edict, based not on legal precedent, but upon a volume, the editor of which said our Constitution is outdated and must be changed and the writers of which, some had admittedly belonged to as many as half a hundred communist-front organizations. It is this theory that led this same group of men to briefly bare the ungodly core of that philosophy in forbidding little school children to say a prayer. And we find the evidence of that ungodliness even in the removal of the words "in God we trust" from some of our dollars, which was placed there as like evidence by our founding fathers as the faith upon which this system of government was built. It is the spirit of power thirst that caused a President in Washington to take up Caesar's pen and with one stroke of it make a law. A law which the law making body of Congress refused to pass...a law that tells us that we can or cannot buy or sell our very homes, except by his conditions...and except at *his* discretion. It is the spirit of power thirst that led the same President to launch a full offensive of twenty-five thousand troops against a university...of all places... in his own country...and against his own people, when this nation maintains only six thousand troops in the beleaguered city of Berlin. We have witnessed such acts of "might makes right" over the world as men yielded to the temptation to play God...but we have never before witnessed it in America. We reject such acts as free men. We do not defy, for there is nothing to defy...since as free men we do not recognize any government right to give freedom... or deny freedom. No government erected by man has that right. As Thomas Jefferson said, "The God who gave us life, gave us liberty at the same time; no King holds the right of liberty in his hands." Nor does any ruler in American government.

We intend, quite simply, to practice the free heritage as bequeathed to us as sons of free fathers. We intend to re-vitalize the truly new and progressive form of government that is less that two hundred years old...a government first founded in this nation simply and purely on faith...that there is a personal God who rewards good and punishes evil...that hard work will receive its just deserts...that ambition and ingenuity and incentiveness...and profit of such... are admirable traits and goals...that the individual is encouraged in his spiritual growth and from that growth arrives at a character that enhances his charity toward others and from that character and that charity so is influenced business, and labor and farmer and government. We intend to renew our faith as God-fearing men... *not* government-fearing men nor any other kind of fearing-men. We intend to roll up our sleeves and pitch in to develop this full bounty

God has given us...to live full and useful lives and in absolute freedom from all fear. Then can we enjoy the full richness of the Great American Dream.

We have placed this sign, "In God We Trust," upon our State Capitol on this Inauguration Day as physical evidence of determination to renew the faith of our fathers and to practice the free heritage they bequeathed to us. We do this with the clear and solemn knowledge that such physical evidence is evidently a direct violation of the logic of that Supreme Court in Washington D.C., and if they or their spokesmen in this state wish to term this defiance...I say... then let them make the most of it.

This nation was never meant to be a unit of one...but a united of the many...that is the exact reason our freedom loving forefathers established the states, so as to divide the rights and powers among the states, insuring that no central power could gain master government control.

In united effort we were meant to live under this government... whether Baptist, Methodist, Presbyterian, Church of Christ, or whatever one's denomination or religious belief...each respecting the other's right to a separate denomination...each, by working to develop his own, enriching the total of all our lives through united effort. And so it was meant in our political lives...whether Republican, Democrat, Prohibition, or whatever political party...each striving from his separate political station...respecting the rights of others to be separate and work from within their political framework...and each separate political station making its contribution to our lives.....

And so it was meant in our racial lives...each race, within its own framework has the freedom to teach...to instruct...to develop...to ask for and receive deserved help from others of separate racial stations. This is the great freedom of our American founding fathers... but if we amalgamate into the one unit as advocated by the communist philosophers...then the enrichment of our lives...the freedom for our development...is gone forever. We become, therefore, a mongrel unit of one under a single all-powerful government...and we stand for everything...and for nothing.

The true brotherhood of America, of respecting the separateness of others...and uniting in effort...has been so twisted and distorted from its original concept that there is a small wonder that communism is winning the world.

We invite the Negro citizens of Alabama to work with us from his separate racial station...as we will work with him...to develop, to grow in individual freedom and enrichment. We want jobs and a good future for *both* races...the tubercular and the infirm. This is the basic heritage of my religion, if which I make full practice...for we are all the handiwork of God.

But we warn those, of any group, who would follow the false doctrine of communistic amalgamation that we will not surrender our system of government...our freedom of race and religion... that freedom was won at a hard price and if it requires a hard price to retain it...we are able...and quite willing to pay it.

The liberals' theory that poverty, discrimination and lack of opportunity is the cause of communism is a false theory...if it were true the South would have been the biggest single communist bloc in the western hemisphere long ago...for after the great War Between the States, our people faced a desolate land of burned universities, destroyed crops and homes, with manpower depleted and crippled, and even the mule, which was required to work the land, was so scarce that whole communities shared one animal to make the spring plowing. There were no government handouts, no Marshall Plan aid, no coddling to make sure that *our* people would not suffer; instead the South was set upon by the vulturous carpet-bagger and federal troops, all loyal Southerners were denied the vote at the point of bayonet, so that the infamous, illegal 14th Amendment might be passed. There was no money, no food and no hope of either. But our grandfathers bent their knee only in church and bowed their head only to God.

Not for a single instant did they ever consider the easy way of federal dictatorship and amalgamation in return for fat bellies. They fought. They dug sweet roots from the ground with their bare hands and boiled them in iron pots...they gathered poke salad from the woods and acorns from the ground. They fought. They followed no false doctrine...they knew what they wanted...and they fought for freedom! They came up from their knees in the greatest display of sheer nerve, grit and guts that has ever been set down in the pages of written history...and they won! The great writer Rudyard Kipling wrote of them that: "There in the Southland of the United States of America, lives the greatest fighting breed of man...in all the world!"

And that is why today, I stand ashamed of the fat, well-fed whimperers who say that it is inevitable...that our cause is lost. I am ashamed *of* them...and I am ashamed *for* them. They do not represent the people of the Southland.

And may we take note of one other fact, with all trouble with communists that some sections of this country have...there are not enough native communists in the South to fill up a telephone booth...and *that* is a matter of public FBI record.

We remind all within hearing of this Southland that a *Southerner*, Peyton Randolph, presided over the Continental Congress in our nation's beginning...that a *Southerner*, Thomas Jefferson, wrote the Declaration of Independence, that a *Southerner*, George Washington, is the Father of our country...that a *Southerner*, James Madison, authored our Constitution, that a *Southerner*, George Mason, authored the Bill of Rights and it was a Southerner who said, "Give me liberty...or give me death," Patrick Henry.

Southerners played a most magnificent part in erecting this great divinely inspired system of freedom...and as God is our witness, Southerners will save it.

Let us, as Alabamians, grasp the hand of destiny and walk out of the shadow of fear...and fill our divine destination. Let us not simply defend...but let us assume the leadership of the fight and carry our leadership across this nation. God has placed us here in this crisis...let is not fail in this...our most historical moment.

You are here today, present in this audience, and to you over this great state, wherever you are in sound of my voice, I want to humbly and with all sincerity, thank you for your faith in me.

I promise you that I will try to make you a good governor. I promise you that, as God gives me the wisdom and the strength, I will be sincere with you. I will be honest with you.

I will apply the old sound rule of our fathers, that anything worthy of our defense is worthy of one hundred percent of our defense. I have been taught that freedom meant freedom from any threat or fear of government. I was born in that freedom, I was raised in that freedom...I intend to live in that freedom...and God willing, when I die, I shall leave that freedom to my children...as my father left it to me.

My pledge to you...to "Stand up for Alabama," is a stronger pledge today than it was the first day I made that pledge. I shall "Stand up for Alabama," as Governor of our State...you stand with me...and we, together, can give courageous leadership to millions of people throughout this nation who look to the South for their hope in this fight to win and preserve our freedoms and liberties.

So help me God.

And my prayer is that the Father who reigns above us will bless all the people of this great sovereign State and nation, both white and black.

I thank you.

ENOCH POWELL
"Rivers of Blood"
Conservative Association Meeting
("How dare I say such a horrible thing? How dare
I stir up trouble and inflame feelings by
repeating such a conversation?")
Birmingham, England
April 20, 1968

*Enoch Powell (1912–1998), a classical scholar, war veteran, and prominent
British politician, campaigned against the immigrants from Great Britain's
former colonies.*

The supreme function of statesmanship is to provide against preventable evils. In seeking to do so, it encounters obstacles which are
deeply rooted in human nature.

One is that by the very order of things such evils are not demon-
strable until they have occurred: at each stage in their onset there is
room for doubt and for dispute whether they be real or imaginary.
By the same token, they attract little attention in comparison with
current troubles, which are both indisputable and pressing: whence
the besetting temptation of all politics to concern itself with the
immediate present at the expense of the future.

Above all, people are disposed to mistake predicting troubles for
causing troubles and even for desiring troubles: "If only," they love
to think, "if only people wouldn't talk about it, it probably wouldn't
happen."

Perhaps this habit goes back to the primitive belief that the word
and the thing, the name and the object, are identical.

At all events, the discussion of future grave but, with effort now,
avoidable evils is the most unpopular and at the same time the most
necessary occupation for the politician. Those who knowingly shirk
it deserve, and not infrequently receive, the curses of those who
come after.

A week or two ago I fell into conversation with a constituent, a
middle-aged, quite ordinary working man employed in one of our
nationalised industries.

After a sentence or two about the weather, he suddenly said: "If I
had the money to go, I wouldn't stay in this country." I made some

deprecatory reply to the effect that even this government wouldn't last for ever; but he took no notice, and continued: "I have three children, all of them been through grammar school and two of them married now, with family. I shan't be satisfied till I have seen them all settled overseas. In this country in 15 or 20 years' time the black man will have the whip hand over the white man."

I can already hear the chorus of execration. How dare I say such a horrible thing? How dare I stir up trouble and inflame feelings by repeating such a conversation?

The answer is that I do not have the right not to do so. Here is a decent, ordinary fellow Englishman, who in broad daylight in my own town says to me, his Member of Parliament, that his country will not be worth living in for his children.

I simply do not have the right to shrug my shoulders and think about something else. What he is saying, thousands and hundreds of thousands are saying and thinking—not throughout Great Britain, perhaps, but in the areas that are already undergoing the total transformation to which there is no parallel in a thousand years of English history.

In 15 or 20 years, on present trends, there will be in this country three and a half million Commonwealth immigrants and their descendants. That is not my figure. That is the official figure given to parliament by the spokesman of the Registrar General's Office.

There is no comparable official figure for the year 2000, but it must be in the region of five to seven million, approximately one-tenth of the whole population, and approaching that of Greater London. Of course, it will not be evenly distributed from Margate to Aberystwyth and from Penzance to Aberdeen. Whole areas, towns and parts of towns across England will be occupied by sections of the immigrant and immigrant-descended population.

As time goes on, the proportion of this total who are immigrant descendants, those born in England, who arrived here by exactly the same route as the rest of us, will rapidly increase. Already by 1985 the native-born would constitute the majority. It is this fact which creates the extreme urgency of action now, of just that kind of action which is hardest for politicians to take, action where the difficulties lie in the present but the evils to be prevented or minimised lie several parliaments ahead.

The natural and rational first question with a nation confronted by such a prospect is to ask: "How can its dimensions be reduced?" Granted it be not wholly preventable, can it be limited, bearing in mind that numbers are of the essence: the significance and consequences of an alien element introduced into a country or population are profoundly different according to whether that element is 1 per cent or 10 per cent.

The answers to the simple and rational question are equally simple and rational: by stopping, or virtually stopping, further inflow, and by promoting the maximum outflow. Both answers are part of the official policy of the Conservative Party.

It almost passes belief that at this moment 20 or 30 additional immigrant children are arriving from overseas in Wolverhampton alone every week—and that means 15 or 20 additional families a decade or two hence. Those whom the gods wish to destroy, they first make mad. We must be mad, literally mad, as a nation to be permitting the annual inflow of some 50,000 dependants, who are for the most part the material of the future growth of the immigrant-descended population. It is like watching a nation busily engaged in heaping up its own funeral pyre. So insane are we that we actually permit unmarried persons to immigrate for the purpose of founding a family with spouses and fiancés whom they have never seen.

Let no one suppose that the flow of dependants will automatically tail off. On the contrary, even at the present admission rate of only 5,000 a year by voucher, there is sufficient for a further 25,000 dependants per annum *ad infinitum*, without taking into account the huge reservoir of existing relations in this country—and I am making no allowance at all for fraudulent entry. In these circumstances nothing will suffice but that the total inflow for settlement should be reduced at once to negligible proportions, and that the necessary legislative and administrative measures be taken without delay.

I stress the words "for settlement." This has nothing to do with the entry of Commonwealth citizens, any more than of aliens, into this country, for the purposes of study or of improving their qualifications, like (for instance) the Commonwealth doctors who, to the advantage of their own countries, have enabled our hospital service to be expanded faster than would otherwise have been possible. They are not, and never have been, immigrants.

I turn to re-emigration. If all immigration ended tomorrow, the rate of growth of the immigrant and immigrant-descended population would be substantially reduced, but the prospective size of this element in the population would still leave the basic character of the national danger unaffected. This can only be tackled while a considerable proportion of the total still comprises persons who entered this country during the last ten years or so.

Hence the urgency of implementing now the second element of the Conservative Party's policy: the encouragement of re-emigration.

Nobody can make an estimate of the numbers which, with

generous assistance, would choose either to return to their countries of origin or to go to other countries anxious to receive the man-power and the skills they represent.

Nobody knows, because no such policy has yet been attempted. I can only say that, even at present, immigrants in my own constituency from time to time come to me, asking if I can find them assistance to return home. If such a policy were adopted and pursued with the determination which the gravity of the alternative justifies, the resultant outflow could appreciably alter the prospects.

The third element of the Conservative Party's policy is that all who are in this country as citizens should be equal before the law and that there shall be no discrimination or difference made between them by public authority. As Mr. Heath has put it we will have no "first-class citizens" and "second-class citizens." This does not mean that the immigrant and his descendent should be elevated into a privileged or special class or that the citizen should be denied his right to discriminate in the management of his own affairs between one fellow-citizen and another or that he should be subjected to imposition as to his reasons and motive for behaving in one lawful manner rather than another.

There could be no grosser misconception of the realities than is entertained by those who vociferously demand legislation as they call it "against discrimination," whether they be leader-writers of the same kidney and sometimes on the same newspapers which year after year in the 1930s tried to blind this country to the rising peril which confronted it, or archbishops who live in palaces, faring delicately with the bedclothes pulled right up over their heads. They have got it exactly and diametrically wrong.

The discrimination and the deprivation, the sense of alarm and of resentment, lies not with the immigrant population but with those among whom they have come and are still coming.

This is why to enact legislation of the kind before parliament at this moment is to risk throwing a match on to gunpowder. The kindest thing that can be said about those who propose and support it is that they know not what they do.

Nothing is more misleading than comparison between the Commonwealth immigrant in Britain and the American Negro. The Negro population of the United States, which was already in existence before the United States became a nation, started literally as slaves and were later given the franchise and other rights of citizenship, to the exercise of which they have only gradually and still incompletely come. The Commonwealth immigrant came to Britain as a full citizen, to a country which knew no discrimination between one citizen and another, and he entered instantly into the possession of the rights of every citizen, from the vote to free treatment under the National Health Service.

Whatever drawbacks attended the immigrants arose not from the law or from public policy or from administration, but from those personal circumstances and accidents which cause, and always will cause, the fortunes and experience of one man to be different from another's.

But while, to the immigrant, entry to this country was admission to privileges and opportunities eagerly sought, the impact upon the existing population was very different. For reasons which they could not comprehend, and in pursuance of a decision by default, on which they were never consulted, they found themselves made strangers in their own country.

They found their wives unable to obtain hospital beds in childbirth, their children unable to obtain school places, their homes and neighbourhoods changed beyond recognition, their plans and prospects for the future defeated; at work they found that employers hesitated to apply to the immigrant worker the standards of discipline and competence required of the native-born worker; they began to hear, as time went by, more and more voices which told them that they were now the unwanted. They now learn that a one-way privilege is to be established by act of parliament; a law which cannot, and is not intended to, operate to protect them or redress their grievances is to be enacted to give the stranger, the disgruntled and the agent-provocateur the power to pillory them for their private actions.

In the hundreds upon hundreds of letters I received when I last spoke on this subject two or three months ago, there was one striking feature which was largely new and which I find ominous. All Members of Parliament are used to the typical anonymous correspondent; but what surprised and alarmed me was the high proportion of ordinary, decent, sensible people, writing a rational and often well-educated letter, who believed that they had to omit their address because it was dangerous to have committed themselves to paper to a Member of Parliament agreeing with the views I had expressed, and that they would risk penalties or reprisals if they were known to have done so. The sense of being a persecuted minority which is growing among ordinary English people in the areas of the country which are affected is something that those without direct experience can hardly imagine.

I am going to allow just one of those hundreds of people to speak for me:

"Eight years ago in a respectable street in Wolverhampton a house was sold to a Negro. Now only one white (a woman old-age

pensioner) lives there. This is her story. She lost her husband and
both her sons in the war. So she turned her seven-roomed house,
her only asset, into a boarding house. She worked hard and did well,
paid off her mortgage and began to put something by for her old
age. Then the immigrants moved in. With growing fear, she saw
one house after another taken over. The quiet street became a place
of noise and confusion. Regretfully, her white tenants moved out.

"The day after the last one left, she was awakened at 7 A.M. by two
Negroes who wanted to use her phone to contact their employer.
When she refused, as she would have refused any stranger at such
an hour, she was abused and feared she would have been attacked
but for the chain on her door. Immigrant families have tried to rent
rooms in her house, but she always refused. Her little store of money
went, and after paying rates, she has less than £2 per week. "She
went to apply for a rate reduction and was seen by a young girl, who
on hearing she had a seven-roomed house, suggested she should
let part of it. When she said the only people she could get were
Negroes, the girl said, 'Racial prejudice won't get you anywhere in
this country.' So she went home.

"The telephone is her lifeline. Her family pay the bill, and help her
out as best they can. Immigrants have offered to buy her house—at a
price which the prospective landlord would be able to recover from
his tenants in weeks, or at most a few months. She is becoming afraid
to go out. Windows are broken. She finds excreta pushed through
her letter box. When she goes to the shops, she is followed by children, charming, wide-grinning piccaninnies. They cannot speak
English, but one word they know. "Racialist," they chant. When the
new Race Relations Bill is passed, this woman is convinced she will
go to prison. And is she so wrong? I begin to wonder."

The other dangerous delusion from which those who are wilfully
or otherwise blind to realities suffer, is summed up in the word
"integration." To be integrated into a population means to become
for all practical purposes indistinguishable from its other members.

Now, at all times, where there are marked physical differences,
especially of colour, integration is difficult though, over a period,
not impossible. There are among the Commonwealth immigrants
who have come to live here in the last fifteen years or so, many
thousands whose wish and purpose is to be integrated and whose
every thought and endeavour is bent in that direction.

But to imagine that such a thing enters the heads of a great and
growing majority of immigrants and their descendants is a ludicrous
misconception, and a dangerous one.

We are on the verge here of a change. Hitherto it has been force of circumstance and of background which has rendered the very idea of integration inaccessible to the greater part of the immigrant population—that they never conceived or intended such a thing, and that their numbers and physical concentration meant the pressures towards integration which normally bear upon any small minority did not operate.

Now we are seeing the growth of positive forces acting against integration, of vested interests in the preservation and sharpening of racial and religious differences, with a view to the exercise of actual domination, first over fellow-immigrants and then over the rest of the population. The cloud no bigger than a man's hand, that can so rapidly overcast the sky, has been visible recently in Wolverhampton and has shown signs of spreading quickly. The words I am about to use, verbatim as they appeared in the local press on 17 February, are not mine, but those of a Labour Member of Parliament who is a minister in the present government:

"The Sikh communities' campaign to maintain customs inappropriate in Britain is much to be regretted. Working in Britain, particularly in the public services, they should be prepared to accept the terms and conditions of their employment. To claim special communal rights (or should one say rites?) leads to a dangerous fragmentation within society. This communalism is a canker; whether practised by one colour or another it is to be strongly condemned."

All credit to John Stonehouse for having had the insight to perceive that, and the courage to say it.

For these dangerous and divisive elements the legislation proposed in the Race Relations Bill is the very pabulum they need to flourish. Here is the means of showing that the immigrant communities can organise to consolidate their members, to agitate and campaign against their fellow citizens, and to overawe and dominate the rest with the legal weapons which the ignorant and the ill informed have provided. As I look ahead, I am filled with foreboding; like the Roman, I seem to see "the River Tiber foaming with much blood."

That tragic and intractable phenomenon which we watch with horror on the other side of the Atlantic but which there is interwoven with the history and existence of the States itself, is coming upon us here by our own volition and our own neglect. Indeed, it has all but come. In numerical terms, it will be of American proportions long before the end of the century.

Only resolute and urgent action will avert it even now. Whether there will be the public will to demand and obtain that action, I do not know. All I know is that to see, and not to speak, would be a great betrayal.

RICHARD M. NIXON

U.S. President

First Watergate Speech

("There can be no whitewash at the White House")

April 30, 1973

The Republican Richard M. Nixon (1913–1994), the 37th President of the United States, served as Dwight D. Eisenhower's vice president in the 1950s. He narrowly lost the presidential election in 1960 to John F. Kennedy. Personally unpleasant but clever and persistent, he defeated his Democratic presidential rivals Hubert Humphrey in 1968 and George McGovern in 1972. The Watergate scandal revolved around his involvement in the cover-up of a break-in of Democratic National Committee offices in the Watergate office complex in Washington, D.C. "In any organization, the man at the top must bear the responsibility," he declares here. "That responsibility, therefore, belongs here, in this office. I accept it." Two weeks later a Senate Committee commenced public hearings on the case. Nixon officially resigned from office, with impeachment proceedings looming in Congress, on August 9, 1974.

Good evening:

I want to talk to you tonight from my heart on a subject of deep concern to every American.

In recent months, members of my Administration and officials of the Committee for the Re-Election of the President—including some of my closest friends and most trusted aides—have been charged with involvement in what has come to be known as the Watergate affair. These include charges of illegal activity during and preceding the 1972 Presidential election and charges that responsible officials participated in efforts to cover up that illegal activity.

The inevitable result of these charges has been to raise serious questions about the integrity of the White House itself. Tonight I wish to address those questions.

Last June 17, while I was in Florida trying to get a few days rest after my visit to Moscow, I first learned from news reports of the Watergate break-in. I was appalled at this senseless, illegal action, and I was shocked to learn that employees of the Re-Election Committee were apparently among those guilty. I immediately ordered an investigation by appropriate Government authorities. On

September 15, as you will recall, indictments were brought against seven defendants in the case.

As the investigations went forward, I repeatedly asked those conducting the investigation whether there was any reason to believe that members of my Administration were in any way involved. I received repeated assurances that there were not. Because of these continuing reassurances, because I believed the reports I was getting, because I had faith in the persons from whom I was getting them, I discounted the stories in the press that appeared to implicate members of my Administration or other officials of the campaign committee.

Until March of this year, I remained convinced that the denials were true and that the charges of involvement by members of the White House Staff were false. The comments I made during this period, and the comments made by my Press Secretary in my behalf, were based on the information provided to us at the time we made those comments. However, new information then came to me which persuaded me that there was a real possibility that some of these charges were true, and suggesting further that there had been an effort to conceal the facts both from the public, from you, and from me.

As a result, on March 21, I personally assumed the responsibility for coordinating intensive new inquiries into the matter, and I personally ordered those conducting the investigations to get all the facts and to report them directly to me, right here in this office.

I again ordered that all persons in the Government or at the Re-Election Committee should cooperate fully with the FBI, the prosecutors, and the grand jury. I also ordered that anyone who refused to cooperate in telling the truth would be asked to resign from Government service. And, with ground rules adopted that would preserve the basic constitutional separation of powers between the Congress and the Presidency, I directed that members of the White House Staff should appear and testify voluntarily under oath before the Senate committee which was investigating Watergate.

I was determined that we should get to the bottom of the matter, and that the truth should be fully brought out—no matter who was involved.

At the same time, I was determined not to take precipitate action and to avoid, if at all possible, any action that would appear to reflect on innocent people. I wanted to be fair. But I knew that in the final analysis, the integrity of this office—public faith in the integrity of this office—would have to take priority over all personal considerations.

Today, in one of the most difficult decisions of my Presidency, I accepted the resignations of two of my closest associates in the

White House—Bob Haldeman, John Ehrlichman—two of the finest public servants it has been my privilege to know.

I want to stress that in accepting these resignations, I mean to leave no implication whatever of personal wrongdoing on their part, and I leave no implication tonight of implication on the part of others who have been charged in this matter. But in matters as sensitive as guarding the integrity of our democratic process, it is essential not only that rigorous legal and ethical standards be observed but also that the public, you, have total confidence that they are both being observed and enforced by those in authority and particularly by the President of the United States. They agreed with me that this move was necessary in order to restore that confidence.

Because Attorney General Kleindienst—though a distinguished public servant, my personal friend for 20 years, with no personal involvement whatever in this matter—has been a close personal and professional associate of some of those who are involved in this case, he and I both felt that it was also necessary to name a new Attorney General.

The Counsel to the President, John Dean, has also resigned.

As the new Attorney General, I have today named Elliot Richardson, a man of unimpeachable integrity and rigorously high principle. I have directed him to do everything necessary to ensure that the Department of Justice has the confidence and the trust of every law-abiding person in this country.

I have given him absolute authority to make all decisions bearing upon the prosecution of the Watergate case and related matters. I have instructed him that if he should consider it appropriate, he has the authority to name a special supervising prosecutor for matters arising out of the case.

Whatever may appear to have been the case before, whatever improper activities may yet be discovered in connection with this whole sordid affair, I want the American people, I want you to know beyond the shadow of a doubt that during my term as President, justice will be pursued fairly, fully, and impartially, no matter who is involved. This office is a sacred trust and I am determined to be worthy of that trust.

Looking back at the history of this case, two questions arise:

How could it have happened?

Who is to blame?

Political commentators have correctly observed that during my 27 years in politics I have always previously insisted on running my own campaigns for office.

But 1972 presented a very different situation. In both domestic and foreign policy, 1972 was a year of crucially important decisions, of intense negotiations, of vital new directions, particularly in working toward the goal which has been my overriding concern throughout my political career—the goal of bringing peace to America, peace to the world.

That is why I decided, as the 1972 campaign approached, that the Presidency should come first and politics second. To the maximum extent possible, therefore, I sought to delegate campaign operations, to remove the day-to-day campaign decisions from the President's office and from the White House. I also, as you recall, severely limited the number of my own campaign appearances.

Who, then, is to blame for what happened in this case?

For specific criminal actions by specific individuals, those who committed those actions must, of course, bear the liability and pay the penalty.

For the fact that alleged improper actions took place within the White House or within my campaign organization, the easiest course would be for me to blame those to whom I delegated the responsibility to run the campaign. But that would be a cowardly thing to do.

I will not place the blame on subordinates—on people whose zeal exceeded their judgment and who may have done wrong in a cause they deeply believed to be right.

In any organization, the man at the top must bear the responsibility. That responsibility, therefore, belongs here, in this office. I accept it. And I pledge to you tonight, from this office, that I will do everything in my power to ensure that the guilty are brought to justice and that such abuses are purged from our political processes in the years to come, long after I have left this office.

Some people, quite properly appalled at the abuses that occurred, will say that Watergate demonstrates the bankruptcy of the American political system. I believe precisely the opposite is true. Watergate represented a series of illegal acts and bad judgments by a number of individuals. It was the system that has brought the facts to light and that will bring those guilty to justice—a system that in this case has included a determined grand jury, honest prosecutors, a courageous judge, John Sirica, and a vigorous free press.

It is essential now that we place our faith in that system—and especially in the judicial system. It is essential that we let the judicial process go forward, respecting those safeguards that are established to protect the innocent as well as to convict the guilty. It is essential that in reacting to the excesses of others, we not fall into excesses ourselves.

It is also essential that we not be so distracted by events such as this that we neglect the vital work before us, before this Nation, before America, at a time of critical importance to America and the world.

Since March, when I first learned that the Watergate affair might in fact be far more serious than I had been led to believe, it has claimed far too much of my time and my attention. Whatever may now transpire in the case, whatever the actions of the grand jury, whatever the outcome of any eventual trials, I must now turn my full attention—and I shall do so—once again to the larger duties of this office. I owe it to this great office that I hold, and I owe it to you—to my country.

I know that as Attorney General, Elliot Richardson will be both fair and he will be fearless in pursuing this case wherever it leads. I am confident that with him in charge, justice will be done.

There is vital work to be done toward our goal of a lasting structure of peace in the world—work that cannot wait, work that I must do.

Tomorrow, for example, Chancellor Brandt of West Germany will visit the White House for talks that are a vital element of "The Year of Europe," as 1973 has been called. We are already preparing for the next Soviet-American summit meeting later this year.

This is also a year in which we are seeking to negotiate a mutual and balanced reduction of armed forces in Europe, which will reduce our defense budget and allow us to have funds for other purposes at home so desperately needed. It is the year when the United States and Soviet negotiators will seek to work out the second and even more important round of our talks on limiting nuclear arms and of reducing the danger of a nuclear war that would destroy civilization as we know it. It is a year in which we confront the difficult tasks of maintaining peace in Southeast Asia and in the potentially explosive Middle East.

There is also vital work to be done right here in America: to ensure prosperity, and that means a good job for everyone who wants to work; to control inflation, that I know worries every housewife, everyone who tries to balance a family budget in America; to set in motion new and better ways of ensuring progress toward a better life for all Americans.

When I think of this office—of what it means—I think of all the things that I want to accomplish for this Nation, of all the things I want to accomplish for you.

On Christmas Eve, during my terrible personal ordeal of the renewed bombing of North Vietnam, which after 12 years of war finally helped to bring America peace with honor, I sat down just before midnight. I wrote out some of my goals for my second term as President.

Let me read them to you:

"To make it possible for our children, and for our children's children, to live in a world of peace.

"To make this country be more than ever a land of opportunity—of equal opportunity, full opportunity for every American.

"To provide jobs for all who can work, and generous help for those who cannot work.

"To establish a climate of decency and civility, in which each person respects the feelings and the dignity and the God-given rights of his neighbor.

"To make this a land in which each person can dare to dream, can live his dreams—not in fear, but in hope—proud of his community, proud of his country, proud of what America has meant to himself and to the world."

These are great goals. I believe we can, we must work for them. We can achieve them. But we cannot achieve these goals unless we dedicate ourselves to another goal.

We must maintain the integrity of the White House, and that integrity must be real, not transparent. There can be no whitewash at the White House.

We must reform our political process—ridding it not only of the violations of the law but also of the ugly mob violence and other inexcusable campaign tactics that have been too often practiced and too readily accepted in the past, including those that may have been a response by one side to the excesses or expected excesses of the other side. Two wrongs do not make a right.

I have been in public life for more than a quarter of a century. Like any other calling, politics has good people and bad people. And let me tell you, the great majority in politics—in the Congress, in the Federal Government, in the State government—are good people. I know that it can be very easy, under the intensive pressures of a campaign, for even well-intentioned people to fall into shady tactics—to rationalize this on the grounds that what is at stake is of such importance to the Nation that the end justifies the means. And both of our great parties have been guilty of such tactics in the past.

In recent years, however, the campaign excesses that have occurred on all sides have provided a sobering demonstration of how far this false doctrine can take us. The lesson is clear: America, in its political campaigns, must not again fall into the trap of letting the end, however great that end is, justify the means.

I urge the leaders of both political parties, I urge citizens, all of you, everywhere, to join in working toward a new set of standards, new rules and procedures to ensure that future elections will be as nearly free of such abuses as they possibly can be made. This is my goal. I ask you to join in making it America's goal.

When I was inaugurated for a second time this past January 20, I gave each member of my Cabinet and each member of my senior White House Staff a special four-year calendar, with each day marked to show the number of days remaining to the Administration. In the inscription on each calendar, I wrote these words: "The Presidential term which begins today consists of 1,461 days—no more, no less. Each can be a day of strengthening and renewal for America; each can add depth and dimension to the American experience. If we strive together, if we make the most of the challenge and the opportunity that these days offer us, they can stand out as great days for America, and great moments in the history of the world."

I looked at my own calendar this morning up at Camp David as I was working on this speech. It showed exactly 1,361 days remaining in my term. I want these to be the best days in America's history, because I love America. I deeply believe that America is the hope of the world. And I know that in the quality and wisdom of the leadership America gives lies the only hope for millions of people all over the world that they can live their lives in peace and freedom. We must be worthy of that hope, in every sense of the word. Tonight, I ask for your prayers to help me in everything that I do throughout the days of my Presidency to be worthy of their hopes and of yours.

God bless America and God bless each and every one of you.

IDI AMIN DADA
President of Uganda

United Nations Speech on Zionism as Racism

("I call for the expulsion of Israel from the
United Nations and the extinction of Israel as a State,
so that the territorial integrity of Palestine
may be ensured and upheld")

New York City

October 1, 1975

Field Marshal Idi Amin Dada (1925–2003) was the Chairman of the Organization of African Unity and, when this address was presented, already notorious for his views on Israel. Amin wanders through various points about economic development in Africa (most of which, for patience's sake, I have left out), and apartheid in South Africa before moving to his attacks on Great Britain Israel, Zionism, and the United States. After Amin prefaced the speech in English, Khalid Younis Kinene, Uganda's Representative to the United Nations, read the speech in the Luganda language. Amin then concluded with a brief summary in English. He became known as "the Butcher of Uganda" for murdering hundreds of thousands of his own people. He fled Uganda in 1979 and died in Saudi Arabia in 2003.

As a pure and proper son of Africa, who does not believe in any colonial and imperialist language, I shall address you in an African language which will be interpreted to you through the good offices of the United Nations Secretariat....

The thirtieth session of the General Assembly is being held at a time when developments in the world are moving fast. Imperialism is being resolutely driven back, and the peoples of the industrialized countries are showing fresh interest in the genuine development of the third world and in its fight for economic independence and construction. The OAU [Organization of African Unity], of which I have the honor to be the current Chairman, wishes this session success in its deliberations, aimed not only at consolidating the political and economic independence and the construction of its members, but also at the cultural and moral development of peoples all over the world. We in Africa, and in Uganda in particular, are fully dedicated and committed to that end....

Except for the southern tip of the African continent and isolated pockets here and there, the worldwide war for self-determination and political independence is almost over now. But the struggle for self-reliance continues. The present stage in this struggle is for economic independence without which, as it has rightly been stated, political freedom is meaningless.

All States Members of the OAU are vigorously waging battles for full economic control over their own affairs. Each State is following a method and a speed that is most suited to its national conditions. We in Uganda, having taken a short and revolutionary cut to economic independence, are now somewhat luckier than many of our sister States members of the OAU. Our experience, among many other things, has taught us that, if the more industrialized countries are genuinely serious about extending technical assistance to the developing countries, they should ensure that the experts they send are dedicated and appreciative of the aspirations and determination of the third-world countries to be masters of their own economies.

These modern technical missionaries should not have that old colonial mentality of their predecessors who came out to Africa with the conviction that they were coming to work with second-rate human beings. The modern expatriates Africa now needs should come with the knowledge that they are employees, not employers; partners for peace, not preachers of political ideologies or builders of foreign empires. If this type of expatriate comes to Africa, and indeed goes to other parts of the third world, the cause of international peace and positive development will be served....

...I should like now to discuss a few points in my capacity as President of Uganda, starting with the very first prerequisite of a State, namely, its land.

Needless to say, land is the greatest gift the Creator has given to man. Its price cannot be estimated in terms of money or any other measure of value. Without it there would be no States and the human race could not exist in the form in which we know it. Land, through the ages, has been the cause of both joys and woes, unity and conflict. When thinking about land in its proper perspective, considerations cut across national boundaries and assume an international character to which nations should give serious priority consideration, commitment and dedication. Today the peoples of the world are very much worried about overpopulation, and those fears are based entirely on the kind and amount of food that can be available to feed the ever-increasing millions of people on earth. As we know it today, food is a product of land. Therefore, land utilization and settlement are subjects of top priority to the human race. In many countries there is no more space left for the growing of food to feed their nationals, and therefore in this regard they face peril. The only hope for survival of such people lies in the amount of food that can be obtained from the new lands which are less populated, endowed with a good climate and soil and which, therefore, can achieve maximum production with the least effort in terms of technology and finance. Nations blessed with the attribute of a large area of arable land therefore stand in a unique position.

I am glad and proud to inform you this Assembly that Uganda is one of the very few countries which occupy that unique position. Uganda realizes its moral responsibility to humanity to hold out the breadbasket to the starving world. In this connexion, the Government of Uganda has recently promulgated three decrees designed to bring about maximum productivity and the better utilization of land within its national territorial boundaries and to increase employment opportunities. By the grace of God, Uganda does boast a wonderful climate rich soil, a healthy energetic people, good means of communication and rich natural resources, all of which, if fully exploited, would benefit the human race and go a long way towards removing the fears in which the world is engulfed today. It is against that background that the Land Reform Decree, the Community Farm Settlement Decree and the Self-Help Projects Decree were promulgated in the middle of this year. Those decrees place all land in the hands of the Government for management, distribution and control, provide for its planned settlement and utilization and encourage the supplementing of financial investment requirements by our time-honoured voluntary communal labour supply for community development.

The following reasons led to the reform of land possession and management law: to enable the Government to make proper plans of land use for maximum productivity: to remove the evils of feudalism which discouraged the farmers of the land and encouraged laziness and exploitation by the absentee landlords; and to provide employment. Under the new decrees, everyone in Uganda now has an equal opportunity to own land and develop it for the benefit of himself, the country and the world at large, since the world expects those who are so favourably placed as regards rich natural resources, like Uganda, to share them with their fellow human beings the world over.

The effect of the new decrees on Uganda's social pattern of life and economic development has been tremendous. Anyone who visits Uganda today will see the great strides that have been taken by the people in the development of land for agriculture and animal husbandry, although it is barely four months since the decrees were promulgated.

The international community has recognized that one of the most serious problems facing the majority of mankind today is the problem of human settlement. The three decrees promulgated in Uganda, already referred to, are meant among things to solve this problem at the national level. It will be appreciated, however, that human settlement is an international problem which can best be solved at the international level. For that reason Uganda supports the proposal for the creation of a United Nations agency or programme to deal specifically with this international problem of human settlement. In this connexion, Uganda offers to be the host country to the secretariat of such an agency or programme of the United Nations, if and when it is created. As is very well known, Uganda has the capacity and the facilities to be host not only to the secretariat of such an agency or programme but even to much bigger ones.

Full exploitation of the land resources requires heavy financial investment. If the world is going to benefit in the shortest possible time from the natural wealth of Uganda, then the world must be prepared to invest in the exploitation of these resources. Uganda invites interested parties on the individual, State and international levels to participate in the exploitation of these rich resources. Our law protects foreign investments and we guarantee fair returns on these foreign investments. We respect in full measure the right to property as a fundamental inalienable right. Our Constitution guarantees this right and the Government and people of Uganda observe this constitutional guarantee strictly; so much so that when I declared the economic war in order to restore to our people their natural rights, dignity and self-respect and save them from callous exploitation by foreigners, I also guaranteed payment of compensation to these exploiters. Negotiations are going on between Uganda and the countries concerned to determine the amount due and the method and programme of payment of compensation. The United Kingdom team was recently in Kampala, our capital city, for this purpose. The United States of America's claim has long since been settled. All that indicates that we are not just interested in making sweet utterances or paying lip service to human rights and law, but that we observe all these principles and back them up with practical, visible action.

Uganda takes strength and gains inspiration from the numerous utterances and resolutions of this venerable house urging the colonial and imperial Powers to make speedy restoration of full economic rights to the hitherto exploited oppressed and enslaved peoples of the third world. My strength and earnestness of purpose is even greater when I stand here delivering my speech on the soil of the United States of America, the country which in our era conceived a new philosophy which has lit, cleansed, inspired and sustained the third world in the pursuit of freedom. The United States colonies resisted exploitation by foreign Powers 200 years ago. They wanted to have the sole right and control over their economy. This is the accepted principle today in this Assembly, in the world of peace-loving and right-thinking peoples and the international law platform. We in Uganda have pursued the same goal.

For the pursuit of our natural rights; for the consolidation of our independence; for the retrieve of our economy; for our struggle for equality, dignity, justice in the world; for our efforts in fostering international brotherhood; for the creation of a world order in which there will be complete independence of States, with freedom for each State to decide on its destiny without regard to size, ethnic grouping, colour or creed; for our unflinching fight against oppression by big or technologically advanced nations, against exploitation and enslavement of the majority by a few powerfully placed reactionary and fascist minority regimes in southern Africa; for our dedicated commitment to the liberation movements in Africa, Asia and the Middle East, we have been subjected to blackmail, vulgar abuse, commercial ostracism, economic strangulation and treachery by imperialists in league with the Fascists and Zionists. Our case has exposed the moral bankruptcy of those powerful nations of the West which through deceit have for so long held themselves up as the bastions of peace, freedom and justice. They have, in their endeavours to distort our image in the eyes of the international community through their powerful news media in order to cover up for their inadequacies at home, not only revealed their hypocrisy but to their chagrin given unprecedented publicity to our nation and the truth we stand for.

While we have liberated our economy to feed our people, unemployment in the United Kingdom has but soared to an all-time record. While we have taken measures to restore our cultural values and establish justice among our people, the United Kingdom has turned to blackmail in order to confuse the world about the terrible situation of an internecine war in the United Kingdom colony of Northern Ireland, where the colonized people live in great fear for their lives. Today, the London-based organization, Amnesty International, continues to pay lip service to the cause of justice and, as shown in its recent publication, has blackmailed over 100 nations of the world as violators of human rights without mentioning the United Kingdom and its role in Northern Ireland. It is impossible to feel secure in the United Kingdom today because of the sporadic bomb blasts which wreck churches, schools, cafes, bars, trains and even hospitals. Kidnappings and murders have long since ceased to shock the British society as hardly a week passes without press reports of such horrible acts. This shows the decadence of a nation which once prided itself before the entire world, a quarter of which it colonized, as the fountain of peace, freedom, justice and tranquility. Amnesty International is fed on rumours and concoctions from discredited criminals in exile and, surprisingly, feels content to continue to be fed on rumours. Where on earth have exiles spoken glowingly of the regime in their country or exposed their own criminality? Amnesty International has taken no trouble to investigate or send a team to Uganda to see for itself. Its report has indicted over 100 States. How can it be said that 95 percent of the entire world does not conform to accepted standards? By what measures does it judge 95 percent of the entire world? What is the justification of the continued existence of Amnesty International if it is so helplessly behind the times? It has lent itself as tools for the smear campaigns perpetuated by the colonial and imperialistic powers that fund its existence. It wishes to divert the attention of those peoples fighting for their freedom, equality and independence in order to subvert the world order. Such tricks have not been accepted by the peoples of the third world, who form the majority of the world society.

We in Uganda are proud and committed to hold the banner of independence for the oppressed peoples to see and follow. We condemn all forms of enslavement and economic exploitation as exhibited by the minority regimes in Rhodesia and South Africa. We salute the new order in Portugal which has seen the truth and committed itself to the liberation of all its colonies which formerly were called overseas Territories. We condemn any form of aggrandizement as practised by the Zionists in the Middle East. We condemn any perpetration of illegalities in the United Nations or sustenance of the bogus State of Israel. Until 1947 there was no State of Israel, but Palestine. The colonial Powers, for their imperialistic motives, created Israel, carved out of the State of Palestine, thus causing an upheaval which, if it is not settled immediately, may throw the world into conflagration. It is reported today that, in spite of the so-called peace accord between peace-loving Egypt and the bogus State of Israel, much more powerful arms have been delivered to Israel by the United States, including missiles capable of carrying nuclear warheads. This has created great uncertainty and fear not only in the Middle East but in all of Africa, which in the northern corner has the Zionists and in the southern corner the Boers of South Africa. It has also accelerated the chances of nuclear confrontation, which may spell the doom of the human race.

Israel, like South Africa, has absolutely ignored the United Nations resolutions commanding it to withdraw from the occupied territories of Egypt, Palestine, Jordan and Syria. It is disappointing to note that some major Powers, notably the United States of America, which are founder Members of this Organization which was established to bring about a world order based upon law, justice and peace, have not only continually supported Israel in flouting United Nations resolutions, but have also equipped it with powerful armaments to make it strong enough to defy, grab and plunder its neighbour's territory. Today, without the United States of America, there would be no Israel.

The United States' persistent support for Israel stems from the sad history of colonization. The United States of America has been colonized by the Zionists who hold all the tools of development and power. They own virtually all the banking institutions, the major manufacturing and processing industries and the major means of communication; and have so much infiltrated the Central Intelligence Agency that they are posing a great threat to nations and peoples which may be opposed to the atrocious Zionist movement. They have turned CIA into a murder squad to eliminate any form of just resistance anywhere in the world. The role of CIA has been revealed to the world community by United States senators and congressmen themselves, as we learn from the United States news media. The top echelon of CIA has made an admission of this. How can we expect freedom, peace and justice in the world when such a powerful nation as the United States of America is in the hands of the Zionists? I call upon the people of the United States of America, whose forefathers founded this State "conceived in liberty and dedicated to the proposition that all men are created equal," to rid their society of the Zionists in order that the true citizens of this nation may control their own destiny and exploit the natural resources of their country to their own benefit. I call for the expulsion of Israel from the United Nations and the extinction of Israel as a State, so that the territorial integrity of Palestine may be ensured and upheld.

When this objective is achieved the Holy City of Jerusalem will once more revert to its holy status. Jerusalem should and will remain the holy place of worship for Christians, Moslems and Jews and must be free of any military activity. When recently I had the honour of being received by His Holiness the Pope, in our discussion we shared this view.

I like the Jews but I do not approve of Zionism. There are many Jews in many countries who do not subscribe to the iniquitous Zionist philosophy. To these, all the peace-loving people of the world extend their hand in friendship. Indeed, Yasser Arafat himself announced at the General Assembly last year that the Palestinian people were prepared, ready and willing to live in partnership and amity with people of all creeds, Christians, Moslems and Jews in one State, the State of Palestine. Zionist Israel has refused this offer. While millions of displaced Palestinians roam without home, without shelter, without food, millions of dollars extracted from the sweat and resources of the American people go to the aid and fatten the Zionists. While the United Nations continues to pass resolutions without sanction, the displaced Palestinian people decay and perish. Their hope and reason are fast running out. To my Arab brothers I wish to give a piece of brotherly advice. If they wish to defeat Israel they must unite. No country should be diverted from the common objective without consulting the other Arab States. Lack of proper consultation causes friction and misunderstandings, to the great benefit of Israel. Arab must stop fighting Arab so that together they may face their enemy, Israel.

I wish to emphasize that I am not a racist. I hate racialism in all its manifestations, as practised in Rhodesia and South Africa. Apartheid, like Zionism, is an enemy to humanity itself. Uganda is totally committed to the liberation of the African peoples under colonial minority regimes. We are baffled by the double standards displayed by imperialists who, in the name of democracy, plundered Viet Nam, Cambodia and many other lands while they support oppression in Rhodesia, South Africa and the Middle East; who veto the admission of gallant Viet Nam in the same way they veto the expulsion of South Africa and Israel from the United Nations; who withhold financial support from peaceful nations and pour investments into South Africa, Rhodesia and Israel.

We welcome investors to come to Uganda as friends, but not as masters, and they will find us active, generous and friendly. Anyone interested in youth programmes, employment programmes, increased productivity programmes, freedom-from-hunger programmes and environmental programmes, whether taken together or separately, will certainly take an interest in our law of reform and the methods we have devised and continue to devise. To this end I wish to restate that we are non-aligned and therefore our doors are open to any country or organization in the world with aims, methods and objectives acceptable to us to participate with us in the development of our land resources for the benefit of the world.

While here in the United States of America, a country that is celebrating its two hundredth year of independence from British colonialism, I should like to mention, without in any way imputing racial bias, the position of the black Americans in this country. In spite of the fact that he was forcibly brought to this country against his will, the black American has contributed as much as, if not more than, most of the other races towards the construction, development and now the economic mightiness of this country. His contribution, to his credit, stands sharply in contrast to the treatment he received from his fellow Americans. Having been in this country for some three centuries now and at present numbering some 30 million or more, one would have expected that of the 50-odd governors in this country at least one, if not several, would be black. As to the top executive policy-makers of the Federal Government, such as Secretaries of State, one would have hoped that at this time and moment in American history this great country, a champion of peace and freedom, would have boasted of having several black faces in that group of policy-makers. But none of these hopes have materialized. Why? This is a challenge that I would like to leave with the American people. It is a challenge whose concern has been beyond United

States boundaries since the United States became a super-Power. Hence my mentioning it here.

While I leave the entire American community with this challenge, I should like to mention specifically that the black Americans themselves are to blame in a way because of the many reported divisions in their own communities. These divisions should certainly become unnecessary in the face of continued and perpetual subjugation of their own lot by their fellow citizens. For our part in Uganda, we have done our best to champion the cause of the black Americans. In the context of the OAU, we have for the last several years now advocated their identification with the continent of their origin in the same way as the other races in this continent take pride in their ancestral homelands.

The international community has committed itself to intensify action in promoting equal rights, opportunities and responsibilities of men and women, to ensure the full integration of women in the total development effort and to involve women widely in international cooperation and in the strengthening of world peace through the proclamation of this year, 1975, as International Women's Year. I am glad to say that as far as Uganda is concerned, under my Government we have already guaranteed, in principle and practice, equality between men and women. Both sexes have equal opportunities and responsibilities to enable them to develop their particular talents and capabilities in the service of Uganda and the rest of the international community. Ugandan women have, like their male counterparts, full opportunities to make maximum contributions in every field and are playing their roles fully and effectively at all levels of decision-making, planning and implementation of all policies, programmes and projects. Our women have been fully integrated. They receive their full share of the benefits of development. In this connexion I wish to mention that there are Ugandan women at all levels of administration, including, at the top, Permanent Secretaries; there are Ugandan women professors; a Ugandan woman ambassador; doctors; lawyers; business women, and women in all areas of our total endeavour.

Our faith in fundamental human rights and in the dignity and worth of the human being is so strong that we have extended it to all spheres of our endeavours, including the prison services. Our view of prisoners is not to inflict punitive punishment on them but to reform and rehabilitate them so as to enable them to become useful and responsible members of society who make maximum contributions to the economic and social development of our country. Prisoners in Uganda are therefore trained in such fields as crop and animal husbandry, where our prison industries are some of the best farming institutions in the country. They are also trained in such other skills as furniture making, shoemaking, tailoring, blacksmithery, metalworking, handicrafts and many other industrial skills. The results we are obtaining are very good indeed in that the majority of our prisoners complete their sentences fully reformed and use the skills attained in prisons in their future lives.

We in Uganda believe that the best and most practical and lasting form of international cooperation is in trade. It is for this reason that I wish to remind representatives, and through them the countries they represent, that Uganda produces some of the world's best coffee, cotton, tea, tobacco, copper and many other forms of trade commodities, which are available for the international community to buy. I express the hope that, under the proposed new world economic order, Uganda, like other developing countries, will receive fair prices for its raw materials, which constitute the major part of its exports.

Uganda, which is in the very heart of Africa, astride the Equator, is renowned as one of the world's tourist paradises. The fabulous beauty of the countryside, with its rich colours; the graciousness of its traditionally friendly, courteous and hospitable people; the mighty Kabalega Falls; the snow-capped, fantastic Mountains of the Moon, carrying permanent glaciers; the source of the immortal River Nile; the unsurpassable magnificence of the equatorial forests; the many lakes and the unequaled scenic beauty; the rolling and terraced hills; the extraordinary concentrations of wild life in its national parks and game reserves, including the rare, huge but extremely shy gorillas, the precious white rhinoceros, the lordly lion, zebras, leopards, cheetahs, herds of elephants, buffaloes, hippopotamuses, huge crocodiles, bewildering varieties of bird life; the famous local dishes, including the Nile perch and the local brand of gin-cum-vodka, unforgettable *waragi*; the elegance of Uganda's traditional crafts; Uganda's rich traditional music, dances and cultural activities; the glorious summer sunshine of the Equator and the coolness of the mountain breezes; Kampala, the capital city, standing on a series of closely-gathered lush green hills—all these tourist attractions, topped with a year-round congenial climate, provide a visitor with the experience of a lifetime. All these God-given fantastic natural treasures are available to the world community as a whole. Ugandans welcome you and your fellow compatriots to come and share them with us in the spirit of international harmony and cooperation.

Long live Africa. Long live the third world. Long live the United Nations. For God and our country.

JAMES JONES
Peoples Temple Leader
Call for Mass Suicide
Jonestown, Guyana
November 18, 1978

James Jones (1931–1978) was the American leader of a socialist cult who built a compound for his followers in the South American country of Guyana. The Peoples Temple had more than nine hundred members, most of whom committed suicide at the urging of Jones, after a few members murdered a U.S. Congressman and three journalists who came to investigate their organization. Someone audiotaped the grisly and pathetic scene wherein Jones exhorts his followers to drink the poison mixed with Flavor Aid: "It's simple. It's simple. There's no convulsions with it. It's just simple. Just, please get it." The excerpts that follow come from Mary McCormick Maaga's transcript of the suicide in her book Hearing the Voices of Jonestown (Syracuse: Syracuse University Press, 1998).

How very much I've tried my best to give you a good life. But in spite of all of my trying a handful of our people, with their lies, have made our lives impossible. There's no way to detach ourselves from what's happened today.

Not only are we in a compound situation, not only are there those who have left and committed the betrayal of the century, some have stolen children from others, and they are in pursuit right now to kill them because they stole their children. And we are sitting here waiting on a powder keg.

I don't think it is what we want to do with our babies—I don't think that's what we had in mind to do with our babies. It is said by the greatest of prophets from time immemorial: "No man may take my life from me; I lay my life down." So to sit here and wait for the catastrophe that's going to happen on that airplane—it's going to be a catastrophe. It almost happened here. Almost happened when the congressman was nearly killed here. You can't steal people's children. You can't take off with people's children without expecting a violent reaction. And that's not so unfamiliar to us either—even if we were Judeo-Christian—if we weren't Communists. The world *(inaudible)* suffers violence, and the violent shall take it by force. If we can't live in peace, then let's die in peace. *(Applause.)*

We've been so betrayed. We have been so terribly betrayed. *(Music and singing)* But we've tried and as *(inaudible)*...if this only works one day it was worthwhile. *(Applause.)* Thank you.

Now what's going to happen here in a matter of a few minutes is that one of those people on that plane is going to shoot the pilot—I know that. I didn't plan it, but I know it's going to happen. They're gonna shoot that pilot and down comes that plane into the jungle. And we had better not have any of our children left when it's over because they'll parachute in here on us.

I'm going to be just as plain as I know how to tell you. I've never lied to you. I never have lied to you. I know that's what's gonna happen. That's what he intends to do, and he will do it. He'll do it.[1]

What's with being so bewildered with many, many pressures on my brain, seeing all these people behave so treasonous—there was too much for me to put together, but I now know what he was telling me. And it'll happen. If the plane gets in the air even.[2]

So my opinion is that you be kind to children and be kind to seniors and take the potion like they used to take in ancient Greece and step over quietly because we are not committing suicide; it's a revolutionary act. We can't go back; they won't leave us alone. They're now going back to tell more lies, which means more congressmen. And there's no way, no way we can survive....

And I'd like to choose my own kind of death for a change. I'm tired of being tormented to hell, that's what I'm tired of. Tired of it. *(Applause.)*

I have twelve hundred people's lives in my hands, and I certainly don't want your life in my hands. I'm going to tell you, Christine,

---

[1] "Jones is referring to Larry Layton and the apparent plan to shoot the pilot of one of the airplanes that was to transport Ryan and his entourage, including the defectors, back to Georgetown from Port Kaituma. In fact, before the plane could take off, the men from Jonestown inside the tractor-trailer opened fire, and Layton never carried out the plan." (Footnote by Mary McCormick Maaga.)

[2] "This line suggests that Jones was aware of the plan for the ambush at the airstrip. Perhaps Larry Layton was sent in case the trailer did not arrive in time, or maybe, Layton was sent as a 'message' for his sister, Debbie Blakey, but his ability to carry out the murder[s] was enough in question that the gunmen in the trailer were sent as a backup plan. Given that Layton was not asked to come to Guyana until after his sister had defected, one wonders if he were sent for to participate in some activity (not necessarily this one) that would demonstrate to his sister and family that Larry Layton was more loyal to Peoples Temple than to his biological family." (Footnote by Mary McCormick Maaga.)

without me, life has no meaning. *(Applause.)* I'm the best thing you'll ever have.

I want, want, I have to pay—I'm standing with Ujara. I'm standing with those people. They are part of me. I could detach myself. I really could detach myself. No, no, no, no, no, no. I never detach myself from any of your troubles. I've always taken your troubles right on my shoulders. And I'm not going to change that now. It's too late. I've been running too long. Not going to change now. *(Applause.)*

Maybe the next time you'll get to go to Russia. The next time round. This is—what I'm talking about now is the dispensation of judgment. This is a revolutionary—a revolutionary suicide council. I'm not talking about self—self-destruction. I'm talking about that we have no other road. I will take your call. We will put it to the Russians. And I can tell you the answer now because I am a prophet. Call the Russians and tell them, and see if they'll take us....

I made my manifestation, and the world was ready, not ready for me. Paul said, "I was a man born out of due season." I've been born out of due season, just like all we are, and the best testimony we can make is to leave this goddamn world. *(Applause.)*

...You asked me about Russia. I'm right now making a call to Russia. What more do you suggest? I'm listening to you. You've yet to give me one slight bit of encouragement. I just now instructed her to go there and do that.

...Some months I've tried to keep this thing from happening. But I now see it's the will—it's the will of Sovereign Being that this happen to us. That we lay down our lives to protest against what's being done. That we lay down our lives to protest at what's being done. The criminality of people. The cruelty of people.

Who walked out of here today? See all those who walked out? Mostly white people. Mostly white people walked. I'm so grateful for the ones that didn't—those who knew who they are. I just know that there's no point—there's no point to this. We are born before our time. They won't accept us. And I don't think we should sit here and take any more time for our children to be endangered. Because if they come after our children, and we give them our children, then our children will suffer forever.

It's all over. The congressman has been murdered. *(Music and singing.)* Well, it's all over, all over. What a legacy, what a legacy. What the Red Brigade doin' that once ever made any sense anyway? They invaded our privacy. They came into our home. They followed us six thousand miles away. Red Brigade showed them justice. The congressman's dead.

Please get us some medication. It's simple. It's simple. There's no convulsions with it. It's just simple. Just, please get it. Before it's too late. The GDF[3] will be here, I tell you. Get movin', get movin', get movin'.

...Don't be afraid to die. You'll see, there'll be a few people land out here. They'll torture some of our children here. They'll torture our people. They'll torture our seniors. We cannot have this.

Are you going to separate yourself from whoever shot the congressman? I don't know who shot him....Let's make our peace.

...It's just too late. It's too late. The congressman's dead. The congressman lays dead. Many of our traitors are dead. They're all layin' out there dead. *(Inaudible.)*

I didn't, but my people did. My people did. They're my people, and they've been provoked too much. They've been provoked too much. What's happened here's been since Tuesday's been an act of provocation.

...Please, can we hasten? Can we hasten with that medication? You don't know what you've done. I tried. *(Applause, music, singing.)*

They saw it happen and ran into the bush and dropped the machine guns. I never in my life. But not any more. But we've got to move. Are you gonna get that medication here? You've got to move. Marceline, about forty minutes.

...All right, it's hard but only at first—only at first is it hard. Hard only at first. Living—you're looking at death and it looks—living is much, much more difficult. Raising up every morning and not knowing what's going to be the night's bringing. It's much more difficult. It's much more difficult. *(Crying and talking.)*

Please. For God's sake, let's get on with it. We've lived—we've lived as no other people lived and loved. We've had as much of this world as you're gonna get. Let's just be done with it. Let's be done with the agony of it. *(Applause.)*

It's far, far harder to have to walk through every day, die slowly—and from the time you're a child 'til the time you get gray, you're dying.

Dishonest, and I'm sure that they'll—they'll pay for it. They'll pay for it. This is a revolutionary suicide. This is not a self-destructive suicide. So they'll pay for this. They brought this upon us. And they'll pay for that. I leave that destiny to them.

(Voices.)

Who wants to go with their child has a right to go with their child. I think it's humane. I want to go—I want to see you go, though. They can take me and do what they want—whatever they

---

[3] "Guyanese Defense Force." (Footnote by Mary McCormick Maaga.)

want to do. I want to see you go. I don't want to see you go through this hell no more. No more. No more. No more.

We're trying. If everybody will relax. The best thing you do to relax, and you will have no problem. You'll have no problem with this thing if you just relax....

It's not to be afeared. It is not to be feared. It is a friend. It's a friend...sitting there, show your love for one another. Let's get gone. Let's get gone. Let's get gone. *(Children crying.)* We had nothing we could do. We can't—we can't separate ourselves from our own people. For twenty years laying in some old rotten nursing home. *(Music.)* Taking us through all these anguish years. They took us and put us in chains and that's nothing. This business—that business—there's no comparison to that, to this.

They've robbed us of our land, and they've taken us and driven us and we tried to find ourselves. We tried to find a new beginning. But it's too late. You can't separate yourself from your brother and your sister. No way I'm going to do it. I refuse. I don't know who fired the shot. I don't know who killed the congressman. But as far as I am concerned, I killed him. You understand what I'm saying? I killed him. He had no business coming. I told him not to come....

I, with respect, die with a degree of dignity. Lay down your life with dignity. Don't lay down with tears and agony. There's nothing to death. It's like Mac said, it's just stepping over to another plane. Don't be this way. Stop this hysterics. This is not the way for people who are Socialists or Communists to die. No way for us to die. We must die with some dignity. We must die with some dignity. We will have no choice. Now we have some choice. Do you think they're gonna allow this to be done—allow us to get by with this? You must be insane.

Look children, it's just something to put you to rest. Oh, God. *(Children crying.)*

Mother, Mother, Mother, Mother, Mother, please. Mother, please, please, please. Don't—don't do this. Don't do this. Lay down your life with your child. But don't do this.

...Free at last. Keep—keep your emotions down. Keep your emotions down. Children, it will not hurt. If you'd be—if you'll be quiet. If you'll be quiet.

(Music and crying.)

It's never been done before, you say. It's been done by every tribe in history. Every tribe facing annihilation. All the Indians of the Amazon are doing it right now. They refuse to bring any babies into the world. They kill every child that comes into the world. Because they don't want to live in this kind of a world.

So be patient. Be patient. Death is—I tell you, I don't care how many screams you hear. I don't care how many anguished cries. Death is a million times preferable to ten more days of this life. If you knew what was ahead of you—if you knew what was ahead of you, you'd be glad to be stepping over tonight.

Death, death, death is common to people. And the Eskimos, they take death in their stride. Let's be digni—let's be dignified. If you quit tell them they're dying—if you adults would stop some of this nonsense. Adults, adults, adults. I call on you to stop this nonsense. I call on you to quit exciting your children when all they're doing is going to a quiet rest. I call on you to stop this now if you have any respect at all. Are we black, proud, and Socialist, or what are we? Now stop this nonsense. Don't carry this on anymore. You're exciting your children.

No, no sorrow—that it's all over. I'm glad it's over. Hurry, hurry my children. Hurry. All I think *(inaudible)* from the hands of the enemy. Hurry, my children. Hurry. There are seniors out here that I'm concerned about. Hurry. I don't want to leave my seniors to this mess. Only quickly, quickly, quickly, quickly, quickly.... Good knowing you.

No more pain now. No more pain, I said *(inaudible)*. No more pain. Jim Cobb is laying on the airfield dead at this moment. *(Applause.)* Remember the Oliver woman said she—she'd come over and kill me if her son wouldn't stop her? These, these are the people—the peddlers of hate. All we're doing is laying down our lives. We're not letting them take our lives. We're laying down our lives. Peace in their lives. They just want peace. *(Music.)* ...

Stop this, stop this, stop this. Stop this crying, all of you....

All they do is taking a drink. They take it to go to sleep. That's what death is, sleep. You can have it *(inaudible)* I'm tired of it all....

Where's the vat, the vat, the vat? Where's the vat with the Green C on it? The vat with the Green C in. Bring it so the adults can begin....

Don't, don't fail to follow my advice. You'll be sorry. You'll be sorry. If we do it, than that they do it. Have trust. You have to step across. *(Music.)* We used to think this world was—this world was not our home—well, it sure isn't—we were saying—it sure wasn't.

He doesn't want to tell them. All he's doing—if they will tell them—assure these kids. Can't some people assure these children of the relaxation of stepping over to the next plane? They set an example for others. We said—one thousand people who said, we don't like the way the world is....

Take our life from us. We laid it down. We got tired. We didn't commit suicide, we committed an act of revolutionary suicide protesting the conditions of an inhumane world.

P. W. BOTHA
"Crossing the Rubicon"
Address by South Africa's State President at the Opening of the National Party Natal Congress

("I am not prepared to lead White South Africans and other minority groups on a road to abdication and suicide")

Durban, South Africa

August 15, 1985

The Afrikaner (that is, Dutch-descended African) Pieter Willem Botha (1916–2006) was the leader of South Africa from 1978 until 1989 (as prime minister and then as president). In 1989, he would eventually meet with but continue to keep Nelson Mandela, the black opposition leader, in jail. At various moments, Botha was ready to make concessions about the separate and unequal legal rights of whites and non-whites—Apartheid—but not to do away with it. This speech demonstrates both his openness to discussion and his stubbornness about Apartheid.

During recent months and particularly the last few weeks, I have received a great deal of advice.

Most of the persons and institutions who offered advice and still offer advice have good and well-meaning intentions. I thank them and where the advice is practical, it is considered.

I almost daily receive hundreds of messages and letters of goodwill and encouragement from all over the Western world and from people in our own country, as well as assurances that people are praying for me. Just before we left for this meeting, a very touching message was received by me from a member of the Greek community from Johannesburg. I sincerely appreciate these gestures of goodwill.

Most of the media in South Africa have already informed you on what I was going to say tonight, or what I ought to say, according to their superior judgment.

Of all the tragedies in the world I think the greatest is the fact that our electorate refrained so far to elect some of these gentlemen as their government. They have all the answers to all the problems.

And these answers differ from day to day and from Sunday to Sunday!

Seldom in our past has there been a party congress of the National Party for which so many expectations were raised as this Congress in Natal. Some of the reasons for this are evident, for example the partial emergency situation in less than 14% of the magisterial districts of the RSA. Other reasons are more sinister, such as the motives of those who have put words in my mouth in advance.

During recent weeks there was an unparalleled scurry from different sources, within and outside South Africa, to predict and prescribe what is to be announced at the Congress. It was also envisaged that worldwide, people are going to be dissatisfied if certain things are not announced as were predicted.

It is of course a well-known tactic in negotiations to limit the other person's freedom of movement about possible decisions, thus forcing him in a direction where his options are increasingly restricted.

It is called the force of rising expectations.

Firstly, an expectation is raised that a particular announcement is to be made. Then an expectation is raised about what the content of the announcement should be. The tactic has two objectives.

Firstly, the target is set so high that, even if an announcement is made, it is almost impossible to fulfill the propagated expectations. Secondly, it is also an attempt to force the one party into negotiations to make the expected decision. If this is not done, public opinion is already conditioned to such an extent that the result is widespread dissatisfaction. If you want to read about these tactics, read the book *Nicaragua Betrayed* and then you will see the history of some of these gentlemen repeated in South Africa.

This is what has been happening over recent weeks. I find it unacceptable to be confronted in this manner with an accomplished fact. That is not my way of doing and the sooner these gentlemen accept it, the better.

I think we should first reconsider the objective of a party congress.

The National Party in each province is connected to the Party in other provinces on a federal basis. The Provincial Congress is the highest authority of the Party in each province. One of the major activities of the Congress is to decide on Party policy. It would thus be unwise of the Leader of the Party to confront the Provincial Congress with certain final decisions.

Moreover, the subject of most of the speculations, namely the constitutional future of the Black peoples in South Africa, is of such a nature that it must be determined in consultation with those concerned. We cannot confront them with certain final decisions.

Over the years, that was exactly the criticism against our Government—that we make decisions about people and not with them. Now, suddenly I'm expected to make the decision for them.

I find the attempts from various sources to compromise me and the Government very unfortunate. It is a very dangerous game, and it definitely does not serve the interest of negotiation and reform in South Africa.

I have used a quotation of Langenhoven earlier. I want to quote him again. He wrote:

"If we are in front we can wait for time. If we are behind, it does not wait for us."

In our relationship with our fellow-South Africans and in our relationship as a multicultural society in South Africa, no spirit of defeatism or hysterical actions will help us to be on time.

We must deal with our relationships and accept future challenges in a balanced way and with devotion. You will find that balance in thinking and devotion in the National Party—the only political party which is representative of the vast majority of White South Africa.

The Party stands for the just and equal treatment of all parts of South Africa, and for the impartial maintenance of the rights and privileges of every section of the population. But, the Party must also deal with the heritage of history. Certain situations in this country were created by history and not by other national parties.

We are not prepared to accept the antiquated, simplistic and racist approach that South Africa consists of a White minority and a Black majority.

We cannot ignore the fact that this country is a multicultural society—a country of minorities—White minorities as well as Black minorities.

While the National Party accepts and respects the multicultural and poly-ethnic nature of South Africa's population, it rejects any system of horizontal differentiation which amounts to one nation or group in our country dominating another or others.

We believe in and uphold the principle of economic interdependence of the population groups as well as the acceptance of the properly planned utilization of manpower.

In this regard we have advanced very far through modernizing our labour laws, the creation of a Development Bank for Southern

Africa, as well as a Corporation for the Development of Small Business Activities. We already co-operate in various ways through multi-national ministerial committees, meeting from time to time and working positively in the interest of South Africa as a whole.

It is true that as a result of serious world recessionary circumstances, South Africa, which was also hit by recessionary conditions and overspending in some fields, could not make progress as we would have preferred.

But it is common knowledge by now that the official economic strategy applied in South Africa during the past twelve months has produced excellent results:

—Overspending by the private and public sectors have been eliminated.
—The money supply is under control.
—Government spending is being effectively curbed and soundly financed.
—The balance of payments on current account is showing a surplus of about R5 billion per year—much larger than anticipated.
—The banking sector and private companies have for months now been repaying substantial amounts of foreign debt.
—Our net gold and foreign exchange reserves increased by R1.4 billion during the second quarter of 1985.
—The prime overdraft rate of the banks has been reduced four times since May, from 25% to 21%. Other interest rates have also declined.
—The rate of inflation is still around 16% but should begin to decline before the end of the year.
—With exports rising strongly and interest rates falling, the domestic economy should move into a new upswing in 1986.

The so-called "economic fundamentals" are therefore at present very favourable in South Africa.

Many of the present perceptions of the South African situation overseas are, of course, quite erroneous. Nobody would deny that we face problems that demand solutions, but every country has. I can name you quite a number of countries who have more problems than S.A.

But the perceptions of many overseas observers bear little relationship to the realities of the situation.

People are flocking to South Africa tonight, from neighbouring countries because they are looking for work and health services.

Only last week I was in the north of our country and there I had the experience that people were flocking from Mozambique into South Africa in their tens of thousands. How do you explain that? Do people flee to hell?

The Republic of South Africa still remains the leading country in the sub-continent of Southern Africa. If the Republic of South Africa suffers from economic setbacks, the whole of Southern Africa will pay a heavy price. For example, at present 90% of the exports of Southern Africa takes place through the transport systems of the Republic of South Africa.

We in the Republic of South Africa, as well as our neighbours, will in the foreseeable future have to find solutions for our fast growing populations and their rightful demands. We have our responsibilities in connection with proper family planning, health services, the provision of clean and fresh water, training of young people and the creation of work opportunities.

The Government, apart from its normal budget this year, made provision for R100 million to provide people with work, and only yesterday we had a report saying that we are succeeding in our efforts. We have such a vast task ahead of us and such great challenges to create a better future, that we can ill afford the irresponsibilities and destructive actions of barbaric Communist agitators and even murderers who perpetrate the most cruel deeds against fellow South Africans, because they are on the payroll of their masters far from this lovely land of ours.

I have the knowledge because I have the facts. As head of this Government I am in the position to tell you tonight what the facts are. No government in this country or elsewhere in the world can solve all the problems in its country in a given time.

But despite our human weaknesses and our limited powers as human instruments, we can attempt to be on time. We can make serious attempts not to be behind time.

We are suffering in some parts of South Africa from two basic problems.

The first is the problem of unemployment—a problem of the entire Western world, with perhaps to a lesser extent the United States—especially a problem of Africa where people die of hunger, where one of the leaders of Africa in the Organisation of African Unity declared: "Africa, it is time."

We believe that the Small Business Corporation we created is of vital importance in this connection to remedy this problem. I am of the opinion that there are too many rules and regulations in our country serving as stumbling blocks in the way of entrepreneurs.

These stumbling blocks must be removed. We are already seriously attending to this problem. Even if I as State President have to take power during the next session of Parliament so as to enable me to deregulize in the interest of the country, I will do so!

The underdeveloped part of the economy is mainly that of different non-White communities. There are historic reasons for this, just as there are historic reasons for the plight of Africa in general. Instead of the Whites paternalistically trying to do everything for the Blacks, they must rather be allowed to help themselves—in the informal as well as the formal sector of the economy.

When I met with President Machel some time ago on the border of South Africa and Mozambique, I told him he must not expect from South Africa the same policy which destroyed Africa under the leadership of the West and Russia. I told him that we are not coming with aid programmes, but we want co-operation and he interrupted immediately and said: "Africa is tired of aid, provide us with co-operation, and help us to help ourselves." Consequently, I shall go out of my way to see to it that more substantial funds are made available to the Small Business Development Corporation.

Secondly, I refer to the problem of housing, caused mainly by our population explosion in Southern Africa, as elsewhere in Africa.

It is a fallacious belief that the Government must do everything for all. We must help the people to help themselves, to build and upgrade their homes through their own efforts. We have decided that land should be made available where possible, and site services supplied. We have already accepted the principle of ownership rights for Blacks in the urban areas rights to people in the National States.

But the State must mainly take responsibility for the infrastructure such as fresh drinking water, sanitation and roads and leave it to the people to provide their own homes.

The Government intends setting aside R1 billion during the next five years to improve underdeveloped towns and cities, not only in metropolitan areas. Our policy of decentralisation will be actively continued, and you know for a fact that we have advanced very fast in this direction. Get the facts, and the people who know the facts will support the Government in its efforts.

On the question of influx control—I can only say that the present system is outdated and too costly. The President's Council assured me that they are at present considering this matter and will probably report on it in the near future, while the Government itself is also at present considering improvements.

But of course we shall need the closest co-operation from the private sector. I hope they will stand up and be counted as they did in the past when I called upon them for their co-operation.

When I was Minister of Defence and the world started an arms boycott against South Africa, I called upon the private sector to support the Government in providing our own arms which they did successfully. I now appeal to them again to stand together for South Africa, not for any other interest.

I now wish to deal with some other aspects of our National Life.

It is my considered opinion that any future constitutional dispensation providing for participation by all South African citizens, should be negotiated.

But let me point out at once that since South Africa freed itself from colonialism, democracy has already been broadened and millions of people who never had a say in Governmental affairs under the British Colonial system, have it today.

I am pressed by some who mean it well and those who wish to destroy orderly government in this country, to make a Statement of Intent. I am not prepared to make it, not now and not tomorrow.

I say it would be wrong to be prescriptive as to structures within which participation will have to take place in the future.

It would also be wrong to place a time limit on negotiations. I am not going to walk into this trap—I am responsible for South Africa's future.

However, I believe that the majority of South Africans as well as independent states, which form our immediate neighbours, have much in common apart from our economic interests.

We believe in the same Almighty God and the redeeming grace of His Son, Jesus Christ.

And I know what I am talking about, because only a few months ago I stood before an audience of three million Black people, proving the truth of what I am saying now. I don't know whether one of our critics ever saw three million people together in a meeting. I did.

We believe and wish to uphold religious freedom in South Africa. This is a country of religious freedom.

We believe in democratic institutions of government and we believe in the broadening of democracy.

We believe our great wealth of divergent population groups must speak to each other through their elected leaders, not self-appointed leaders.

We believe that our peace and prosperity is indivisible.

We believe in the protection of minorities. Is there anybody in this hall who would get up and say he is not for the protection of minorities? Let me see how such a fool looks.

We know that it is the hard fact of South African life, that it will not be possible to accommodate the political aspirations of our various population groups and communities in a known defined political system, because our problems are unique.

We have often found that our efforts to find solutions have been impeded and frustrated because of different interpretations of the terminology that we use to describe our particular form of democratic solutions.

Some years ago, with the best intentions on my part, I advocated a confederation of Southern African states to co-operate with one another. The idea was belittled and prejudice was created against it and that is why I say I am not going to fall into that trap again, before I had the opportunity to discuss with the elected leaders of other communities in South Africa the structures we jointly agree on.

Now let me state explicitly that I believe in participation of all the South African communities on matters of common concern. I believe there should exist structures to reach this goal of co-responsibility and participation.

I firmly believe that the granting and acceptance of independence by various Black peoples within the context of their own statehood, represent a material part of the solution. I believe in democratic neighbours, not neighbours that call out elections and then stop them in their mysterious ways.

I would, however, like to restate my Government's position in this regard, namely that independence cannot be forced upon any community. Should any of the Black National States therefore prefer not to accept independence, such states or communities will remain a part of the South African nation, are South African citizens and should be accommodated within political institutions within the boundaries of the Republic of South Africa. This does not exclude that regional considerations should be taken into account and that provision be made for participation in institutions on a regional and/or group basis. We must be practical in this regard.

But I know for a fact that most leaders in their own right in South Africa and reasonable South Africans will not accept the principle of one-man-one-vote in a unitary system. That would lead to domination of one over the other and it would lead to chaos. Consequently, I reject it as a solution.

Secondly, a so-called fourth chamber of Parliament is not a practical solution and I do not think responsible people will argue in favour of it.

We must rather seek our solutions in the devolution of power and in participation on common issues.

But I admit that the acceptance by my Government of the permanence of Black communities in urban areas outside the National States, means that a solution will have to be found for their legitimate rights.

The future of these communities and their constitutional arrangements will have to be negotiated with leaders from the National States, as well as from their own ranks.

But let me be quite frank with you—you must know where you stand with me. I have no unfulfilled ambitions in political life in South Africa. I am standing where I am standing because people asked me to stand here. Let me be quite frank with you tonight, if you do not like my way of thinking, if you do not like the direction I am going in, it is the right of the Party Congresses to state whether they agree with their leader or not.

I am not prepared to lead White South Africans and other minority groups on a road to abdication and suicide.

Destroy White South Africa and our influence, and this country will drift into faction strife, chaos and poverty.

Together with my policy statements earlier this year in Parliament, I see this speech of mine as my Manifesto for a new South Africa.

In my policy statements in January and June of this year, I indicated that there would be further developments with regard to the rights and interests of the various population groups in Southern Africa.

Since then we have had to contend with escalating violence within South Africa, and pressure from abroad in the form of measures designed to coerce the Government into giving in to various demands.

Our enemies—both within and without—seek to divide our peoples. They seek to create unbridgeable differences between us to prevent us from negotiating peaceful solutions to our problems. Peaceful negotiation is their enemy. Peaceful negotiation is their enemy, because it will lead to joint responsibility for the progress and prosperity of South Africa. Those whose methods are violent, do not want to participate. They wish to seize and monopolize all power. Let there be no doubt about what they would do with such power.

One has only to look at their methods and means. Violent and brutal means can only lead to totalitarian and tyrannical ends.

Their actions speak louder than their words. Their words offer ready panaceas such as one-man-one-vote, freedom and justice for all. Their actions leave no doubt that the freedoms that we already have—together with the ongoing extension of democracy in South

Africa—are the true targets of their violence. Is this type of Government really such a wonderful example that they wish to have? Why do they not organise the investors of the Western world to invest in Lesotho and Mozambique? Why do I have to appeal to people to invest in Mozambique?

I have a specific question I would like to put to the media in South Africa: How do they explain the fact that they are always present, with cameras et cetera, at places where violence takes place? Are there people from the revolutionary elements who inform them to be ready? Or are there perhaps representatives of the reactionary groups in the ranks of certain media?

My question to you is this: Whose interests do you serve—those of South Africa or those of the revolutionary elements? South Africa must know, our life is at stake.

From certain international as well as local quarters, appeals are being made to me to release Mr. Nelson Mandela from jail.

I stated in Parliament, when put this question, that if Mr. Mandela gives a commitment that he will not make himself guilty of planning, instigating or committing acts of violence for the furtherance of political objectives, I will, in principle, be prepared to consider his release.

But let me remind the public of the reasons why Mr. Mandela is in jail. I think it is absolutely necessary that we deal with that first of all. When he was brought before court in the sixties, the then Attorney General, Dr. Yutar, set out the State's case inter alia as follows:

"As the indictment alleges, the accused deliberately and maliciously plotted and engineered the commission of acts of violence and destruction throughout the country... The planned purpose thereof was to bring about in the Republic of South Africa chaos, disorder and turmoil.... They (Mr. Mandela and his friends) planned violent insurrection and rebellion."

The saboteurs had planned the manufacture of at least seven types of bombs: 48,000 anti-personnel mines, 210,000 hand grenades, petrol bombs, pipe bombs, syringe bombs and bottle bombs.

A document was produced during the Court case in Mandela's own handwriting in which he stated:

"We Communist Party members are the most advanced revolutionaries in modern history.... The enemy must be completely crushed and wiped out from the face of the earth before a Communist world can be realised."

In passing sentence at the time, the Judge, Mr. Justice De Wet, remarked:

"The crime of which the accused have been convicted that is

the main crime, the crime of conspiracy, is in essence one of high treason. The State has decided not to charge the crime in this form. Bearing this in mind and giving the matter very serious consideration, I have decided not to impose the supreme penalty which in a case like this would usually be the proper penalty for the crime."

The violence of our enemies is a warning to us. We, who are committed to peaceful negotiation, also have a warning to them. Our warning is that our readiness to negotiate should not be mistaken for weakness.

I have applied much self-discipline during the past weeks and months. I have been lenient and patient. Don't push us too far in your own interests, I tell them. Reform through a process of negotiation is not weakness. Talking, consulting, bargaining with all our peoples' leaders is not weakness. Mutual acceptance of and joint responsibility for the welfare and stability of our country is not weakness. It is our strength.

Our strength is the courage to face and accommodate the problems bequeathed to us by history. The reality of our diversity is a hard reality. We face it, because it is there. How do we accommodate it? How do we build a better future out of cultures, values, languages which are demonstrably real in our heterogeneous society?

We are resolved, we are committed, to do so in two fundamental ways.

Firstly—by letting the people speak. By letting the people speak through their leaders.

By negotiation between all these leaders. I go out of my way, and my colleagues know that I am working all hours every day of my life. Negotiation in which we will all endeavour to improve our common well being. Negotiation in which there will be give and take. We will not prescribe and we will not demand—to do so would be to take only. We will give so that others can also give—towards a better future for each and everyone.

Secondly—the overriding common denominator is our mutual interest in each other's freedoms and well being. Our peace and prosperity is indivisible. Therefore, the only way forward is through co-operation and co-responsibility.

If we ignore the existence of minorities; if we ignore the individual's right to associate with others in the practice of his beliefs and the propagation of his values; if we deny this in favour of a simplistic "winner-takes-all" political system—then we will diminish and not increase the freedoms of our peoples. Then we would deny the right of each and everyone to share in the decisions which shape his destiny.

Between the many and varied leaders in this country, in the

National States and the independent states neighbouring on our borders, in our urban areas I recognise this, but I also know that their love for South Africa is intense as my own. I am therefore in no doubt that working together, we shall succeed in finding the way which will satisfy the reasonable social and political aspirations of the majority of us.

The work of the Special Cabinet Committee is bearing fruit. At the correct time other heads of Governments and I, together with other leaders of goodwill, will also be able to take part more directly in this process. But it cannot be solved overnight, not in South Africa.

We have never given in to outside demands and we are not going to do so now. South Africa's problems will be solved by South Africans and not by foreigners.

We are not going to be deterred from doing what we think best, nor will we be forced into doing what we don't want to do. The tragedy is that hostile pressure and agitation from abroad have acted as an encouragement to the militant revolutionaries in South Africa to continue with their violence and intimidation. They have derived comfort and succour from this pressure.

My Government and I are determined to press ahead with our reform programme, and to those who prefer revolution to reform, I say they will not succeed. If necessary we will use stronger measures but they will not succeed.

We prefer to resolve our problems by peaceful means: then we can build, then we can develop, then we can train people, then we can uplift people, then we can make this country of ours a better place to live in. By violence and by burning down schools and houses and murdering innocent people, you don't build a country, you destroy it.

Despite the disturbances, despite the intimidation, there is more than enough goodwill among Blacks, Whites, Coloureds and Asians to ensure that we shall jointly find solutions acceptable to us.

But I say it is going to take time. Revolutionaries have no respect for time, because they have no self-respect. Look what they have done to Africa, a continent that is dying at present. I can tell you, because I know what is happening in many of these countries. I have the facts and I am not going to hand South Africa over to these revolutionaries to do the same to this lovely country.

I am encouraged by the growing number of Black leaders who are coming forward to denounce violence. Any reduction of violence will be matched by action on the part of the Government to lift the State of Emergency and restore normality in the areas concerned.

Moreover, as violence diminishes, as criminal and terrorist activities cease, and as the process of dialogue and communication acquires greater momentum, there would be little need to keep those affected in detention or prison.

The implementation of the principles I have stated today can have far-reaching effects on us all. I believe that we are today crossing the Rubicon. There can be no turning back. We now have a manifesto for the future of our country, and we must embark on a programme of positive action in the months and years that lie ahead. The challenges we face call for all concerned to negotiate in a spirit of give and take. With mutual goodwill we shall reach our destination peacefully.

We undertake to do all that man can possibly do. In so saying, I pray that Almighty God would grant us the wisdom and the strength to seek to fulfill His Will.

I thank you.

DENG XIAOPING

Address to the Martial Units—Tiananmen Square

("America has criticized us for suppressing students....
What qualifications do they have to criticize us?")

Beijing, China

June 9, 1989

In the spring of 1989, China's leaders responded to the largest peaceful protest movement in Communist China's history with a violent crackdown at Beijing's Tiananmen Square. Students and other citizens staged hunger strikes and pro-democracy demonstrations. On June 3, army units, apparently directed by Deng Xiaoping to "shed some blood," began their removal of the protesters. Deng Xiaoping (1904–1997), head of the Central Military Commission, had this speech delivered to the soldiers who had cleared the square. In spite of the hundreds of deaths of protesters (possibly more than a thousand deaths, but the Chinese government did not share its numbers, and the imprisonment of hundreds more), Deng here declares: "All in all, this was a test, and we passed."

Comrades, you have been working very hard. First, I express my profound condolences to the commanders and fighters of the People's Liberation Army [PLA], commanders and fighters of the armed police force, and public security officers and men who died a heroic death; my cordial sympathy to the several thousand commanders and fighters of the PLA, commanders and fighters of the armed police force, and public security officers and men who were injured in this struggle; and cordial regards to all commanders and fighters of the PLA, commanders and fighters of the armed police force, and public security officers and men who took part in this struggle. I propose that we all rise and stand in silent tribute to the martyrs.

I would like to take this opportunity to say a few words.

This storm was bound to come sooner or later. This is determined by the major international climate and China's own minor climate. It was bound to happen and is independent of man's will. It was just a matter of time and scale. It is more to our advantage that this happened today. What is most advantageous to us is that we have a large group of veteran comrades who are still alive. They have experienced many storms and they know what is at stake. They support the use of resolute action to counter the rebellion. Although some comrades may not understand this for a while, they will eventually understand this and support the decision of the Central Committee.

The April 26 Renmin Ribao editorial ascertained the nature of the problem as that of turmoil. The word turmoil is appropriate. This is the very word to which some people object and which they want to change. What has happened shows that this judgment was correct. It was also inevitable that the situation would further develop into a counterrevolutionary rebellion.

We still have a group of veteran comrades who are alive. We also have core cadres who took part in the revolution at various times, and in the army as well. Therefore, the fact that the incident broke out today has made it easier to handle. The main difficulty in handling this incident has been that we have never experienced such a situation before, where a handful of bad people mixed with so many young students and onlookers. For a while we could not distinguish them, and as a result, it was difficult for us to be certain of the correct action that we should take. If we had not had the support of so many veteran party comrades, it would have been difficult even to ascertain the nature of the incident.

Some comrades do not understand the nature of the problem. They think it is simply a question of how to treat the masses. Actually, what we face is not simply ordinary people who are unable to distinguish between right and wrong. We also face a rebellious clique and a large number of the dregs of society, who want to topple our country and overthrow our party. This is the essence of the problem. Failing to understand this fundamental issue means failing to understand the nature of the incident. I believe that after serious work, we can win the support of the overwhelming majority of comrades within the party concerning the nature of the incident and its handling.

The incident became very clear as soon as it broke out. They have two main slogans: One is to topple the Communist Party, and the other is to overthrow the socialist system. Their goal is to establish a totally Western-dependent bourgeois republic. The people want to combat corruption. This, of course, we accept. We should also take the so-called anticorruption slogans raised by people with ulterior motives as good advice and accept them accordingly. Of course, these slogans are just a front: The heart of these slogans is to topple the Communist Party and overthrow the socialist system.

In the course of quelling this rebellion, many of our comrades were injured or even sacrificed their lives. Their weapons were also taken from them. Why was this? It also was because bad people mingled with the good, which made it difficult to take the drastic measures we should take.

Handling this matter amounted to a very severe political test for our army, and what happened shows that our PLA passed muster. If we had used tanks to roll across [bodies?], it would have created a confusion of fact and fiction across the country. That is why I have to thank the PLA commanders and fighters for using this attitude to deal with the rebellion. Even though the losses are regrettable, this has enabled us to win over the people and made it possible for those people who can't tell right from wrong to change their viewpoint. This has made it possible for everyone to see for themselves what kind of people the PLA are, whether there was bloodbath at Tiananmen, and who were the people who shed blood.

Once this question is cleared up, we can seize the initiative. Although it is very saddening to have sacrificed so many comrades, if the course of the incident is analyzed objectively, people cannot but recognize that the PLA are the sons and brothers of the people. This will also help the people to understand the measures we used in the course of the struggle. In the future, the PLA will have the people's support for whatever measures it takes to deal with whatever problem it faces. I would like to add here that in the future we must never again let people take away our weapons.

All in all, this was a test, and we passed. Even though there are not very many senior comrades in the army and the fighters are mostly children of eighteen or nineteen years of age—or a little more than twenty years old—they are still genuine soldiers of the people. In the face of danger to their lives, they did not forget the people, the teachings of the party, and the interests of the country. They were resolute in the face of death. It's not an exaggeration to say that they sacrificed themselves like heroes and died martyrs' deaths.

When I talked about passing muster, I was referring to the fact that the army is still the People's Army and that it is qualified to be so characterized. This army still maintains the traditions of our old Red Army. What they crossed this time was in the true sense of the expression a political barrier, a threshold of life and death. This was not easy. This shows that the People's Army is truly a great wall of iron and steel of the party and state. This shows that no matter how heavy our losses, the army, under the leadership of the party, will always remain the defender of the country, the defender of socialism, and the defender of the public interest. They are a most lovable people. At the same time, we should never forget how cruel our enemies are. We should have not one bit of forgiveness for them.

The fact that this incident broke out as it did is very worthy of our pondering. It prompts us cool-headedly to consider the past and the future. Perhaps this bad thing will enable us to go ahead with reform and the open policy at a steadier and better—even a faster—pace, more speedily correct our mistakes, and better develop our strong points....

[A long digression on economic policy.]

The problems we face in the course of reform are far greater than those we encounter in opening our country to the outside world. In reform of the political system, we can affirm one point: We will persist in implementing the system of people's congresses rather than the American system of the separation of three powers. In fact, not all Western countries have adopted the American system of the separation of three powers. America has criticized us for suppressing students. In handling its internal student strikes and unrest, didn't America mobilize police and troops, arrest people, and shed blood? They are suppressing students and the people, but we are quelling a counterrevolutionary rebellion. What qualifications do they have to criticize us? From now on, we should pay attention when handling such problems. As soon as a trend emerges, we should not allow it to spread.

What do we do from now on? I would say that we should continue to implement the basic line, principles, and policies we have already formulated. We will continue to implement them unswervingly. Except where there is a need to alter a word or phrase here and there, there should be no change in the basic line and basic principles and policies....

SADDAM HUSSEIN

Arab Cooperation Council Speech

("America must respect the Arabs and respect
their rights, and should not interfere in their
internal affairs under any cover")

Amman, Jordan

February 24, 1990

*Saddam Hussein (1937–2006) was the ruthless, genocidal Iraqi leader, who
took power as president in 1979 by murdering hundreds of potential opponents. As president, he murdered hundreds of thousands of Kurds and Shias
and allowed the starvation of a half-million children. One of his long-time
heroes was, appropriately enough, Josef Stalin. At a council of Arab leaders he attacks American interference with his right to do whatever he likes,
including, presumably, his right to use chemical weapons against his own
citizens. Soon after this summit meeting in 1990, he will order the invasion
of neighboring Kuwait. He was brought to trial in an Iraqi court in 2006,
found guilty of numerous crimes, and executed.*

Since it is difficult in a meeting such as this to deal with all that is
negative or positive in international developments during 1989 and
prior to then, and during the period from the beginning of 1990,
you might share my opinion that discussions should deal with the
most urgent and important of these issues and within the limits of
time allowed us.

Among the most important developments since the international
conflict in World War II has been the fact that some countries which
used to enjoy broad international influence, such as France and Britain, have declined, while the influence and impact of two countries
expanded until they became the two superpowers among the countries of the world—I mean the United States and the Soviet Union.
Of course, with these results, two axes have developed: the Western
axis under the leadership of the United States, with its known capitalist approach and its imperialist policy; and the East bloc under the
leadership of the Soviet Union and its communist philosophy.

Among the results of World War II: The Zionist state has become
a reality, and the original owners of the land, the Palestinians, have
become refugees. While the imperialist Western world helped the

expansionist scheme and aggression of the Zionist entity in 1967, the communist bloc sided with the Arabs in the concept of balance of interests in the context of the global competition between the two blocs, and sought to secure footholds for the East Bloc against the Western interests in the Arab homeland. The East bloc, led by the U.S.S.R., supported the Arabs' basic rights, including their rights in the Arab–Zionist conflict. The global policy continued on the basis of the existence of two poles that were balanced in term of force. They are the two superpowers, the United States and the U.S.S.R.

And suddenly, the situation changed in a dramatic way. The U.S.S.R. turned to tackle its domestic problems after relinquishing the process of continuous conflict and its slogans. The U.S.S.R. shifted from the balanced position with the United States in a practical manner, although it has not acknowledged this officially so far. The U.S.S.R. went to nurse the wounds that were inflicted on it as a result of the principles and mistaken policy it followed for such a long time, and as a result of the wave of change it embarked on, which began to depart from the charted course. It has become clear to everyone that the United States has merged in a superior position in international politics. This superiority will be demonstrated in the United States readiness to play such a role more than in the predicted guarantees for its continuation.

We believe that the world can fill the vacuum resulting from the recent changes and find a new balance in the global arena by developing new perspectives and reducing or adding to this or that force. The forces that laid the ground for filling the vacuum and for the emergence of the two superpowers, the United States and the U.S.S.R., after World War II at the expense of France, Britain, and Germany can develop new forces, which we expect will be in Europe or Japan. America will lose its power just as quickly as it gained it by frightening Europe, Japan, and other countries through the continuous hinting at the danger of the U.S.S.R. and communism. The United States will lose its power as the fierce competition for gaining the upper hand between the two superpowers and their allies recedes.

However, we believe that the United States will continue to depart from the restrictions that govern the rest of [the] world throughout the next five years until new forces of balance are formed. Moreover, the undisciplined and irresponsible behavior will engender hostility and grudges if it embarks on rejected stupidities....

We all remember, as does the whole world, the circumstances under which the United States deployed and bolstered its fleets in the Gulf. Most important of these circumstances: The war that was raging between Iraq and Iran; Iranian aggression had extended to other Arabian Gulf countries, most notably the sisterly state of Kuwait. At the time, beyond the conflicting views regarding the presence of foreign fleets in Arab territorial waters and foreign bases on their territory and their repercussions for pan-Arab security, that excessive deployment was somehow comprehensible. But now, and against the background of the recent world developments and the cessation of hostilities between Iraq and Iran, and with Kuwait no longer being the target of Iranian aggression, the Arabian Gulf states, including Iraq, and even the entire Arabs would have liked the Americans to state their intention to withdraw their fleets.

Had they said that under the same circumstances and causes they would have returned to the Gulf, it might have been understandable also. But U.S. officials are making such statements as if to show that their immediate and longer-term presence in Gulf waters and, maybe, on some of its territory, is not bound to a time frame. These suspect policies give Arabs reason to feel suspicious of U.S. policies and intentions as to whether it is officially and actually interested in a termination of the Iraq-Iran war and thus in contributing to much needed regional stability.

The other side is the immigration of Soviet Jews to the occupied Palestinian land. How can we explain the Americans' support and backing for Jewish immigration to the occupied Arab territories, except that the United States does not want peace as it claims and declares. If it really and actually wants peace, the United States would not have encouraged Israel and the aggressive trends in it to adopt such policies, which enhance Israel's capability to commit aggression and carry out expansion.

We the Arabs, proceeding from a long-standing friendship with the Soviet Union, did not expect that the Soviets would give in to this U.S. pressure in such a way that it would lead to these grave consequences for the Arabs and their pan-Arab security. As we tackle these challenges, it would be just as compromising to the destiny and cause of the Arabs to feel fear as it would be to be lax in our evaluating and working out a reaction to them. Therefore, there is no place among the ranks of good Arabs for the faint hearted who would argue that as a superpower, the United States will be the decisive factor, and others have no choice but to submit. At the same time, there is no place in our midst for those who fail to take note of recent developments that have added to U.S. strength, thus prompting it to the possible commission of follies against the interests and national security of the Arabs—either directly or by fanning and encouraging conflicts detrimental to the Arabs, irrespective of their source. We are only making the point that the Arabs seek peace and justice throughout the world and want to forge relations of friendship with those who show respect to what friendship is all about—be it the United States or any other nation. It is only natural that the Arabs take a realistic approach to the new posture and power of the United States that has led the Soviet Union to abandon its erstwhile position of influence. However, America must respect the Arabs and respect their rights, and should not interfere in their internal affairs under any cover....

Against the backdrop of the vital issue related to the substance of national Arab security, the question arises as to what we the Arabs have to do....It has been proven that Arabs are capable of being influential when they make a decision and set their minds to it for actual application purposes. We have much evidence of how effective they can be; for example, the joint Iraqi–Saudi resolution of August 6, 1980, and the warning the two countries issued together that embassies must not be moved to Jerusalem, one of whose direct results in less than a month—the duration of the warning—was not only that the concerned countries did not transfer their embassies to Jerusalem, but also that embassies that had already long been transferred to the city returned to Tel Aviv.

The reason the United States stays in the Gulf is that the Gulf has become the most important spot in the region and perhaps the whole world due to developments in international policy, the oil market, and increasing demands from the United States, Europe, Japan, Eastern Europe, and perhaps the Soviet Union, for this product. The country that will have the greatest influence in the region through the Arab Gulf and its oil will maintain its superiority as a superpower without an equal to compete with it. This means that if the Gulf people, along with all Arabs, are not careful, the Arab Gulf region will be governed by the United States's will. If the Arabs are not alerted and the weakness persists, the situation could develop to the extent desired by the United States; that is, it would fix the amount of oil and gas produced in each country and sold to this or that country in the world. Prices would also be fixed in line with a special perspective benefitting U.S. interests and ignoring the interests of others.

If this possibility is there and it is convincing, those who are convinced by it must conclude that peace in the Middle East is remote from the United States' point of view because U.S. strategy, according to this analysis, needs an aggressive Israel, not a peaceful one. Peace between Iraq and Iran could be far off as long as Iran does not react favorably from an aware and responsible position and with the peace initiatives proposed by Iraq. The region could witness inter-Arab wars or controlled wars between the Arabs and some of their neighbors, if tangible results are not achieved on the basis of the principles of noninterference in others' internal affairs and non use of military force in inter-Arab relations.

Agreement should be reached over clear and widespread pan-Arab cooperation programs among Arab countries in the economic, political, and educational fields, as well as other fields. Love and peace of mind will take the place of suspicion, doubt, mistrust, and giving in to information and speculation propagated by rumormongers, such as prejudiced Westerners and some rootless Arabs.

Brothers, the weakness of a big body lies in its bulkiness. All strongmen have their Achilles' heel. Therefore, irrespective of our known stand on terror and terrorists, we saw that the United States as a superpower departed Lebanon immediately when some Marines were killed, the very men who are considered to be the most prominent symbol of its arrogance. The whole U.S. administration would have been called into question had the forces that conquered Panama continued to be engaged by the Panamanian armed forces. The United States has been defeated in some combat arenas for all the forces it possesses, and it has displayed signs of fatigue, frustration, and hesitation when committing aggression on other peoples' rights and acting from motives of arrogance and hegemony. This is a natural outcome for those who commit aggression on other peoples' rights. Israel, once dubbed the invincible country, has been defeated by some of the Arabs. The resistance put up by Palestinian and Lebanese militia against Israeli invasion forces in 1982 and before that the heroic Egyptian crossing of the Suez Canal in 1973 have had a more telling psychological and actual impact than all Arab threats.

Further, the threat to use Arab oil in 1973 during the October war proved more effective than all political attempts to protest or to begat the gates of American decision-making centers. The stones in occupied Palestine now turn into a virtual and potentially fatal bullet if additional requirements are made available. It is the best proof of what is possible and indeed gives us cause to hold our heads high.

Just as Israel controls interests to put pressure on the United States administration, hundreds of billions invested by Arabs in the United States and the West may be similarly deployed. Indeed, for instance, some of these investments may be diverted to the U.S.S.R. and East European countries. It may prove even more profitable than investment in the West, which has grown saturated with its national resources. Such a course of action may yield in estimable benefits for the Arabs and their national causes. Our purported weakness does not lie in our ideological and hereditary characteristics. Contemporary experience has shown our nation to be distinguished and excellent, just as our nation's history over the centuries has shown this to be the case. Our purported weakness lies in a lack of mutual trust among ourselves, our failure to concentrate on the components of our strength, and our failure to focus on our weaknesses with a view to righting them. Let our motto be: All of us are strong as long as we are united, and all of us are weak as long as we are divided.

SLOBODAN MILOSEVIC
President of the Federal Republic of Yugoslavia
Address to the Nation on the NATO Bombings
("NATO isn't attacking Serbia because of Milosevic; it is attacking Milosevic because of Serbia")
Belgrade, Serbia
October 2, 2000

Milosevic (1941–2006), born in Serbia, became a Marxist during Josip Broz Tito's Yugoslavian reign. During the dissolution of Yugoslavia as a unified country in the 1980s, Milosevic garnered power as a Serbian nationalist by appealing to the Serbian minorities in Kosovo, the Albanian Muslim region of the country. He became president of Serbia in 1989 and instigated wars and persecutions against regions dominated by non-Serbs. In 1999, he invaded Kosovo and spurred violence against the ethnic Albanians. NATO forces bombed Serbia to end Milosevic's attempt at ethnic cleansing. Having just lost the election for president the week before, Milosevic here demands another election. Milosevic was later tried for war crimes by United Nations and charged with, among other things, genocide. He died of heart failure while in custody of the court.

Honored citizens, in the expectation of a second round of election, I'd like to take the opportunity to explain my views on the political situation in our country, especially in Serbia. As you know, efforts have been underway for a whole decade to put the whole Balkan Peninsula under the control of certain Western powers. A big part of that job was accomplished by establishing puppet governments in some countries, by transforming them into countries with limited sovereignty or no sovereignty at all.

Because we resisted, we have been subjected to all the pressures that can be applied to people in today's world. The number and intensity of these pressures multiplied as time went by.

All the experience that the big powers gained in the second half of the 20th century in overthrowing governments, causing unrest, instigating civil wars, disparaging or liquidating national freedom fighters, bringing states and nations to the brink of poverty—all this was applied to our country and our people.

The events unfolding around our elections are part of the organized persecution of our country and our people because we constitute a barrier to the full domination of the Balkan Peninsula.

For a long time there has been a grouping among us which, under the guise of being pro-democratic, have in fact represented the interests of the governments attacking Yugoslavia, especially Serbia.

During the elections that group called itself the "Democratic" Opposition of Serbia. Its boss is not its presidential candidate.

Its boss is the president of the Democratic Party. For years he has collaborated with the military alliance that attacked our country. He could not even hide his collaboration. In fact, our entire public knows that he appealed to NATO to bomb Serbia for as many weeks as necessary to break its resistance.

So the "democratic" grouping organized for these elections represents the armies and governments which recently waged war against Yugoslavia.

At the behest of these foreign powers our "democrats" told the people that they would make Yugoslavia be free of war and violence, that Yugoslavia would prosper, the living standard would improve visibly and fast, that Yugoslavia would rejoin international institutions, and on and on.

Honored citizens, it is my duty to warn you publicly, while there is time, that these promises are false. The situation is quite different.

It is precisely our policy which allows peace and theirs which guarantees lasting conflict and violence, and I shall tell you why.

With the establishment of an administration supported or installed by NATO, Yugoslavia would quickly be dismembered.

These are not NATO's intentions alone. These are the pre-election promises of the Democratic Opposition of Serbia. We have heard from its representatives that [the section of Serbia known as the] Sandzak would get the autonomy advocated by one of its coalition members, Sulejman Ugljanin, leader of a separatist Muslim organization. This autonomy, which Sulejman Ugljanin has been advocating for ten years, would in fact mean a definite separation of Sandzak from Serbia.

Their promises also include giving [the Serbian Province of] Vojvodina an autonomy that would not only separate it from Serbia and Yugoslavia but would in fact make it an integral part of neighboring Hungary.

In a similar manner other areas would be separated from Serbia, especially its border areas.

The annexation of these areas by neighboring states has for a long time been a hot issue in those states which have continuously incited their minorities in Yugoslavia to help integrate parts of our country into neighboring states.

Within this policy of dismembering Yugoslavia, Kosovo would be the first victim. Its present status would be proclaimed legal and final. It is the first part of Serbian territory to which Serbia would have to bid farewell, without even a hope that we could reclaim this part of our country.

The territory that would be left to bear the name Serbia would be occupied by international forces, U.S. or some other. They would treat our land as their military training ground, as their private preserve, to be controlled in accord with the interests of the occupying power.

We have been looking at cases of such control and its consequences for decades, and especially in this past decade, in many countries around the world, unfortunately lately even in Europe, for instance in Kosovo, Republic of Srpska and Macedonia, in our immediate neighborhood.

The people of Serbia would know the fate of the Kurds, with a prospect of being exterminated more speedily than the Kurds since they are less numerous, and since their movements would be limited to a much smaller area than the one in which Kurds have been present for decades.

As for Montenegro, its fate would be left in the hands of the Mafia, whose rules of the game should be made well known to the citizens: any breach of discipline and especially any opposition to Mafia interests is punishable by death without any right to appeal.

I have presented you the fate of Yugoslavia in the event that the NATO option were accepted in order to warn you that, in addition to loss of land and the humiliation of the people, all would live under a regime of ceaseless violence.

The new owners of what had been Yugoslavia's state territory and the occupiers of what was left of Serbian territory would, predictably, terrorize the population whose territory they had seized. The Serbian people would be forced to fight continuously for the re-establishment of a Serb state in which the people could reassemble.

These Imperial powers do not want peace or prosperity in the Balkans. They want this to be a zone of permanent conflicts and wars which would provide them with an alibi for maintaining a lasting presence.

A puppet administration therefore guarantees violence, possibly many years of war, anything but peace. Only self-administration makes peace possible.

And there is more. All countries finding themselves with limited sovereignty and with governments controlled by foreign powers, speedily become impoverished in a way that destroys all hope for more just and humane social relations.

A great division into a poor majority and a rich minority, this has been the picture in Eastern Europe for some years now that we can all see.

That picture would also include us. Under the control of the new owners of our country we too would quickly have a tremendous majority of the very poor, whose prospects of coming out of their poverty would be very uncertain, very distant.

The rich minority would be made up of the black marketeering elite, which would be allowed to stay rich only on condition that it was fully loyal to the outside, controlling powers.

Public and social property would quickly be transformed into private property, but its owners, as demonstrated by the experience of our neighbors, would be foreigners. Among the few exceptions would be those who would buy their right to own property by their loyalty and submission, which would lead to the elimination of elementary national and human dignity.

The greatest national assets in such circumstances become the property of foreigners, and the people who used to manage them continue to do so, but as employees of foreign companies in their own country.

National humiliation, state fragmentation and social misery would necessarily lead to many forms of social pathology, of which crime would be the first. This is not just a supposition; this is the experience of all countries which have taken the path that we are trying to avoid at any cost.

The capitals of European crime are no longer in the West, they were moved to Eastern Europe a decade ago.

Our people find it hard to bear even the present crime incidence, because for a long time, from World War II to the nineties we lived in a society which knew hardly any crime. This tremendous increase in crime, such as cannot be avoided in a society such as we would become with the loss of our sovereignty and a large part of our territory, such wider crime would be as dangerous for our people, few in numbers and unused to crime, just as war is dangerous for society and its citizens.

One of the essential tasks of a puppet government in any country, including ours, were we to have such a government, is loss of identity.

Countries under foreign command quickly forget their history, their past, their tradition, their national symbols, their way of living, often their own literary language.

Our national identity would be scrutinized, invisibly at first, but very efficiently and mercilessly, and certain aspects of national identity would be selected, reducing it to a few local dishes, a few songs and folk dances, with the names of national heroes used as brand names for food products or cosmetics.

One of the really obvious consequences of the takeover of countries by the big powers in the 20th century is the annihilation of the people's national identity.

The experience of other countries shows that people can hardly come to terms with the speed with which they must start using a foreign language as their own, identifying with foreign historic figures while forgetting their own, becoming better acquainted with the literature of their occupiers than with their own, glorifying the history of others while mocking their own, so that they come resemble others instead of themselves.

The loss of national identity is the greatest defeat a nation can know, and it is inevitable under the contemporary form of colonization.

Besides, by its very nature, this new form of colonization rules out any possibility of free speech or free will, and especially rules out creativity of any kind. Countries that are not free deny to the people who live in them the right to free speech; free speech would cause problems in the absence of freedom.

This is why torture over wrong thoughts is the most consistent and essential form of torture in a country that has lost its freedom. As for exercising free will, it is, naturally, out of the question. Free will is allowed only as a farce. It is allowed only to the lackeys of foreign masters, whose simulated free will is used by the occupiers as a justification for establishing a 'democracy' in whose name they take and hold another people's country.

I would like to stress particularly to young people, intellectuals, scientists, that countries deprived of sovereignty are as a rule deprived of the right to creative work, and especially creative work in the field of science.

Large centers and large powers finance scientific work, control its attainments and decide about the application of its results. Even if dependent states do have scientific laboratories and scientific institutes, these are not independent ones; rather they operate as branches controlled by one center. Their attainments must remain within definite limits so as not to introduce in occupied countries and occupied peoples the seed of rebellion and emancipation.

Now we are in the period before the run-off elections. The "Democratic" Opposition of Serbia doubts it can achieve the result it needs. Therefore leaders of this Opposition are trying to stop production, all work, all activity. Using money that's being shipped into the country, they are bribing some, blackmailing or harassing others, organizing strikes, unrest and violence.

The idea is to stop life in Serbia while offering the bait that life can start again and prosper if only it is organized by those who represent, within Serbia—what do they represent? The plans and interests of the would-be occupiers.

Our country is a sovereign state. It has its laws. Its own Constitution and institutions. Serbia deserves and is duty bound to defend itself from this invasion which has begun with these staged disruptions and false promises of quick improvement.

And citizens should know, that if some do participate in this subversion whose objective is foreign domination over and occupation of their country then they will shoulder the historical responsibility not only of denying to their country the right to exist but also of losing control over their own lives.

By giving up their country to others, to a foreign will, they will also surrender to a foreign will their own lives and the lives of their children and many other people.

I considered it my duty to warn the citizens of our country about the consequences of the activities financed and supported by the NATO governments.

Citizens, you must make up your own minds whether to believe me or not. My only wish is that they do not realize I am telling the truth when it is too late, that they do not realize after it has become so much more difficult to correct mistakes that some people have made, naively, superficially or erroneously. Some of those mistakes would be difficult to rectify and some would never be rectified.

My motive in expressing my opinion in this way is not personal; not at all. I was twice elected president of Serbia and once president of Yugoslavia. It should be clear to all, after the past ten years, that NATO isn't attacking Serbia because of Milosevic; it is attacking Milosevic because of Serbia.

My conscience in that respect is clear. But my conscience would not be clear if I did not tell my people, after all these years as their leader, what I think will happen if they let their fate be imposed by a hostile, outside force, even if it appears that they have chosen that fate for themselves.

The misjudgment they would make by "choosing" what has been chosen for them, is the most dangerous misjudgment possible. That is why I am publicly addressing the citizens of Yugoslavia today.

Thank you.

OSAMA BIN LADEN
Al-Qaeda Leader
Broadcast on al-Jazeera

("O American people, I address these words
to you regarding the best way of avoiding
another Manhattan")

October 29, 2004

The most famous terrorist in the world was born in 1957 to a wealthy family in Saudi Arabia. Educated at a university there, he became radicalized by the Soviet war in Afghanistan and later, as he says in this speech, in 1982, as a result of the war between Israel and Lebanon. He has been accused of being responsible for, or a contributor to, the bombings of U.S. Embassies in East Africa in 1998. He organized the 9/11 attack on the World Trade Center towers and the Pentagon. At large, he periodically releases videotaped speeches. Here, he challenges President George W. Bush's assertions about Al-Qaeda and explains, among the organization's other acts of violence, the attack in 2001 (for which he claims responsibility for the first time), and warns of further violence should concessions not be made.

O American people, I address these words to you regarding the best way of avoiding another Manhattan, and regarding the war, its causes and its consequences. But before this, I say to you: Security is one of the important pillars of human life, and free men do not take their security lightly, contrary to Bush's claim that we hate freedom. Let him explain why we did not attack Sweden, for example. Clearly, those who hate freedom—unlike the 19, may Allah have mercy on them—have no self-esteem. We have been fighting you because we are free men who do not remain silent in the face of injustice. We want to restore our [Islamic] nation's freedom. Just as you violate our security, we violate yours. Whoever toys with the security of others, deluding himself that he will remain secure, is nothing but a foolish thief. One of the most important things rational people do when calamities occur is to look for their causes so as to avoid them.

But I am amazed at you. Although we have entered the fourth year after the events of 9/11, Bush is still practicing distortion and deception against you and he is still concealing the true cause from you. Consequentially, the motives for its reoccurrence still exist. I will tell you about the causes underlying these events and I will tell you the truth about the moments this decision was taken, to allow you to reflect.

I say to you, as Allah is my witness: We had not considered attacking the towers, but things reached the breaking point when we witnessed the iniquity and tyranny of the American-Israeli coalition against our people in Palestine and Lebanon—then I got this idea.

The events that had a direct influence on me occurred in 1982, and the subsequent events, when the U.S. permitted the Israelis to invade Lebanon with the aid of the American sixth fleet. They started shelling, and many were killed and wounded, while others were terrorized into fleeing. I still remember those moving scenes—blood, torn limbs, and dead women and children; ruined homes everywhere, and high-rises being demolished on top of their residents; bombs raining down mercilessly on our homes. It was as though a crocodile swallowed a child, and he could do nothing but cry. But does a crocodile understand any language other than arms? The entire world saw and heard, but did not respond.

In those critical moments, I was overwhelmed by ideas that are hard to describe, but they awakened a powerful impulse to reject injustice and gave birth to a firm resolve to punish the oppressors. As I was looking at those destroyed towers in Lebanon, I was struck by the idea of punishing the oppressor in the same manner and destroying towers in the U.S., to give it a taste of what we have tasted and to deter it from killing our children and women. That day I became convinced that iniquity and the premeditated murder of innocent children and women is an established American principle, and that terror is [the real meaning of] "freedom" and "democracy," while they call the resistance "terrorism" and "reaction." America stands for iniquity and for imposing sanctions on millions of people, resulting in the death of many, as Bush, Sr., did, causing the mass slaughter of children in Iraq, [the worst] that humanity has ever known. It stands for dropping millions of pounds of bombs and explosives on millions of children in Iraq again, as Bush Jr. did, in order to depose an old agent and to appoint a new agent to help him steal Iraq's oil, and other sorts of horrible things.

It was against the backdrop of these and similar images that 9/11 came in response to these terrible iniquities. Should a man be blamed for protecting his own? And is defending oneself and punishing the wicked an eye for an eye—is that reprehensible terrorism? Even if it is reprehensible terrorism, we have no other choice. This is the message that we have tried to convey to you, in words and in deeds, more than once in the years preceding 9/11. Observe it, if you will, in the interview with Scott in *Time Magazine* in 1996, and with Peter Arnett on CNN in 1997, then John Wiener in 1998; observe it, if you will, in the deeds of Nairobi and Tanzania and Aden, and observe it in my interview with Abd Al-Bari Atwan and in interviews with Robert Fisk. The latter is of your own and of your religious affiliation, and I consider him to be unbiased.

Would those who claim to stand for freedom in the White House and in the TV stations that answer to them, would they conduct an interview with him [Fisk] so that he might convey to the American people what he has understood from us concerning the causes of our fight against you? For if you were to avoid these causes, you would take America in the right path to the security it knew before 9/11. So much for the war and its causes.

As for its results, they are very positive, with Allah's grace. They surpassed all expectations by all criteria for many reasons, one of the most important of which is that we had no difficulty dealing with Bush and his administration, because it resembles the regimes in our [Arab] countries, half of which are ruled by the military, and the other half are ruled by the sons of kings and presidents with whom we have had a lot of experience. Among both types, there are many who are known for their conceit, arrogance, greed, and for taking money unrightfully.

This resemblance began with the visit of Bush, Sr., to the region. While some of our people were dazzled by the U.S. and hoped that these visits would influence our countries, it was he who was influenced by these monarchic and military regimes. He envied them for remaining in their positions for decades, while embezzling the nation's public funds with no supervision whatsoever. He bequeathed tyranny and the suppression of liberties to his son and they called it the Patriot Act, under the pretext of war on terrorism.

Bush, Sr., liked the idea of appointing his sons as state [*wilaya*] governors. Similarly, he did not neglect to import to Florida the expertise in falsifying [elections] from the leaders of this region in order to benefit from it in difficult moments.

As previously mentioned, it was easy for us to provoke this administration and to drag it [after us]. It was enough for us to send two *Jihad* fighters to the farthest east to hoist a rag on which "Al-Qa'ida" was written—that was enough to cause generals to rush off to this place, thereby causing America human and financial and political losses, without it accomplishing anything worthy of mention, apart from giving business to [the generals'] private corporations. Besides, we gained experience in guerilla warfare and in conducting a war of attrition in our fight with the iniquitous, great power, that is, when we conducted a war of attrition against Russia with *Jihad* fighters for ten years until they went bankrupt, with Allah's grace; as a result, they were forced to withdraw in defeat, all praise and thanks to Allah. We are continuing in the same policy—to make America bleed profusely to the point of bankruptcy, Allah willing. And that is not too difficult for Allah.

Whoever says that Al-Qa'ida triumphed over the White House administration, or that the White House administration lost this war—this is not entirely accurate, for if we look carefully at the results, it is impossible to say that Al-Qa'ida is the only cause for these amazing gains. The White House policy, which strove to open war fronts so as to give business to their various corporations—be they in the field of armament, of oil, or of construction–also helped in accomplishing these astonishing achievements for Al-Qa'ida. It appeared to some analysts and diplomats as though we and the White House play as one team to score a goal against the United States of America, even though our intentions differ. Such ideas, and some others, were pointed out by a British diplomat in the course of a lecture at the Royal Institute for International Affairs; for example, that Al-Qa'ida spent $500,000 on the event [9/11] while America lost in the event and its subsequent effects more than 500 billion dollars; that is to say that each of Al-Qa'ida's dollars defeated one million American dollars, thanks to Allah's grace. This is in addition to the fact that America lost a large number of jobs, and as for the [federal] deficit, it lost a record number estimated at a trillion dollars.

Even more serious for America is the fact that the *Jihad* fighters have recently forced Bush to resort to an emergency budget in order to continue the fighting in Afghanistan and in Iraq, which proves the success of the plan of bleeding [America] to the point of bankruptcy, Allah willing.

Indeed, all of this makes it clear that Al-Qa'ida won gains; but on the other hand, it also makes it clear that the Bush administration won gains as well, since anyone who looks at the scope of the contracts won by large dubious corporations like Halliburton and other similar ones that have ties to Bush and to his administration will become convinced that the losing side is in fact you, the American people, and your economy.

We agreed with the general commander Muhammad Atta, may Allah have mercy on him, that all operations should be carried out within 20 minutes, before Bush and his administration would become aware. We never imagined that the Commander in Chief of the American armed forces would abandon 50,000 of his citizens in the Twin Towers to face this great horror alone when they needed him most. It seemed to him that a girl's story about her goat and its butting was more important than dealing with planes and their "butting" into skyscrapers. This allowed us three times the amount of time needed for the operations, Allah be praised.

It should be no secret to you that American thinkers and intellectuals warned Bush before the war: all that you [Bush] need in order to assure America's security by ridding [Iraq] of weapons of mass destruction, assuming there were any, is at your disposal, and all the countries of the world are with you in the matter of carrying out inspections, and the U.S.'s interest does not require you to drive it into an unjustified war, whose end you cannot know.

However, the blackness of black gold blinded his sight and his perception and he gave preference to private interests over America's public interest. And so there was war and many died. The American economy bled and Bush became embroiled in the quagmire of Iraq, which now threatens his future.

His case is like that [described in the parable]:

"He is like the ill-tempered goat that dug out of the ground the sharp knife [with which it would be slaughtered]."

I say to you: more than 15,000 of our people were killed and tens of thousands were wounded, just as more than 1,000 of you were killed and more than 10,000 wounded, and Bush's hands are sullied with the blood of all of these casualties on both sides, for the sake of oil and to give business to his private companies. You should know that a nation that punishes a weak person if he is instrumental in killing one of that nation's sons for money, while letting go free a high-class man who was instrumental in killing more than 1,000 of its sons, also for money [sic]. Similarly your allies in Palestine intimidate women and children and murder and imprison men. [*inaudible*]

Keep in mind that every action has a reaction, and finally you should consider the last wills and testaments of the thousands who left you on 9/11, waving their hands in despair. These are inspiring wills, which deserve to be published and studied thoroughly. One of the most important things I have read regarding their hand-waving signals before they fell is that they were saying, "We were wrong to let the White House carry out unchecked its aggressive foreign policy against oppressed people." As though they were telling you, the American people, "You should call to task those who caused our death." Happy is he who learns a lesson from the experience of others. A verse that I have read is also relevant to their [last] signals:

> Evil kills those who perpetrate it,
> And the pastures of iniquity are harmful.

There is a saying: a small amount spent on prevention is better than a great amount spent on treatment. You should know that it is better to return to that which is right than to persist in that which is wrong. A rational man would not neglect his security, property, or home for the sake of the liar in the White House.

Your security is not in the hands of Kerry or Bush or Al-Qa'ida. Your security is in your own hands, and any [U.S.] state [*wilaya*] that does not toy with our security automatically guarantees its own security.

Allah is our guardian but you have none.

Peace be upon whoever follows the true guidance.

HUGO CHAVEZ
President of Venezuela
"We are Rising Up Against the Empire"
Address to the United Nations
("The devil, the devil himself, is right in the house")
New York City
September 20, 2006

Hugo Chavez (b. 1954), the revolutionary and socialist leader of Venezuela since 1998, became a socialist while serving in the Venezuelan army. After participating in a coup attempt in 1992, he went to jail. On his release, he organized a socialist reform platform and won the presidency. Reelected in 2000, he took over much of Venezuela's private land- and oil-holdings. In 2002, during public protest and violence, he resigned the presidency but two days later was restored to power. He began his third term as president in 2006. A professed Marxist, he has enjoyed tweaking his international political enemies. In this speech, he mocks U.S. President George W. Bush, who, the day before, had spoken to the same audience at the United Nations.

Representatives of the governments of the world, good morning to all of you. First of all, I would like to invite you, very respectfully, to those who have not read this book, to read it.

Noam Chomsky, one of the most prestigious American and world intellectuals, Noam Chomsky, and this is one of his most recent books, *Hegemony or Survival: The Imperialist Strategy of the United States.*

[*Holds up book, waves it in front of General Assembly.*]

It's an excellent book to help us understand what has been happening in the world throughout the 20th century, and what's happening now, and the greatest threat looming over our planet.

The hegemonic pretensions of the American empire are placing at risk the very survival of the human species. We continue to warn you about this danger and we appeal to the people of the United States and the world to halt this threat, which is like a sword hanging over our heads. I had considered reading from this book, but, for the sake of time—[*flips through the pages, which are numerous*]—I will just leave it as a recommendation.

It reads easily, it is a very good book, I'm sure Madame [U.N. President Haya Rashed Al-Khalifa] you are familiar with it. It appears in English, in Russian, in Arabic, in German. I think that the first people who should read this book are our brothers and sisters in the United States, because their threat is right in their own house.

The devil is right at home. The devil, the devil himself, is right in the house.

And the devil came here yesterday. Yesterday the devil came here. Right here. [*crosses himself*] And it smells of sulfur still today.

Yesterday, ladies and gentlemen, from this rostrum, the president of the United States, the gentleman to whom I refer as the devil, came here, talking as if he owned the world. Truly. As the owner of the world.

I think we could call a psychiatrist to analyze yesterday's statement made by the president of the United States. As the spokesman of imperialism, he came to share his nostrums, to try to preserve the current pattern of domination, exploitation and pillage of the peoples of the world.

An Alfred Hitchcock movie could use it as a scenario. I would even propose a title: "The Devil's Recipe."

As Chomsky says here, clearly and in depth, the American empire is doing all it can to consolidate its system of domination. And we cannot allow them to do that. We cannot allow world dictatorship to be consolidated.

The world parent's statement—cynical, hypocritical, full of this imperial hypocrisy from the need they have to control everything.

They say they want to impose a democratic model. But that's their democratic model. It's the false democracy of elites, and, I would say, a very original democracy that's imposed by weapons and bombs and firing weapons.

What a strange democracy. Aristotle might not recognize it or others who are at the root of democracy.

What type of democracy do you impose with marines and bombs?

The president of the United States, yesterday, said to us, right here, in this room, and I'm quoting, "Anywhere you look, you hear extremists telling you can escape from poverty and recover your dignity through violence, terror and martyrdom."

Wherever he looks, he sees extremists. And you, my brother—he looks at your color, and he says, oh, there's an extremist. Evo Morales, the worthy president of Bolivia, looks like an extremist to him.

The imperialists see extremists everywhere. It's not that we are extremists. It's that the world is waking up. It's waking up all over. And people are standing up.

I have the feeling, dear world dictator, that you are going to live the rest of your days as a nightmare because the rest of us are standing up, all those who are rising up against American imperialism, who are shouting for equality, for respect, for the sovereignty of nations.

Yes, you can call us extremists, but we are rising up against the empire, against the model of domination.

The president then—and this he said himself, he said: "I have come to speak directly to the populations in the Middle East, to tell them that my country wants peace."

That's true. If we walk in the streets of the Bronx, if we walk around New York, Washington, San Diego, in any city, San Antonio, San Francisco, and we ask individuals, the citizens of the United States, what does this country want? Does it want peace? They'll say yes.

But the government doesn't want peace. The government of the

United States doesn't want peace. It wants to exploit its system of exploitation, of pillage, of hegemony through war.

It wants peace. But what's happening in Iraq? What happened in Lebanon? In Palestine? What's happening? What's happened over the last 100 years in Latin America and in the world? And now threatening Venezuela—new threats against Venezuela, against Iran?

He spoke to the people of Lebanon. Many of you, he said, have seen how your homes and communities were caught in the crossfire. How cynical can you get? What a capacity to lie shamefacedly. The bombs in Beirut with millimetric precision?

This is crossfire? He's thinking of a western, when people would shoot from the hip and somebody would be caught in the crossfire.

This is imperialist, fascist, assassin, genocidal, the empire and Israel firing on the people of Palestine and Lebanon. That is what happened. And now we hear, "We're suffering because we see homes destroyed."

The president of the United States came to talk to the peoples—to the peoples of the world. He came to say—I brought some documents with me, because this morning I was reading some statements, and I see that he talked to the people of Afghanistan, the people of Lebanon, the people of Iran. And he addressed all these peoples directly.

And you can wonder, just as the president of the United States addresses those peoples of the world, what would those peoples of the world tell him if they were given the floor? What would they have to say?

And I think I have some inkling of what the peoples of the south, the oppressed people think. They would say, "Yankee imperialist, go home." I think that is what those people would say if they were given the microphone and if they could speak with one voice to the American imperialists.

And that is why, Madam President, my colleagues, my friends, last year we came here to this same hall as we have been doing for the past eight years, and we said something that has now been confirmed—fully, fully confirmed.

I don't think anybody in this room could defend the system. Let's accept—let's be honest. The U.N. system, born after the Second World War, collapsed. It's worthless.

Oh, yes, it's good to bring us together once a year, see each other, make statements and prepare all kinds of long documents, and listen to good speeches, like Abel's yesterday, or President Mullah's. Yes, it's good for that.

And there are a lot of speeches, and we've heard lots from the president of Sri Lanka, for instance, and the president of Chile.

But we, the assembly, have been turned into a merely deliberative organ. We have no power, no power to make any impact on the terrible situation in the world. And that is why Venezuela once again proposes, here, today, 20 September, that we re-establish the United Nations.

Last year, Madam, we made four modest proposals that we felt to be crucially important. We have to assume the responsibility our heads of state, our ambassadors, our representatives, and we have to discuss it.

The first is expansion, and Mullah talked about this yesterday right here. The Security Council, both as it has permanent and non-permanent categories, (inaudible) developing countries and LDCs must be given access as new permanent members. That's step one.

Second, effective methods to address and resolve world conflicts, transparent decisions.

Point three, the immediate suppression—and that is something everyone's calling for—of the anti-democratic mechanism known as the veto, the veto on decisions of the Security Council.

Let me give you a recent example. The immoral veto of the United States allowed the Israelis, with impunity, to destroy Lebanon. Right in front of all of us as we stood there watching, a resolution in the council was prevented.

Fourthly, we have to strengthen, as we've always said, the role and the powers of the secretary general of the United Nations.

Yesterday, the secretary general practically gave us his speech of farewell. And he recognized that over the last 10 years, things have just gotten more complicated; hunger, poverty, violence, human rights violations have just worsened. That is the tremendous consequence of the collapse of the United Nations system and American hegemonistic pretensions.

Madam, Venezuela a few years ago decided to wage this battle within the United Nations by recognizing the United Nations, as members of it that we are, and lending it our voice, our thinking.

Our voice is an independent voice to represent the dignity and the search for peace and the reformulation of the international system; to denounce persecution and aggression of hegemonistic forces on the planet.

This is how Venezuela has presented itself. Bolivar's home has sought a nonpermanent seat on the Security Council.

Let's see. Well, there's been an open attack by the U.S. government, an immoral attack, to try and prevent Venezuela from being freely elected to a post in the Security Council.

The imperium is afraid of truth, is afraid of independent voices. It calls us extremists, but they are the extremists.

And I would like to thank all the countries that have kindly announced their support for Venezuela, even though the ballot is a secret one and there's no need to announce things.

But since the imperium has attacked, openly, they strengthened the convictions of many countries. And their support strengthens us.

Mercosur, as a bloc, has expressed its support, our brothers in Mercosur. Venezuela, with Brazil, Argentina, Paraguay, Uruguay, is a full member of Mercosur.

And many other Latin American countries, CARICOM, Bolivia have expressed their support for Venezuela. The Arab League, the full Arab League has voiced its support. And I am immensely grateful to the Arab world, to our Arab brothers, our Caribbean brothers, the African Union. Almost all of Africa has expressed its support for Venezuela and countries such as Russia or China and many others.

I thank you all warmly on behalf of Venezuela, on behalf of our people, and on behalf of the truth, because Venezuela, with a seat on the Security Council, will be expressing not only Venezuela's thoughts, but it will also be the voice of all the peoples of the world, and we will defend dignity and truth.

Over and above all of this, Madame President, I think there are reasons to be optimistic. A poet would have said "helplessly optimistic," because over and above the wars and the bombs and the aggressive and the preventive war and the destruction of entire peoples, one can see that a new era is dawning.

As Silvio Rodriguez says, the era is giving birth to a heart. There are alternative ways of thinking. There are young people who think differently. And this has already been seen within the space of a mere decade. It was shown that the end of history was a totally false assumption, and the same was shown about Pax Americana and the establishment of the capitalist neo-liberal world. It has been shown, this system, to generate mere poverty. Who believes in it now?

What we now have to do is define the future of the world. Dawn is breaking out all over. You can see it in Africa and Europe and Latin America and Oceanea. I want to emphasize that optimistic vision.

We have to strengthen ourselves, our will to do battle, our awareness. We have to build a new and better world.

Venezuela joins that struggle, and that's why we are threatened. The U.S. has already planned, financed and set in motion a coup in Venezuela, and it continues to support coup attempts in Venezuela and elsewhere.

President Michelle Bachelet reminded us just a moment ago of the horrendous assassination of the former foreign minister, Orlando Letelier.

And I would just add one thing: Those who perpetrated this

crime are free. And that other event where an American citizen also died were American themselves. They were CIA killers, terrorists.

And we must recall in this room that in just a few days there will be another anniversary. Thirty years will have passed from this other horrendous terrorist attack on the Cuban plane, where 73 innocents died, a Cubana de Aviacion airliner.

And where is the biggest terrorist of this continent who took the responsibility for blowing up the plane? He spent a few years in jail in Venezuela. Thanks to CIA and then government officials, he was allowed to escape, and he lives here in this country, protected by the government.

And he was convicted. He has confessed to his crime. But the U.S. government has double standards. It protects terrorism when it wants to.

And this is to say that Venezuela is fully committed to combating terrorism and violence. And we are one of the people who are fighting for peace.

Luis Posada Carriles is the name of that terrorist who is protected here. And other tremendously corrupt people who escaped from Venezuela are also living here under protection: a group that bombed various embassies, that assassinated people during the coup. They kidnapped me and they were going to kill me, but I think God reached down and our people came out into the streets and the army was too, and so I'm here today.

But these people who led that coup are here today in this country protected by the American government. And I accuse the American government of protecting terrorists and of having a completely cynical discourse.

We mentioned Cuba. Yes, we were just there a few days ago. We just came from there happily.

And there you see another era born. The Summit of the 15, the Summit of the Nonaligned, adopted a historic resolution. This is the outcome document. Don't worry, I'm not going to read it.

But you have a whole set of resolutions here that were adopted after open debate in a transparent matter—more than 50 heads of state. Havana was the capital of the south for a few weeks, and we have now launched, once again, the group of the nonaligned with new momentum.

And if there is anything I could ask all of you here, my companions, my brothers and sisters, it is to please lend your good will to lend momentum to the Nonaligned Movement for the birth of the new era, to prevent hegemony and prevent further advances of imperialism.

And as you know, Fidel Castro is the president of the nonaligned for the next three years, and we can trust him to lead the charge very efficiently.

Unfortunately they thought, "Oh, Fidel was going to die." But they're going to be disappointed because he didn't. And he's not only alive, he's back in his green fatigues, and he's now presiding the nonaligned.

So, my dear colleagues, Madam President, a new, strong movement has been born, a movement of the south. We are men and women of the south.

With this document, with these ideas, with these criticisms, I'm now closing my file. I'm taking the book with me. And, don't forget, I'm recommending it very warmly and very humbly to all of you.

We want ideas to save our planet, to save the planet from the imperialist threat. And hopefully in this very century, in not too long a time, we will see this, we will see this new era, and for our children and our grandchildren a world of peace based on the fundamental principles of the United Nations, but a renewed United Nations.

And maybe we have to change location. Maybe we have to put the United Nations somewhere else; maybe a city of the south. We've proposed Venezuela.

You know that my personal doctor had to stay in the plane. The chief of security had to be left in a locked plane. Neither of these gentlemen was allowed to arrive and attend the U.N. meeting. This is another abuse and another abuse of power on the part of the Devil. It smells of sulfur here, but God is with us and I embrace you all.

May God bless us all. Good day to you.